ONE WEEK LOAN

Trading in futures

Trading in futures
Why markets in education don't work

Hugh Lauder and David Hughes,
and Sue Watson, Sietske Waslander,
Martin Thrupp, Rob Strathdee,
Ibrahim Simiyu, Ann Dupuis, Jim McGlinn
and Jennie Hamlin

Open University Press
Buckingham · Philadelphia

Open University Press
Celtic Court
22 Ballmoor
Buckingham
MK18 1XW

email: enquiries@openup.co.uk
world wide web: http://www.openup.co.uk

and
325 Chestnut Street
Philadelphia, PA 19106, USA

First Published 1999

ISBN   0 335 20277 2 (pb)   0 335 20278 0 (hb)

A catalogue record of this book is available from the British Library

Library of Congress Cataloging-in-Publication Data
Trading in futures: why markets in education don't work / David Hughes ... [et al.].
    p. cm.
  Includes bibliographical references and index.
  ISBN 0-335-20278-0. – ISBN 0-335-20277-2 (pbk.)
  1. Education–New Zealand–Finance–Longitudinal studies. 2. School choice–New Zealand–Longitudinal studies. 3. Free markets–New Zealand–Longitudinal studies. I. Hughes, David, 1944–
  LB2826.6.N45T73   1999
  379.3'2'0993–dc21   98–55533
                                                                          CIP

Copy-edited and typeset by The Running Head Limited, London and Cambridge
Printed in Great Britain by Biddles Ltd, Guildford and King's Lynn

Contents

Acknowledgements

This research could not have been undertaken without the support and cooperation of the families, the teachers and the schools in this study. We cannot name them for obvious reasons, but we would like to take this opportunity to express our gratitude.

We are indebted to the New Zealand Ministry of Education who funded this project and, in particular, to Hans Wagemaker, formerly of the Ministry, who acted as a critical friend to the project and who was instrumental in initiating the research. We are well aware that, from time to time, our findings have proved uncomfortable for educational policy makers and politicians in New Zealand and we would wish to place on record our appreciation of their continued financial support for this project. It says something about their commitment to a democratic ethos in the public sector.

Professor John Gray of Cambridge University read and commented on the Year 10 HLM study, and Professor Doug Willms of the University of New Brunswick refereed this study for the Ministry of Education (NZ). We are grateful for their time and the insights they provided. Dr Tony Robinson of the University of Bath did some long-haul flying at a crucial time to help us out, while participants of the King's seminar on parental choice, under the aegis of Professor Stephen Ball, were insightful and supportive in their comments on various aspects of the project.

We should also acknowledge the members of the Project Advisory Board: Jacky Burgon, Ron Crawford, Kahu Katene, Struan Little, Ken Rae, Miriama Vaega and Lynne Whitney; also the cultural liaison advisors: Lanuola Asiasiga, Rinna Cheakong, Mihn Lamb, Onsy Phomevilay, Tuaine Robati and Mr Sopoaga. Many others toiled away at different times on the project, including, Sefulu Hermens, Cherilyn Mills, Mieke Scott, and Sarah Thawley; we are also in their debt.

Finally we would like to thank our editor at the Open University Press, Shona Mullen, who first approached us about this project four years ago and has had the infinite patience to nurture it through to conclusion; and also Carmel Smith, who formatted the MS under great pressure.

Introduction

The introduction of markets into state education has caused intense debate. Advocates of markets in education have claimed that they will raise standards and promote equality of opportunity at a time when economic competitiveness is seen to depend on the performance of educational systems. In the United States the Chief Executive of IBM has gone so far as to write a book extolling the virtues of education markets as the means to halt America's economic decline. In their best-selling book (endorsed by President Clinton), *Reinventing Government*, Osborne and Gaebler (1993) see education markets as the key to promoting efficiency and creativity in education. These arguments have been taken up enthusiastically by national and local governments in the United States, Britain, New Zealand, Canada and Australia. Elements of market policies are also being introduced in Europe and considered in the Pacific Rim, while supranational agencies like the World Bank and the IMF have nailed their colours to the market cause.

The belief in the effectiveness of education markets has become orthodoxy in official policy circles, but many researchers in these countries have taken an opposing view. To date, the debate has gone through two cycles. Initially, it was conducted at an abstract level involving arguments from first principles and inferences as to likely market outcomes from microeconomic theory and research into school effectiveness and social exclusion. Subsequently, aspects of market policies have been the subject of research which has shown that there is considerable inequality of parental choice based on social class, gender and ethnicity. Although these results are important they do not count decisively against market policies in education.

This book initiates a third phase in the debate over markets. At the heart of the debate is the question of whether markets do what market advocates hope, which is to improve school performance. Critics of education markets take the contrary position, arguing that markets will polarize school performance and exacerbate social and educational inequalities. The research findings of our long-term study of education markets (the Smithfield Project) in New Zealand enables us to test the claims at the centre of the debate. To our knowledge this is the first longitudinal study to be able to report on the effects of education markets on school perform-ance, and we hope it will shed some more light on a debate which has so far caused intense heat.

The initial phases of the debate have produced a coherent set of testable propositions both for and against markets. In Chapters 1 and 2 we outline these propositions and the thinking behind them. There are many kinds of educational systems and a variety of ways in which choice policies can be implemented. Our concern is to test the claims of those who champion mar-kets characterized by open enrolments where parents are, in principle, able to send their children to the state school of their choice and where popular schools, in which demand exceeds supply, can choose their students. In Chapter 3 we discuss the way education markets are structured, since the rules which govern them will have an effect on their outcomes, and we pro-vide a brief history of the political genesis of education markets in New Zealand. Chapters 4 through to 7 test the competing propositions of the two camps. Within each camp the propositions are systematically related to one another so that each claim presupposes the one which precedes it. These chapters should therefore be read as a progression, with Chapter 7 providing the focal point of the book, for it is here that the key question of the link between education markets and school performance is examined.

Inevitably with such a complex social phenomenon we have had to develop related data bases to test the various propositions. In order to make the study more accessible to all those interested in the debate we have left the technical details of the sampling and statistical techniques out of the main body of the text. For those interested these are reported in the Appendix.

The study shows that (contrary to current orthodoxy) markets are likely to lead to a decline in overall educational standards because they have a negative effect on the performance of working class schools, while leaving middle class schools untouched. It is for this reason that we have called the book *Trading in Futures* because in effect education markets trade off the opportunities of less privileged children to those already privileged. In these terms markets don't work because they are neither efficient nor equitable.

This finding takes us beyond the specific debate about education markets to question the rationality of policy making. What has led nation states and federal governments to overturn education systems so readily for the untried promises and policies of the market?

Since the research in this book was undertaken in New Zealand a brief note is necessary on some of the Maori terms used in the book. Maori are the indigenous people of what is properly called Aotearoa/New Zealand. Some words of the Maori language have become part of mainstream New Zealand English, particularly the word *Pakeha*, which has come to refer to New Zealanders of European descent. Readers should note that throughout the book we use the terms *social class* and *socioeconomic status* (SES) interchangeably. For a detailed discussion of how we have measured SES, see the Appendix.

A note about the Smithfield Project

The Smithfield Project was conducted in two cities in New Zealand which we have called Central City and Green City. Details of the methodology employed in this study can be found in the Appendix.

one

The magic of the market?

Education is seen throughout the developed world as the royal road to economic competitiveness in the twenty-first century. It is brain power not brawn which generates greater added value; the more educated individuals are the more they will add to a nation's prosperity in the global economy. Or so the argument goes.[1]

Just as there is now a consensus over the importance of education to the economy, so there is also an emerging consensus that market forces will raise the performance of educational systems. Governments from across the political spectrum have been introducing markets into state education, and where they have not yet been implemented they are being considered. What is surprising about this sudden turn towards markets is that belief in their effectiveness is a matter of faith rather than hard evidence. This book is about why this faith is misplaced.

The most dramatic statement of the view that improved educational performance is vital to national survival was made in the *Nations at Risk* report from the United States which saw the threat of the Soviet Union being replaced by the threat of economic decline. The report specifically blamed poor educational standards as the cause of this economic decline in the face of intense global competition. In the authors' view,

> If an unfriendly foreign power had attempted to impose on America the mediocre educational performance that exists today, we might well have viewed it as an act of war. As it stands, we have allowed this to happen to ourselves . . . We have, in effect been committing an act of unthinking, unilateral educational disarmament.
> (National Commission on Excellence in Education 1983: 5)

The same sentiment – if not quite the colourful language – has been common to governments, their agencies and advisors in most of the advanced economies.

Viewed from the perspective of the New Right politicians of the day, the issue was and is not just a question of sharpening a population's technical skills to meet the economic challenge but of using education as a form of national and cultural revitalization. In the period of economic stagnation of the late seventies and early eighties and the right-wing revolutions of Thatcher and Reagan that followed, bureaucratic educational systems were seen as part of a wider problem of state-induced dependency among the population. The New Right intellectuals who advised the Thatcher and Reagan administrations assumed that by liberating education from the state, teachers, parents and students would be released to express the very qualities that had once made these nations great: self-reliance, initiative and creativity.

The background to the concern with cultural and economic revitalization was the decline in levels of economic growth, rising inflation and the perceived threat of the Asian Tiger economies, particularly that of Japan. In the United States economic growth had fallen from 3 per cent in the period 1960–8 to under 2 per cent between 1968–73. A similar trend was found in Britain, while Japan's growth, in contrast, had been spectacular at close to 10 per cent in the sixties. While it declined in the seventies to around 2.5 per cent, it still remained above that of the United States and Britain. Accompanying the decline in growth in the United States and Britain was a decline in productivity (DTI 1997). By the early eighties this economic downturn, when coupled with the new challenge from the Pacific Rim, led to a preoccupation, on both sides of the Atlantic, with the broader issue of the decline of these once great powers. The seemingly poor performance of education, along with that of the economy, lent credence to the idea that these nations were becoming moribund.

In looking for a scapegoat for this decline, right-wing intellectuals in both countries pointed the finger very firmly at the state. It was argued in the United States that the period of intense state intervention which marked Lyndon Johnson's attempt to build the great society had failed because, far from alleviating poverty, state intervention had merely created dependency (Murray 1984). Once that claim was firmly lodged in the imagination of the Reagan and Thatcher administrations it was but a short step to embrace Gilder's (1981) credo that all the poor needed was the spur of their own poverty for them to escape poverty. In other words, without the shackles of the state those in poverty could rise like Lazarus to take their place in consumer society.

In Britain, a similar propaganda role was played by Anthony Flew, who could write in prose as lurid and colourful as anything coming from across the Atlantic. Flew (1987) was highly critical of the common or comprehensive school, arguing that these schools were an example of state attempts at socially engineering equality of opportunity:

This truly radical reorganisation [into the comprehensive system] has sometimes been described as a great experiment; just as, in the 1920s and 1930s the operations of the regime established by the Bolshevik coup of October 1917 were regularly characterised as 'that great social experiment in Russia'.

(Flew 1987: 27)

A similar round of polemic was loosed by a prominent education ginger group, the Hillgate Group:

the deterioration in British education has arisen partly because schools have been treated as instruments for equalising, rather than instructing, children. Merit, competition and self-esteem have been devalued or repudiated; the teaching of facts has given way to the inculcation of opinion; education has often been confounded with indoctrination; and in many places there is a serious risk of disciplined study being entirely swamped by an amorphous tide of easy-going discussion and idle play.

(Hillgate Group 1987: 2)

This kind of rhetoric – which echoed Powell, Farrar and Cohen's (1985) *The Shopping Mall High School* study of American schools – travelled around the globe, with similar sentiments being expressed in New Zealand (NZ Treasury 1987).

The panacea which was hailed as bringing renewal to these beleaguered powers was the market, and nowhere more so than in education. As Chubb and Moe, two of the higher acolytes of market doctrine argued (1992: 10–11), so long as the framework for education markets was carefully designed, 'markets can be allowed to work their wonders . . . for everyone's benefit'. It was not only intellectuals and policy makers who lent credence to the ideology of markets: business executives in the United States and New Zealand, in particular, were vocal in their advocacy. In their book *Reinventing Education: Entrepreneurship in America's Public Schools*, Lou Gerstner, Chief Executive Officer of IBM, and former executive colleagues from Nabisco, opened their tract with this dramatic statement about state schools: 'This is a book about public schools – and their last, best chance to save themselves. They must reinvent themselves in order to survive. The "discipline of the market" provides the key' (Gerstner *et al.* 1994: 19).

Behind the attacks on bureaucratic state education systems were several assumptions which were welded together into a powerful and coherent myth as to how education could aid the revitalization of nations, once released from the chains of the state.

Marketizing education and cultural renewal

The first assumption had to do with the connection between competition and human beings' essential nature. State interference, especially to promote equality of opportunity, was seen as a way of stifling initiative and talent, particularly for the most able. When nations' economic survival was threatened, excellence needed to manifest itself; it could only do so under the 'natural' condition of human existence, competition. Competition was needed to stimulate the most talented students and it was needed to raise the level of schools' performance. State education insulated schools from competition because most had zones or catchment areas which guaranteed them a supply of students irrespective of how they performed. Critics of the comprehensive system argued that this lack of competition was the root cause of the decline of state education.

The thinking behind this argument comprised a coalition of traditions under the banner of the New Right. As Brown (1997b) has noted, for the authoritarian Right, educational standards are as much a moral as an educational issue. Social engineering for equality undermines the traditional moral order because it promotes a shift from elite to mass culture and the erosion of respect for authority. For the liberal Right, it is the freedom of the individual to choose coupled with the efficiency of the market which leads them to the view that education markets are the key to revitalizing the economy. The two traditions are not always compatible, but over the question of education markets they found common ground.

Competition would also lead to cultural renewal through the diffusion of greater initiative and creativity in society. The mechanism for achieving this was parental choice. Linking competition, choice, creativity and initiative produces a potent myth that transcends national borders and cultures. Nevertheless it is a myth in two senses. The obvious point is that it is enormously difficult to test because what we mean by ideas like creativity and initiative is contestable. No two people will come up with the same definitions. Even if agreed definitions could be arrived at, the causal story to be told in linking these concepts is rather vague. At its most convincing the argument will claim that choice allows for the expression of individuality, in that the selection of a school can be made on the basis of the best fit between what the school provides and a particular personality. It will then be claimed that, for the school system as a whole, competition will enable the flowering of diversity as schools seek niche markets which cater for the development of particular personalities. Initiative enters the story because it is needed by parents, students and schools to ensure that demand and supply are matched. In contrast, it will be claimed that a state system based on zoning will produce uniformity rather than diversity and make no demands on parents' initiative and schools' creativity.

If this is the way the story holds together, then parts of this myth are open to testing – as we shall see. Nevertheless, the potency of these ideas clearly transcends the rational (in the sense of testable ideas), raising the possibility that at the heart of policy making there is a founding myth which people have to accept or reject on the basis of faith.

If competition and cultural renewal were at the heart of the initial motivation for the creation of markets in education, then the key issue in establishing them was the idea of declining standards. It was necessary to show that educational standards were indeed in decline if a convincing argument for change was to be made. The question of whether standards were declining at least remained more open to rational debate.

Raising standards through education markets

In the United States there were two principal indicators that excited public attention over the issue of standards: the decline in Scholastic Aptitude Test scores (SATs) and poor performance on comparative international measures in science and maths relative to Pacific Rim nations. SATs are taken by high school students in the United States seeking admission to college. Scores on the SAT began to decline in the mid-sixties, and although there have been variations in the trend, overall scores have not returned to their pre-1975 levels. While there has been considerable debate about the causes of this decline (which we will discuss later), the conclusion drawn by pro-market critics of the system was that education was failing due to lack of competition between schools. Further evidence for this view was extracted from international comparative studies of education performance. One of the first comprehensive reviews in 1977 showed that the United States lagged behind Japan and many of its European competitors in science. This was also true of mathematics. Subsequent results from a 1981 survey showed that the United States fell consistently behind these countries and was close to the bottom of the league tables on algebra and calculus for twelfth-grade students. For school leavers the average Japanese student achieved better results than the top 5 per cent of US students who took college preparatory mathematics.[2]

A further round of comparative tests in OECD countries in 1991 revealed that while US students were now performing back to 1970 levels, they were still behind their international competitors. Among 13-year-olds they were ninth among member countries for maths and eighth in science (although these differences were not statistically significant) and seventh in English. However, these data need to be heavily qualified, not least because there is considerable variation between states within America. For example, in mathematics proficiency scores for 13-year-olds in 1991, Taiwan was the leader, followed by Iowa and North Dakota. At the other end of the table were 14 states where performance is comparatively low, although even here there can be considerable variation in the spread of scores. We make this point simply because the only characteristic shared by these 'low performing' states is that their current expenditure per student is below the United States average (OECD 1994: 93–110). However, it is also true that the 'leaders' Iowa and North Dakota received below-average expenditure, although they still received more funding than the majority of the low performing states. Given such variations in expenditure and performance, it is hard to understand the leap of faith made by market advocates as anything but an expression of what Mrs Thatcher called conviction politics. There are many measures to improve performance that could have been considered without recourse to a wholesale change in the education system.

In the countries where conviction politics were perfected, Britain and New Zealand, the use of comparative international achievement data did not play such a prominent role in the justification of markets. Deductions from first ideological principles showing that markets would *obviously* raise standards appeared to be sufficient for policy makers. In New Zealand, however, it was academics sceptical of the marketization of education who turned to comparative data to demonstrate that the picture of a general decline in standards was false (Elley 1991; Irving 1991b). In particular, New Zealand's achievements in literacy were among the world's highest.

The use of comparative studies by the New Right provides a clear example of how an apparently rational appeal to research can mask the political expedience of conviction politics. Margaret Brown (1998) has cogently argued that, in Britain, governments have been cavalier in using them for their own ideological purposes. Yet the critical literature over the use of such data has, for over a decade, stressed that they need to be treated with caution (Theisen *et al.* 1983; Mislevy 1995).

Moreover, a sensitive comparison of the performance of educational systems would have quickly shown policy makers on both sides of the Atlantic that some of the most highly centralized – such as Japan, Singapore, France and Korea – are also the most 'successful' (Green 1997). In *Politics, Markets and America's Schools*, the authors Chubb and Moe (1990), who we have seen are among the most ideologically committed of market proponents, acknowledge this inconvenient fact in a footnote as follows: 'we think it is important not to jump to conclusions about how our analysis of American education might generalize to – or be modified by – the experiences of other nations . . . Japan and France (among others) seem to do a better job of promoting academic excellence despite being "highly bureaucratic"' (p. 289). Having raised the problem Chubb and Moe dismiss it with the following 'get out' clause: 'Nations are different and appearances can be deceiving' (p. 289). Clearly, this kind of myopia should not have carried weight. Nevertheless, it typified the promotion of the market cause.

On its own the conviction politics of the New Right would have carried the day, but there was also a broader constituency of support and more plausible grounds for thinking that markets in education might have their virtues.

Markets as a vehicle for promoting equality of opportunity

The proponents of greater parental choice and hence markets in education have included some of the most respected US educational researchers. Christopher Jencks, principal author of *Inequality*, one of the most renowned analyses of US inequality, developed a choice model which was applied in Alum Rock, Arkansas between 1969 and 1973. The aim was 'to improve the education of children, particularly disadvantaged children and to give parents, and particularly disadvantaged parents, more control over the kind of education that children get' (Glovinsky 1971: 4).

The concern was that disadvantaged parents and their children were trapped, by zones, in inner city ghetto schools. It appeared that zoning, by concentrating poor children in their neighbourhood schools, simply exacerbated the hopelessness that disadvantage brought. By removing zones it was hoped that some children would move to schools beyond their local area, thereby decreasing segregation. It was anticipated that choice would empower parents to take heart and hope in their children's education. In the event, the Alum Rock experiment was taken to be a failure. Evaluation of the outcomes of the experiment showed that parents did not utilize choice to the degree expected, and where they did, their children did not perform as well as others in the district (Snook 1987).

Underlying the argument for choice, as a means of equalizing opportunities, was an analysis by James Coleman of why social change had rendered the zoned common or comprehensive school redundant. James Coleman was the principal author of *Equality of Opportunity*, a seminal report in the mid-sixties which suggested that social class mix was a key factor in school performance. Coleman's standing as a researcher and interest in equity issues makes what he has to say about choice particularly interesting. His argument is that the nature of communities has changed since the rationale for common schools was advanced a hundred years ago. Then, communities were bound by the ties of neighbourhoods, shared values and often ethnicity. In today's world, communities are not tied to neighbourhoods because of improved transportation and electronic communications. Even more significantly, communities have become economically stratified so that common schools now neither represent the common values of a community nor do they have a wide range of intake from different socioeconomic classes. In such a world Coleman (1990a: xix) argues that 'parental choice of school cannot destroy the common school; it has already been destroyed by residential stratification'. Moreover, the public purposes for which the common school was initially established no longer retain the significance they once had. According to Coleman, a hundred years ago the purpose of public schooling was to break the hold of the family: to promote the talents and opportunities of children rather than serving the immediate economic interests of families and to integrate diverse ethnic groups into the American 'melting pot'. Now, he argues, schools need to co-opt parents as co-educators in their children's learning because research has established how important this is to their educational success. For Coleman, choice establishes the possibility of a 'win win' scenario. In relation to equity he takes the view that choice will release students from ghetto schools. Even if choice leads to the creation of all-black schools he regards this with equanimity so long as parents have been able to make choices:

> Recognition that all-black schools are not inherently inferior has important implications. Perhaps the most significant is the realization that the ethnically and culturally pluralistic society of the United States has room for schools of all sorts. What is essential . . . is that if a child is in an all-black school it is because he [sic] wants to be there and his parents want him to be there, not because it is the only school he has a reasonable chance to attend.
>
> (Coleman 1990b: 216)

In his view, the key justification for choice is the commitment to education resulting from it. Furthermore, this applies as much to teachers as it does to parents and students. Markets can generate this motivation because they create the appropriate incentives:

> The movement toward choice is the first step in a movement toward getting the incentives right in education – incentives for both the suppliers of educational services, that is, schools and their teachers and for the consumers of education, that is, parents and children. The incentives for schools . . . would include an interest in attracting and keeping the best students they could. The incentives for parents and students would include the ability to get into schools they find attractive and remain in those schools.
>
> (Coleman 1992: 260)

Coleman's view summarizes the arguments in favour of choice; we shall have cause to return to it, for the picture he paints hides a fundamental conflict of interest between parents and schools. However, in the light of the current polarization of incomes, levels of child poverty and documented inequalities of opportunity in the Anglo-Saxon-dominated nations like the United States, Britain and New Zealand, the question of how educational equality of opportunity can be promoted among so-called disadvantaged students is an important one.

The views of researchers like Coleman are effectively hypotheses which predict that there will either be an improvement in the performance of traditionally underperforming groups in society and/or that schools will become less segregated ethnically and socioeconomically through the introduction of market mechanisms. The key question then is, once we have stripped away the prejudices of conviction politics, what empirical research was there to support these hypotheses?

The research evidence for markets in education

The research evidence suggesting that the marketization of education might lead to greater diversity of educational provision, higher standards and greater equality of opportunity, was of two kinds. The first derived from the idea that schools are not islands unto themselves but that their performance is related to the overall system of education of which they are a part. Here, researchers attempted to show that it is the political control of public schools which causes their low performance. The second kind of evidence related to the findings that private schools performed better than state schools. If this was so, then according to proponents of education markets, what distinguished private from public schools was precisely that they operated in a market. Hence it followed that if a market system could be created for public schools, their performance should be improved. There is an intuitive plausibility to both these positions but we need to examine them more closely to see how well they stand up under scrutiny.

The political control of public education

The idea that it is the democratic control of public schooling which causes underperformance in schools was first given systematic expression through what is known in the research community as *public choice theory*. This theory harboured grand aspirations, which were directly linked to the idea that America was facing decline, because it could explain the Western economic crisis of the seventies and early eighties. Fundamental to this explanation is the idea that the roots of the crisis were political and related to the growth of state expenditure. According to this theory, welfare state expenditure grows because the democratic process enables pressure groups to assert their interests over the wider and more prudent economic interests of the state by demanding increases in state expenditure, in return for votes. Middle class state workers, such as teachers, who have an interest in gaining higher incomes and expanded job opportunities, are one of the principal villains in this theory. By linking interest group politics to national debt the theory provided an explanation for the increasing government expenditure of the seventies which led to high national debt and high levels of inflation in the early eighties.

The general message underlying public choice theory is that democratic politics and processes are not to be trusted. As James Buchanan, the leading theorist of this school of thought, has commented in relation to national debt, 'budgets cannot be left adrift in a sea of democratic politics' (Buchanan and Wagner 1977: 175). There is, of course, a strong resonance between this theory and the kinds of intuition and prejudice about the causes of economic decline described earlier. In fact Buchanan's work, for which he was awarded the Nobel prize, started much earlier than the concern about America's imminent demise as a great power (Buchanan and Tullock 1962). But the theory became popular in the late seventies because it chimed so well with right-wing sentiment.

This broad theoretical framework has been applied to education in different ways by Hanushek (1986, 1989, 1994), Peltzman (1993) and more famously by Chubb and Moe (1990). What links their studies to the public choice framework is a scepticism about the effectiveness of democratic politics and the behaviour of interest groups like teacher unions. As a research tradition in education, these studies are imaginative in seeking to apply elements of public choice theory to education, but for that reason they are less convincing when their theories are tested against empirical data.

In 1986 Eric Hanushek published an extended paper, while at the Congressional Budget Office, which purported to show that the costs of education had risen while standards of education had declined. The clear inference from his research was that while most of the increase in educational expenditure had been a result of rises in teacher income and conditions, these rises were unjustified in terms of the results they produced.

Hanushek began by arguing that during the period 1960–83 there had been a significant decline in teacher–pupil ratios, an increase in the experience of teachers and an increase in the qualifications of teachers, and that while educational expenditure had increased, student achievement had declined. His choice of variables is significant because they are often associated with improving school performance. So, for example, most people expect improved student learning to result from smaller class sizes and increases in teacher experience and qualifications.

In order to substantiate this argument Hanushek reviewed the results of 147 studies on the impact of these variables on student outcomes. Of these, only a small proportion found a positive significant relationship between student performance and class size, expenditure on students and teachers' education, experience and salaries. The majority of studies found no statistically significant relationship.

Hanushek's conclusion on the basis of this review is that 'schools are economically inefficient because they pay for attributes that are not systematically related to achievement' (1986: 1160). More positively, he made the assumption, which was not subjected to the same kind of testing as the other variables, that there are good and bad teachers. These, he argues, cannot be identified, either by experience or educational qualification. The task of the school, therefore, is to be able to hire good teachers and fire bad teachers. On the basis of two studies he suggested that head teachers are reliable judges in identifying good and bad teachers and that they should be able to reward teachers according to performance. But to do this, the education system would need to strip away many of the regulations which prevent such policies and deal with the issue of teacher union power. Unions help protect teachers through these regulations while extracting more public finance to improve teachers' pay and working conditions. Hanushek does consider the evidence on the superiority of private schooling, but in this paper stopped short of advocating the marketization of education. Nevertheless, his research pointed in that direction because it challenged teachers' existing work conditions and raised questions about the appropriate sanctions and incentives necessary to raise their performance.

There are various criticisms that have been made of Hanushek's research. He has been taken to task for the techniques he adopts in reviewing the evidence, what is called in the jargon, 'meta-analysis' (Hedges *et al.* 1994). The problem with Hanushek's methodology is that both the theory and method in each of the studies in his sample may be quite different, and only the barest judgements are made about their quality and sophistication. So it is hard to understand how legitimate conclusions can be drawn by this methodology.[3] Added to this, reviews of more recent research suggest that the quality of teachers and their knowledge of teaching and learning is a decisive factor in student performance (Darling-Hammond 1997).

Our particular concern with Hanushek's review, in the light of our own research, is that he selects studies which seek to make judgements about the relationship between teacher and expenditure variables and student performance in isolation from the overall school context. For any study in his sample it would be impossible to say whether, for example, teacher experience or class size had any causal effect on student performance, because we do not know how school policies and organization have impacted on the variables that he examines. Take a school or department which poorly resources teachers: however well qualified or experienced they are, the outcome may be that students underperform. In this case the cause may not be the teacher's experience but the school's resourcing policy. Given this, we cannot tell how the blame and praise should be distributed. We would need to know far more about the relationship between school policy, organization and culture before we could more confidently assert that there was or was not a causal link between, say, teacher experience and student performance. The fact is that there are now more powerful analytic techniques available, discussed in Chapter 7, which enable us to shed more light on these complex relationships.

Nevertheless in the climate of the times Hanushek's contribution was seminal. He suggested that governments did not have to spend more money on education to raise performance. Rather, by stripping away regulations and addressing the question of union power, schools would have the freedom to raise standards. These conclusions could be described as the first step in conjuring the illusion that education markets were a panacea to avert national decline.

The next step was provided by Chubb and Moe (1990, 1997), who attacked the idea that 'the one best system' of democratically controlled common schooling was either the only possible system or indeed the best. True to the spirit of public choice theory they saw democratic control rooted in the bureaucracy of the district office as the source of America's educational decline, and explained the perpetuation of a now ailing system in terms of vested interests: 'The winners were elements of business, the middle class and educational professionals – especially the latter because they would be running the new bureaucratic system' (Chubb and Moe 1990: 4). The losers, predictably, would include

> a sizeable portion of the less powerful segments of the American popu-
> lation: the lower classes, ethnic and religious minorities and citizens of
> rural communities. Their traditional control over local schools was
> now largely transferred to the new system's political and administra-
> tive authorities who, according to what soon became official doctrine,
> knew best what kind of education people needed and how it could be
> provided most effectively.
>
> (Chubb and Moe 1990: 4)

From this set of assumptions Chubb and Moe set out a complex theory connecting the structure of school governance to low performance. The theory is in three parts. First, the hierarchy of democratic and bureaucratic constraints imposed on public schools impairs their performance because schools lack the ability to set their own goals, the administrative ability to hire and fire, and the ability to determine the curriculum, instruction and discipline. Second, the greater the absence of external constraint the more schools can set their own goals, use the initiative and autonomy of teachers and create a team spirit which sets a positive ethos for the school. Third, they assume that market modes of incentive provide the kind of autonomy that teachers need to raise performance, citing the evidence of the apparently superior performance of private and Catholic schools in support of this conclusion.

As with Hanushek's research, Chubb and Moe should be credited for an imaginative application of public choice theory to education. But their argument is conceptually flawed, while the empirical evidence they adduce for their thesis has left them with little credibility. Harvey Goldstein, one of the leading statisticians in educational research, described their major work (*Politics, Markets and America's Schools*) as 'an ideological treatise masquerading as serious empirical research' (1993: 118). In saying this he was not alone: many of the major figures in educational research had come to similar conclusions (see, for example, Glass and Matthews 1991).

If we examine the three elements of Chubb and Moe's theory we can gain some understanding as to why the research community was so critical of their attempt to legitimize education markets. For a start, there is a philosophical problem with the idea that schools should set their own goals. If the community believes that there are certain things all students should learn because they are essential to the development of rationality or to the aim of producing a well rounded character, then it is unclear as to why schools, rather than society, ought to set educational goals. The aim of 'goal specialization' is an essential part of the language of markets and is about creating a niche by selling a distinctive product. Chubb and Moe are well aware of this issue but either side-step it (1997: 367) or resort to a populism based on consumer choice (1990: 33).

As to the second element of their theory, it does not follow that bureaucratic systems necessarily generate less autonomy for teachers. For example, prior to 1989, New Zealand had a highly centralized and – by common definitions of the word – bureaucratic system of education. Yet teachers had a high degree of professional autonomy (Lauder and Yee 1987). A similar point can be made in relation to France (Broadfoot *et al.* 1988). Part of the problem here is, as Rosario *et al.* (1992) noted, that Chubb and Moe use the term 'bureaucratic control' so widely that virtually any non-market system of education can be so labelled. More problematic for the theory is Green's suggestion (1997) that highly centralized systems by and large are likely to produce higher levels of academic performance. This clearly tells against the public choice argument that democratic control threatens to lower educational standards.

Perhaps the most powerful argument in Chubb and Moe's locker is that private schools perform better than state schools, even when the socio-economic background of the students is taken into account. To support this part of their theory they rely on the work of Coleman, Hoffer and Kilgore's (1982) and Coleman and Hoffer's (1987) research. The conclusions of this research were that test scores were higher among Catholic and non-Catholic private schools in their sample than among state schools even after taking student characteristics like social background and ethnicity into account. However, the prior achievement of students on entering high school, which is a key predictor of their future performance, was significantly absent from the research design. The authors concluded that Catholic schools in particular did better in educating students from a variety of backgrounds and hence came closer to approaching the common school ideal than state common or comprehensive schools. This was especially so for disadvantaged students.

These results, according to Chubb and Moe, 'set off shockwaves in the educational community' (1997: 367). Certainly they attracted close attention and were the subject of detailed criticism and response in some of the leading educational journals. In reviewing the conflicting evidence produced by Coleman and his associates and the re-analyses undertaken by their critics, Jencks (1985: 134) concluded that on balance it was probably the case that Juniors and Seniors learn slightly more in Catholic than state high schools; also, that the evidence that Catholic schools might be more helpful to disadvantaged students than state schools was 'suggestive, but not conclusive'.

The evidence generated by Coleman's study is interesting but it provides a weak basis for advocating wholesale change in the way education is funded and provided, not least because in his subsequent research with Hoffer (1987), Coleman explained the superior performance of Catholic schools as a function of the community in which they are embedded rather than in terms of their status as private schools; he argued that there is a set of values and expectations that Catholic parents hold which creates a form of social capital supportive of their children's education. In contrast to the American evidence, research from Halsey, Heath and Ridge (1984) in Britain reported that there was a small difference in favour of private schools compared to state schools, once various factors, including student background characteristics, were taken into account. In New Zealand, Lauder, Hughes and Fitzgerald (Lauder *et al.* 1992a) in a study of outcomes for 13 private and state schools in 1982 and 1988, found nonsignificant differences between the school types each year once student background and the nature of a school's socioeconomic composition were taken into account.[4] We do not cite this international evidence to attempt to disprove the claim that private schools perform better than state schools. Rather, we simply wish to record that there is insufficient evidence to demonstrate that private schools, everywhere, are superior to state schools.

However, for staunch supporters of markets in education, the merits of Chubb and Moe's case took second place to the fact that they had written the right book at the right time. Until then, systematic attempts to justify the role of markets in education had amounted to little more than philosophical flag waving which made much of the freedom of the individual (for example Friedman and Friedman 1980) but gave little by way of insight as to why markets could produce superior outcomes in education. Chubb and Moe showed how, in *theory*, the magic of the market could work.

Testing the theory

The evidence on which markets in education were advocated was thin but it was made weaker because it was, at best, indirect. With the exception of the failed voucher experiments it was based on inferences as to why education markets *ought* to deliver rather than on an evaluation as to whether they had delivered.

That said, we should be grateful to the advocates of markets for two reasons. They did echo and reinforce the many concerns that had already been raised about the performance of state education, especially in relation to social class and ethnic groups who had traditionally underperformed. But in pressing their case, they also generated a series of testable hypotheses as to the effects of education markets. To those wishing to evaluate education markets this work has been helpful.

From the literature we have reviewed we can identify the following related hypotheses:

1 Parents will have equal knowledge about schools and the power to send their children to the school of their choice.
2 Schools will become more ethnically and socially mixed because less well-off parents will escape the iron cage of zoning.
3 Schools will become more diverse as they accommodate to parental demands.
4 Education markets will drive up school performance through competition for students.
5 The quality of teaching will be raised in an education market. Bad teachers will be fired while good teachers' morale, motivation and performance will be raised.

As testable hypotheses these need some elaboration. Formally they are the closest possible fit to the assumptions underlying the economic model of perfect competition. Under this model it can be shown that markets produce optimal outcomes in terms of quantity and quality. In the above hypotheses it is assumed that parents can make rational preferences and hence informed choices. While it may take some time, all parents will eventually acquire the knowledge needed in an education market since they will do what is in their children's best interests. They will be aided in this by a set of quality indicators, usually league tables and reports from school inspectors, which will inform parents of the 'best' schools available. It follows from this that parents may not send their children to the local school if they judge that it is not performing well. Hence schools will become more socially and ethnically mixed as inner city students escape the iron cage of zoning. Parents will also demand diverse kinds of school as they seek to match their children's characters to the schools that will maximize their educational performance.

The consequences of this combination of parental knowledge and consumer power is that school performance will be driven up by the competition for students because school income will be determined by student numbers.

Accordingly, 'good' schools will enrol more students while 'bad' schools will improve or close down. The moment a school's performance indicators decline parents will switch schools, thereby sending a signal to the school that if it does not improve it will perish. A school will only expand to the point where the quality of its education doesn't suffer: similarly a school will only alter its staff–student ratio to improve educational 'outputs'. If it seeks to cut costs by reducing staff and this leads to poorer educational performances, the market mechanism will ensure that more staff are hired.

There are several reasons why this 'market' mechanism can only work crudely at best in education. For a start, there is no price system to reconcile demand and supply. If there was it would militate against universal schooling as some parents would not or could not afford schooling for their children. Proxies such as vouchers have been mooted but this only addresses the demand side of the market. On the supply side, there should, in theory, be many producers so that consumers can choose from a wide range of schools. But government funding is finite and the numbers of schools on offer are by and large restricted. The upshot is that demand and supply have to be regulated by other means and, as we shall see, this is a key issue.

However, this is not the only problem with the application of the theory to education. In a perfectly competitive market it is assumed that products are private goods in that one person's consumption of a good does not affect the welfare of other consumers. In education this is a point at issue since, as we explain in Chapter 2, there is sound evidence to believe that the social class and ethnic characteristics of students within a school have a significant impact on its performance. If parents remove some of the students because they would consider them better off in another school, this may have harmful consequences for those that remain.[5]

For these reasons market proponents have placed much more emphasis on the motivational factors associated with markets, rather than suggesting that education markets can approximate to the formal properties and optimal outcomes associated with a perfectly competitive market. In this sense it is the educational variants of public choice theory that have been in the vanguard of justifications for introducing what are, in reality, quasi or proxy market mechanisms into education. It is for this reason that issues relating to teachers' vested interests and the appropriate sanctions and incentives to motivate them have assumed such a high profile in the debate. It is from this theory that the fifth hypothesis is derived. Teachers would be confronted with a Faustian bargain: they would have greater autonomy under a market system but they could also be threatened with unemployment if they did not perform. According to their advocates, what education markets do is to clear the motivational road blocks identified by public choice theorists, and enable parents and teachers to engage in raising educational standards.

Testing these hypotheses opens the way to examining the key assumptions underlying the market model. These coalesce around the question of whether in a highly unequal society there can be equality of choice in a market for education. If there is, then market proponents may be vindicated. If there is not, then they stand open to the charge that they are apologists for the enhanced opportunities education markets afford the children of the more affluent. It is precisely because the issues surrounding markets in education are so intimately related to questions of power and opportunity that the debate, to date, has been so intense.

Conclusion

The appeal to markets was and is extremely attractive to policy makers. The idea that markets could improve educational performance without having to increase government expenditure showed, in theory, how something could be got for nothing, and that was the message that the research of Hanushek, Chubb and Moe and others was giving. At the same time parents could become more involved with their children's education through greater choice: clearly a good selling point at elections. Expressed in these terms the magic promise of the market had obvious attractions. However, critics see no magic in the market but an attempt to shift the nature of the educational competition in favour of the middle class. It is to their views that we now turn.

two

Revealing the magician's tricks: the hidden hand of political conflict

The social and economic world has changed dramatically in the past 30 years, with the consequence that education has assumed increasing importance in providing security and opportunity to those in the labour market. The underlying explanation for the attractiveness of markets to policy makers lies in the nature of these changes.

During the post-war period social progress was built on the pillars of economic prosperity for all, security, and opportunity for social advancement (Brown and Lauder 1999). Prosperity was shared as wages across the board rose with GNP. Security was achieved through policies which ensured full employment. Where there was unemployment, people were protected by the welfare state. Opportunity was achieved through two routes. Education was systematically expanded on the meritocratic principle that the abilities and the motivation of the child were the key to educational success. Alongside apparently meritocratic competition within education was a system of social mobility based on the great bureaucratic organizations of the state and the corporate sector. Upward social mobility was a possibility for the sons and (later) the daughters of the working class. But there was a considerable gap between the principles of meritocracy and the practice. As the middle class expanded, the relative chances of reaching the 'top' were still much greater for the children of the professional and managerial classes (Halsey *et al*. 1980; Goldthorpe 1997).

Prosperity for all, coupled to the security of full employment, came to an end during the prolonged economic crisis of the late seventies and early eighties. Ordinary people in the Western world came through this crisis to find that the world had fundamentally changed. Economic prosperity for all became economic prosperity for a minority: the incomes of the richest rose significantly, while there was stagnation for others or, for the poor, a decline. This was especially marked in the United States, Britain and New Zealand (Hills 1995; Gottschalk and Smeeding 1997). Two-parent families have made up for this decline in wages, where possible, by both parents working. Even so, there is a sense in which the majority of families are running faster to stand still. Some of the costs of major items such as houses, cars and, more recently, day care have risen faster than wages in the United States, even for higher income earners (Hacker 1997; Morris 1997).

At the same time as wages were polarizing, unemployment started to rise and remains at historically high levels. Much is made of the trending down of unemployment in the economies like the United States, Britain and New Zealand, which were restructured by a return to primitive capitalism (Brown and Lauder 1999), but the figures need to be taken with a large dose of scepticism. For example, in the United States, Richard Freeman (1995) estimates that two percentage points have been taken off the unemployment statistics by the policy of increasing the incarceration of young black males. While Britain apparently has the lowest unemployment rate in the European Community it also has one of the highest number of households where no one works: at a conservative estimate about 15 per cent of households (Goodman et al. 1997). In addition, approximately 20 per cent of those in work in Britain receive wages which are so low that they are entitled to tax credits. In essence they are working for poverty wages.

The advent of greater polarization of income and unemployment was coupled with reduced job security. During the eighties the bureaucratic structure of corporations was replaced by 'flatter' organizations. Middle management positions were stripped out, and many of the functions of middle managers were replaced by electronic systems of accounting and surveillance. Organizations also became leaner as corporations shed or contracted out non-core business and created a dual labour market. The jobs of those on the inside (who had specialist experience and knowledge) were relatively safe, but for those on the outside, much of their work was on a contract or casualized basis. Will Hutton (1995: 14) suggests that the workforce can be divided into three groups. Around 40 per cent enjoy full-time tenured work, 30 per cent are insecurely self-employed and approximately 30 per cent are working for poverty wages. Added to this was a wave of mergers and take-overs which continues to this day, albeit for different reasons (Thurow 1993; Hutton 1995; Whitford 1997), which have increased job insecurity. The significance of job insecurity is shown up in the data on inequality of earnings within occupational groups. Gottschalk (1997: 33) explains this inequality in terms of the numbers in any occupational group who are on short-term or 'casual' contracts:

> the increase in inequality partially reflects greater instability in earnings among people . . . with short term transitory increases or decreases in their earnings . . . about a third of the increase in within-group

inequality reflects such instability of earnings . . . Jobs were becoming less stable as well as less equal.

It is against this background of greater economic insecurity and polarization of income that education assumes critical importance. Figures are published on almost a monthly basis showing that better educated individuals have higher incomes. This almost universal fact was well captured by Bill Clinton's 1992 'They are all our children' speech in Los Angeles, when he said:

> The key to our economic strength in America today is productive growth . . . In the 1990s and beyond, the universal spread of education, computers and high speed communications means that what we earn will depend on what we can learn . . . That's why, as we know, a college graduate this year will earn 70 per cent more than a high school graduate in their first year of work.

These are sentiments that are echoed around the world. George Bush wanted to be the education President; Tony Blair, the British Prime Minister, sees 'education, education, education' as the foundation for the future; in New Zealand and Australia the same refrain is heard.

Although it is the case that college graduates earn substantially more than high school graduates there is considerable debate as to why this is. The assumption made by Bill Clinton and most government officials is that the higher premiums for graduates are a return for their higher levels of skill. This idea has been linked to the development of a global economy in which there is something close to perfect competition for skills (Reich 1991). Under these conditions individuals and nations that have high skills will earn high incomes, while those that do not are condemned to a low wage existence.

Reich's idea is controversial (Brown and Lauder 1997, 1999). There is a debate as to whether graduate incomes have risen since the 1970s in real terms and, if they have, whether this reflects an increased demand for skills (Gottschalk and Smeeding 1997; Levin and Kelly 1997). Nevertheless, both rhetoric and government policies around the world have assumed that the picture painted by Robert Reich, once Clinton's Labor Secretary, is accurate. The consequence has been the expansion of higher education, in Western and Pacific Rim nations, into mass systems in which between 30 and 40 per cent of any age cohort now expect to attend university. The result is credential inflation.

Credential inflation

As a good traded in the labour market, educational credentials are unusual. They are often called positional goods (Hirsch 1977) because they are scarce in a socially imposed sense. When too many individuals hold that good or credential at that particular level, it loses value and individuals will try to gain advantage by studying for a credential at an even higher or more prestigious level. So, if ever-larger numbers of students gain first degrees then advantage can only accrue by taking that degree at a highly prestigious university or gaining an even higher qualification.

This turn of the screw of the 'diploma disease' (Dore 1976) has affected all the Western nations and some on the Pacific Rim, like Korea and Japan, where 'exam hell' characterizes students' educational experience. One further factor has added to the upward spiral of credentials: winner-take-all markets.

In their book, *The Winner-Take-All Society*, Robert Frank and Philip Cook (1995) make the point that mega-dollar salary packages are the result of what they call winner-take-all markets. These have long been known in the sporting and entertainment industries but have now been extended to corporate management, medicine, financial and legal services and even universities. They are characterized by the disproportionate earnings of a new class of 'superstars', key players who they argue, 'spell the difference between corporate success and failure. Because their performance is crucial and because modern information technology has helped build consensus about who they are, rival organizations must compete furiously to hire and retain them' (Frank and Cook 1997: 2).

But these winner-take-all markets have unfortunate consequences. They attract large numbers of individuals to compete for the 'glittering prizes', although the majority will fail to attain them. This causes a massive wastage of money, time and effort as students struggle through the professional postgraduate schools of business, law and medicine in order to enter this high stakes competition. Worse still, professions which don't have such conspicuous winner-take-all labour markets, such as engineering, may experience a shortage of skilled labour. That is certainly currently the case in electronics, which may also miss out on the most talented as they pursue the chimera of riches.

Matters are made worse because winner-take-all markets also distort the competition for credentials. As the numbers going into higher education increase so the elite institutions raise their entry requirements and tuition fees. At the same time, because the role of the elite schools as the gatekeepers to society's most prized jobs has been thrown into even sharper relief by winner-take-all markets, only the students from the most prestigious schools and universities are recruited to them. Frank and Cook tell the story of an applicant to Harvard's graduate programme in economics from a small Florida college with a straight-A transcript who, like many others from similar colleges, has been rejected in favour of straight-A students from Stanford, Princeton and MIT. The student from Florida may have been as good as or better than those from these prestigious universities, but clearly selecting those from the likes of MIT is a 'better bet'. Once, students could compete for entry to the top jobs on equal terms by going to their local state universities, but no more. The threat to the principle of meritocracy is clear: equal talent does not necessarily mean equal opportunities under such a system. Critics of the marketization of education argue that this threat is extended by the introduction of markets into primary and secondary education.

If changes in the labour market driven by changes in technology, the global economy and the winner-take-all markets constitute a 'pull factor' in intensifying the competition for credentials, the 'push factor' is caused by the insecurities of the labour market.

Labour market insecurity and the struggle for credentials

Critics of the marketization of education share the view, with their opponents, that education is a site of conflict. But they draw the fault lines of conflict across different sectors of the social topography. For them, the key divisions are those of social class rooted in the power and status that is conferred by organizational hierarchies, gender and ethnicity. This is in contrast to the view taken by public choice theorists, who see class resulting from monopolies in the labour market. They consider teachers in state schools with zones as unjustifiably privileged because they are guaranteed students and tenure.

Across these fault lines it is assumed by critics of marketization that education is a site of struggle for the positional advantage that credentials can confer. The assumption is made on the basis of the research findings we mentioned previously, which have consistently shown that students from professional and managerial families have far greater chances of entering professional and managerial occupations than those from lower middle class white collar or working class blue collar families. One response to these findings is to argue, as Herrnstein and Murray (1994) have, that these results are not in the least surprising because they reflect the genetic inheritance of intelligence. The weight of evidence is against Herrnstein and Murray on this issue, for even if we accept the notion that there is a significant genetic component to intelligence and that it can be measured by IQ tests, the data show that there is a substantial social effect on educational outcomes and labour market destination. Fischer and his colleagues (1996) re-analysed Herrnstein and Murray's data and found that they had exaggerated the impact of IQ. This re-analysis demonstrates that if everyone had the same IQ scores but came from different social backgrounds, the impact of equalizing IQ is a 10 per cent reduction in income inequality. If everyone had the same social background but different IQ scores, Fischer and his colleagues claim that inequality in income would be reduced by 37 per cent.

Similar conclusions about the importance of the social environment have been reached by Jencks *et al.* (1972) and Bowles and Gintis (1976) in the United States, and Lauder and Hughes (1990a) and Hughes and Lauder (1991) in New Zealand.

As Fischer notes, such calculations only tell half the story because they fail to explain the way that income, wealth and life-chances are embedded in the social structure. The argument of the critics of the marketization of education is that educational success represents the triumph of the professional and managerial white middle class and (until recently) male students and their families in the struggle over who wins and who loses in education. We should emphasize that much of this struggle is not consciously intended but is a result of the history, social position, income and education of parents who hold professional or managerial positions. The phrase which is used to capture the complex make-up of the advantage that middle class parents can confer is that of *cultural capital* (Bourdieu 1997).

Class wisdom in the conflict over education

The concept of cultural capital is used to explain the success of middle class students in terms of the informal education received at home through the language employed within the family, books and other cultural artefacts. Allied to this, studies have shown also that children raised in middle class families have far higher educational aspirations and expectations of being able to act upon the world (Kohn 1969). When these elements of class are taken together they combine to create quite different frames of reference within which education is understood by the different classes. We have coined the term *wisdom of the class* to describe these different frames. One of the clearest examples of their impact on students comes from research undertaken by Lauder, Hughes, Dupuis and McGlinn (1992b). In this study we interviewed a sub-sample of students from different class backgrounds, who had university entrance qualifications. We knew, from the overall sample of 2400 students from which they were drawn, that low socio-economic students with university entrance qualifications were far less likely to go to university than their professional middle class counterparts (Lauder and Hughes 1990a), and we wanted to know why.

We asked Terri, the daughter of a university professor why she had decided to go to university. Here is her answer:

> like I never considered doing anything else but coming to university . . .
> it just seemed natural to go to university after school, just like part of
> school really.
>
> (Lauder *et al.* 1992b: 15)

We then asked her to consider what her parents' reaction might have been if she had not gone to university but had become a check-out person in a supermarket. She replied:

> It's up to me what I want to do. They . . . give me advice but they never tell me I should do anything in particular [but] they would have tried to tell me education is a bit more important than that.
>
> (p. 15)

The idea that the decision to go to university is automatic is common-place for students from middle class backgrounds. As Terri noted, parents do not need explicitly to push their children, there is simply a climate of expectation which may be unspoken. In this sense it is a matter of class, not only family background, because it is the school, the peer group and the family which all hold these expectations.

Terri's experience should be contrasted with that of Delia, a working class student. Neither of her parents had educational qualifications but they valued education. Delia says:

> They always wanted us to do well so that we had qualifications when we left [school]. I knew I'd have to stay until I got university entrance. Mum said, 'if you don't get it you're going back until you do.'
>
> (p. 28)

For Delia, as for many working class students, getting the university entrance exam was the means of getting a good working class job (Brown 1987). Her view of school was entirely instrumental and her dislike of it clearly emerged in the interview:

> I hated school. I was glad to be rid of it, having to do stupid things. All the things we learned, oh what was the good of learning half the things we learned.
>
> (p. 28)

When we asked her about going to university she replied:

> I didn't see the point in going to university unless I wanted to be a vet or something. I don't see the point in going. Look at all the others who go, they just waste time, mess around. And I see the ones who go to uni-versity to be teachers and they didn't pass. One went to be a vet and they didn't pass so that's a year wasted. They're on the dole now.
>
> (p. 29)

Her parents would have approved had she gone to university but Delia said:

> But you'd be pretty disappointed if you failed and wasted all that time.

In our view this was a crucial comment by Delia because it indicated the degree of risk she thought was involved in going to university. Her parents had little education and she knew few people who had gone to university; it was, in effect, a foreign place to her, hence she feared the unknown.

These interviews illustrate the different class frames of reference and they are supported by other qualitative studies from the United States, Britain and New Zealand which draw similar conclusions (Sennett and Cobb 1972; Willis 1977; Brown 1987; Jones 1989). These studies were undertaken in the seventies and eighties, and it might be argued that fundamental changes in education and the economy have brought about changes in class frames of reference. Such a conclusion is doubtful. The polarization of income and high unemployment has entrenched elements of an underclass in our societies. For example in Britain, Johnson and Reed (1996) have shown that over 40 per cent of sons whose fathers were either unemployed or in the lowest income bracket in the early seventies have themselves either been unemployed or are in the lowest income bracket. A similar conclusion has been reached in the United States (Solon 1992).

If the different class frames of reference give middle class students an advantage throughout their schooling then it has also been shown that their parents will actively intervene to sustain or enhance that advantage. For example, Annette Lareau (1997) has described in detail how middle class parents fashion a 'customized' education for their children while working class parents within the same primary school receive what she calls a 'generic' education. Middle class parents do this through the subtle pressure they can apply to schools in a way that blue collar parents, by and large, can not. The difference between the groups is one of knowledge of the 'rules of the game' and having the confidence to challenge them.

Amy Stuart Wells and Irene Serna (1997) have documented another aspect of the way middle class parents achieve the kind of schooling they want for their children through concerted pressure. They studied ten racially and socioeconomically mixed state schools introducing mixed ability teaching (de-tracking). What they found was that local elites of professional middle class parents successfully exerted pressure to ensure that de-tracking was modified by 'bribes' or compromises which enabled their children to continue to receive a customized education.

The key point about these studies is that they undermine the long-held view that so-called disadvantaged students underperform because of their home background and neighbourhood. The other side of the coin is that middle class parents, in part unintentionally, and in part actively, seek to maintain the advantage of their own children. That they do so is understandable, but we should not, therefore, simply see what happens to blue collar students as resulting from a deficient family background that they have been unlucky enough to have inherited.

So long as professional middle class parents could use their cultural capital and knowledge of the 'rules of game' to sustain an advantage for their children in an era of full employment and opportunity, the state system of education based on the common or comprehensive school addressed their interests. But once they understood that the security and opportunities afforded by mid-century labour markets were being stripped away, the stakes in the struggle for credentials were raised.

Shifting the goal posts of the credential competition

In a series of books and papers, Phil Brown (1994, 1997a, 1997b) has argued that the key to understanding the introduction of markets in education is the attempt, by the middle class, to change the rules of educational competition in the light of the greater insecurities confronting their children. By changing the process of selection to schools, middle class parents can raise the stakes in creating stronger mechanisms of exclusion for blue collar and post-colonial peoples in their struggle for equality of opportunity. The principle of selection under state common schooling was, as we have noted, that of *meritocracy* captured in the equation: $IQ + Effort = Success$. But the introduction of markets in education changes this principle to one where selection is determined by the wealth and wishes of parents, what Brown (1997b) calls the ideology of *parentocracy*. In essence, his argument is that we are returning to principles of selection which ruled prior to the advent of meritocracy when money was a key factor determining educational success. In the process the yardstick of meritocracy, however imperfect the practice, is being discarded, thereby legitimizing educational advantage captured through the potent combination of material capital (money and time) and cultural capital.

In contemporary education markets cultural capital is needed to determine which schools are best. Material capital is needed to cover the time and transport costs needed to get children to these schools. In both cases it could be predicted that middle class parents would hold the advantage. It is important to emphasize that these inequalities cannot be remedied by providing blue collar parents with information about schools, nor is it a matter of giving them travel subsidies (as the proponents of markets often assume). If the critics of education markets are correct, the issues here run far deeper to ones relating to social and cultural identity, to knowledge of the rules of the game and the confidence to move easily between social class and ethnic contexts. These differences are rooted in history and the social and economic structures of society, and will not be easily changed.

The radical shift from meritocracy to parentocracy can be seen as part of the reconstruction of primitive capitalism engendered by the Reagan and Thatcher eras. After all, both elevated the principle of freedom of choice; in Britain, choice of school went hand in hand with a package of policies aimed at privatizing many of the state's functions. Individuals were encouraged to buy state houses, private pensions and health care. But to see these changes as simply a step back in history would be a mistake.

Although Reagan and Thatcher tried to reconstruct their societies according to their ideological precepts they had to connect with some of the common experiences of everyday life. If they had not they would have been rejected decisively at the polls. Neither was. The key to the appeal of choice as a guiding principle of society was the fact that individuals had changed in their relationship to one another. In the post-war period individuals were confined by pre-given roles. The war had helped to sustain a society where deference to military authority was replaced by deference to corporate authority (Reich 1991). In the home, men and women had separate roles defined by the concept of the male breadwinner. However, as Basil Bernstein (1997) so presciently observed in the early seventies, social interaction based on pre-defined roles was changing to one in which roles were negotiated. Clearly, the changing nature of work and the role of women in paid employment allied to the Feminist movement had much to do with this change. As the nature of social interaction has changed, so notions of identity have come to the fore. Role conflict and negotiation are based on an understanding of individuals' identities and aspirations.

Parents and consumer choice in education

These changes create a quite different dynamic between the individual and the state, making it much harder for a paternalistic state to exist. Deference, which made paternalism possible, has given way to greater awareness of the self in relation to society and a greater emphasis on individual rights. Translated into the debate about school choice, this suggests that parents are unlikely to accept a policy of zoning without question. In the past zoning appeared to be common sense on the part of both state policy and parental understanding. Now, taken-for-granted assumptions have to be justified. Even if individuals are now far more self-conscious or reflexive (Giddens 1991) it does not mean that they can only be so as *consumers*. What the Thatcher, Reagan and (in New Zealand) Douglas revolution did was to structure the development of a human potential for reflexivity into a political project based on consumer choice. Potentially knowledgeable citizens have been encouraged to channel their understanding into becoming 'smart' consumers. The result, as Richard Wilkinson (1996: 226) has acutely observed, is that

> Whenever we leave our homes, we face the world with two perfect symbols of the nature of social relations on the street. Cash equips us to take part in transactions mediated by the market, while keys protect our private gains from each other's envy and greed.

What this political project has done in education is to convert a partially meritocratic competition relying on a degree of civic mindedness and trust in the state into a largely private competition between families. Of course, as Coleman has argued, there are two fundamental contradictory principles involved here: the interests of the nation and the natural interest of parents in wanting the best for their children. The problem, as critics of education markets see it, is that parental choice shifts the balance too far towards private interest, enabling those with more cash to unlock the doors to gaining credentials.

Testing the hypotheses of the critics of markets in education

Looked at in this way the debate over education markets is actually a clash of competing visions of society, economic efficiency and social justice. It is not surprising that the debate has been so intense.

But these differing views of the role of education in society are mirrored in some of the details of the debate, particularly in relation to the specific predictions that proponents and critics of the market would make about the outcomes of education markets.

Critics of the market have a fundamental concern that educational opportunities will become polarized, just as incomes have been polarized. This could occur if middle class families use their advantage in the market to send their children to popular schools because such schools attract children from similar backgrounds, leaving once socially well-mixed schools as working class ghettos.

There are two reasons for thinking socially well-mixed schools are desirable. Since Dewey (1916) there has been a view shared by social democrats that schools have a signal role to play in creating the foundations for democracy. One important way in which they do this is by bringing children from different social backgrounds together, so that by learning together they also learn about and develop tolerance for one another's lifestyles and cultures.

There is also a strong body of evidence (McPherson and Willms 1987; Lauder and Hughes 1990b; Steinberg et al. 1996; Thrupp 1996, 1997, 1999) which suggests that the better the social balance of school intakes is, the better, overall, students will achieve. Hence, polarization would have two undesirable consequences: it would erode one of the educational foundations of democracy and reduce educational achievement. New Right proponents of education markets may not be unduly concerned about the question of democracy because they see the essence of human freedom as being consumer sovereignty (Lauder 1997). However, they would be acutely concerned if markets led to a reduction in educational achievement, since their major justification for them is that they will lead to standards rising. With these issues in mind we should turn to the specific sequence of hypotheses that can be developed from the position proposed by the critics of education markets:

1 Choice in education markets will be determined by social class, gender and ethnicity.
2 Education markets will polarize school intakes.
3 Polarization will cause schools in working class areas to enter a spiral of decline as better off students leave for middle class schools. In turn this will cause a decline in funding, teacher and student morale and, therefore, student performance.
4 Polarization of school intakes will, therefore, lead to a decline in achievement for the children of blue collar workers and the unemployed.
5 Where demand for popular schools exceeds supply and schools are able to choose their students, they will do so on the basis of social class and ethnicity.
6 For blue collar and unemployed parents, notional choice of school will not add to their interest and involvement in their children's education because they will have, in effect, little choice.
7 Schools will not become more diverse. As the diploma disease intensifies, schools will be judged mainly on their credential outcomes.

Not surprisingly these hypotheses are almost the mirror image of those of market proponents. Both sets of hypotheses are at a fairly general level; the task in seeking to test them is to be able to translate them into far more specific claims about the effects of markets. In the process, both sets will become refined and modified. As with the hypotheses advanced by the proponents of markets some of the assumptions underlying the claims made by critics of marketization need elaboration.

The starting point is that these claims reflect the view of a society divided by social class, ethnicity and gender. Critics predict that society will become more polarized as a result of education markets. The source of this polarization will be that choice of school will largely be determined by social class. Polarization of intake in this case means *over and above* that which would be predicted from residential segregation according to social class and ethnicity. Schools are already divided by intake caused by residential segregation, as Coleman (1990a) noted. The issue, then, is whether education markets exacerbate the situation. Under market systems of education, school funding is determined by the number of students a school can attract. If numbers decline, so does funding, with predicted effects on the morale of the school. In such cases it is the very students about whom governments most express concern who would be most adversely affected by education markets. These include underperforming students from blue collar and unemployed homes, and post-colonial peoples who would be trapped in ghetto schools because it would be in the interests of middle class parents and schools to keep them there.

The reason for this is that the middle class would gravitate to schools populated with children with similar backgrounds. This would be quite 'rational' in that the social class intake of a school is the best predictor of a school's exam performance (Lauder 1997). Equally, it would be 'rational' for oversubscribed schools to choose white middle class students, where they were able to (Moore and Davenport 1990). It is for this reason that Coleman's (1992) view that markets would get the incentives right for parents *and* schools is open to challenge. If the parents and schools are middle class his view might be correct, but if the school is middle class and the applicants are working class there is a conflict of interest, as we document in Chapters 4 and 5.

Before we can judge whether critics of marketization should give pro-market policy makers pause for thought we need to consider some of the factors which influence the way markets are created, for the way they are structured will have a determinant effect on their outcomes. There is a world of difference between abstract models of market competition and the way they are applied in practice. Inevitably, their introduction is as much a matter of political conflict as it is of applying a rational blueprint. Certainly in New Zealand the nature of the market that was introduced can only be understood in these terms. It is these issues that we discuss in the following chapter.

three

Structuring the market: global orthodoxies, local politics

Among many policy advisors around the globe, the idea that markets can provide optimal outcomes in education has become orthodoxy. Recently, one of the Smithfield team (see the Appendix) was in Jakarta interviewing the Director of Secondary Education, on whose desk was a copy of Lou Gerstner's *Reinventing Education: Entrepreneurship in America's Public Schools*. Ideas may travel quickly around the globe but they do not travel at random. Powerful global agencies such as the World Bank, the IMF and the OECD are sympathetic to such concepts as decentralization, privatization and markets in state education (see, for example, World Bank 1995) and help spread them around the world. Indeed, the World Bank has sought to impose these ideas in the so-called Third World. The problem is that it is one thing to entertain an ideal notion of how markets should work and it is another thing altogether to realize that ideal when markets are actually introduced.

Some proponents of the marketization of education assume that markets are the natural expression of what they perceive to be the dominant and inherent characteristics of human beings: the pursuit of self-interest (Lauder 1990). Not all intellectuals of the New Right take this view. Indeed, Hayek (1976), one of the most influential political economists in this tradition, expressly argued that market systems have to be imposed in order to make individuals 'rational' in the sense of pursuing their self-interest. For Hayek it is the advent of market societies that will produce human progress. Markets, therefore, need to be constructed. But as Polanyi (1957) has argued, it is inevitable that the construction of markets will involve the expression of political interests. Markets are neither 'natural' nor can they be constructed to exclude cultural and political influences.

If the case for the introduction of education markets was as clear-cut, because rational, as many of its proponents assume, we would expect a general trend towards market policies throughout the world. But that is not the case, despite much rhetoric to that effect. The predominant trends are towards de-centralizing education systems (Whitty *et al.* 1998) and encouraging pluralism within them. In some cases this involves the introduction of market mechanisms and in others it does not. For example, the United States has moved from 'the one best system', that of comprehensive education, to one where a variety of 'experiments' are being conducted, some of which involve parental choice. The same can be said of France, where nearly half the schools are involved in a system of limited parental choice (Ambler 1994). In Germany, which retains a strong egalitarian commitment, only one Länd or province has developed a major initiative in school autonomy and parental participation in school decision making (Weiss 1993). In contrast, some countries like Japan have ignored this trend altogether; it is most unlikely that its highly centralized education system, based on egalitarian principles, will change.

These examples illustrate that there is a diversity of responses to the political and economic forces now confronting governments and educational systems. How states respond will be governed, to some extent, by whether they see markets as a 'solution' to their political problems. In countries with strong egalitarian commitments this is unlikely, but in others, like America or Britain where there is a strong emphasis on individualism, markets may well be seen as the answer to their economic and political problems in education. Codd, Gordon and Harker (1997) argue that faced with the current pressures on the financing of education, the state has to contend with a crisis of legitimacy. In other words, it has to rationalize why it will not spend more on education to the electorate while seeking to reduce the demand for greater educational expenditure. Decentralization and parental choice fit the bill. If schools have the autonomy to set wages and hire and fire teachers, trade union solidarity may be broken because each school will have different work conditions: in some schools teachers could be paid a lot more than in others, and better paid teachers would have little reason to support their poorer colleagues. At the same time the power of teachers' unions to press for more educational resources would be weakened. Community and parental involvement is introduced to cover the problem of legitimacy. Parents are offered a trade-off between the promise of greater power over their children's education and the provision of fewer resources. In our view, this is a bargain that professional middle class parents may readily accept because they have the resources to make up the shortfall in state funding while the rules of the educational competition are shifted in their favour; it is another matter for working class parents.

There are other factors promoting pluralism and diversity in educational provision which present governments with a dilemma. For example, we pointed out in Chapter 2 that the social class mix of schools may have a significant influence on their performance. However, the development of identity politics, especially in relation to those groups who, historically, have suffered the many varieties of colonialism, has introduced a new dynamic into the politics of education. Members of these groups, whether they be Afro-Americans, Maori in New Zealand or Muslims in Britain, have demanded culturally autonomous schools for their children. This demand runs counter to the idea that educational performance can be raised for all if schools take children from diverse social class and ethnic backgrounds. For post-colonial people, the hope is that the power of cultural autonomy in education, coupled with the energy and commitment associated with the renewal of cultural identity, will raise educational outcomes. In this case the state's capacity to act 'in policy areas where the passions, identities, collectively shared meanings . . . are the essential parameters which need to be changed' (Offe 1990: 247) is severely limited.[1] Under these circumstances pluralism within educational systems appears a rational response.

This discussion has suggested that whether markets are introduced into education and (if so) the shape they will take will be determined by the history, culture and politics of that particular society. It is therefore naive to argue as some have (for example Tooley 1996) that a 'genuine' market system of education can be established. In such thinking the 'genuine' market is identical in its appeal to right-wing idealists as communism was to the Left.

It follows from this analysis that it is part of the essential background to our research that we describe the political struggle determining the nature of education markets in New Zealand. For the way markets are constructed will have a determinant effect on their outcomes.

Local policies: the political struggle over education markets in New Zealand

Since 1987 education in New Zealand has been fundamentally restructured. This restructuring should be seen against the backdrop of attempts by successive governments to create a market society in New Zealand according to New Right principles. The changes in New Zealand were implemented faster and have gone further than anywhere else in the world. New Zealand has a reputation as a country of social experiment. It was the first country to give women the vote and also developed a welfare state system in advance of that in Britain or the United States. The new social experiment of creating a market society gave the nation the soubriquet of the New Right laboratory of the world (Kelsey 1995).

The key features of educational change were the speed with which it was effected, the exclusion of teachers from policy development concerning the 'reforms', and – perhaps most significantly – the fact that in its first four years the model of educational organization was changed three times. These changes occurred against a background of constant criticism about the educational system from influential New Right state agencies such as the Treasury and New Right pressure groups like the Business Round Table, a grouping of leading industrialists. In 1987 the New Zealand Treasury, which had become convinced by the rhetoric of markets as a panacea for New Zealand's economic problems, published one of the most extensive manifestos extolling the virtues of markets in education to be found anywhere in the Western world (The Treasury 1987). This document effectively formed the blueprint which has been used by successive administrations to press educational policy ever further in the direction of the 'pure' market.

The struggle for ownership of educational change: 1988–91

Prior to 1987, New Zealand education was run by a centralized bureaucratic system of education. Approximately 90 per cent of school expenditure was determined by the Department of Education in New Zealand's capital, Wellington. The rules and procedures which governed the conduct of school administration were also centrally determined, often by discussions between the teacher unions and the Department of Education. There was centralized bargaining over teachers' work conditions, and schools were zoned. In addition there was an intermediate tier of regional boards between the Department of Education and the schools; this provided a system of services to the schools in their areas.

Several criticisms of this system were made by educational practitioners: the system tended to be slow and inflexible; it didn't encourage innovation (although it certainly didn't preclude it); and it was elitist in that a third of students left school at the age of 15 having failed the national School Certificate examination, while only roughly 13 per cent went on to university. The system also tolerated high degrees of inequality with respect to women, Maori and working class students – although, of course, research has demonstrated quite clearly that these inequalities are not primarily caused by the educational system, although it may exacerbate or ameliorate them.

Despite these problems, there was a high degree of support for the primary and secondary school systems as shown by a survey published in 1988 by the Royal Commission on Social Policy.

In 1987, the Minister of Education, David Lange, appointed a task force, under the leadership of Auckland supermarket magnate Brian Picot, to review educational administration. In 1988 it produced its report, *Administering for Excellence*. The document can be considered a compromise between two different views about the path educational reform should take. The first path, one endorsed by teachers, advocated devolution but on the basis of a partnership between teachers and the local community. It promised to provide teachers with greater control over their resources and hence greater professional autonomy, with a resulting improvement in the educational outcomes of their students. The second path signalled by Picot was of an altogether different nature: this was the path of the marketization of education, by which schools would be modelled on small businesses and would have to compete with one another. The relationship between schools and parents would thus become that of producer and consumer. In a sense, then, Picot set up the terms of struggle, which continues to this day, between educationists and parents on the one hand, and the New Right-inspired vision of a 'pure' education market on the other.

What Picot advocated was a decentralized system of education in which elected parents, the principal, a teacher and a student representative would constitute a Board of Trustees for each school and would have oversight over the general principles governing that school's policy. These principles would be encapsulated in a charter of objectives which had to be ratified by the Ministry of Education and which constituted a quasi-legal contract between the state and individual schools. Boards of Trustees and their schools would be empowered to achieve their objectives through the devolution of approximately 90 per cent of funding to schools, which would then be able to set priorities and determine how the money could best be spent. This meant that the middle tier of state-provided services would be abolished and schools could buy their services from private providers. In addition, Picot held that there were no good grounds for zoning: parental choice should govern where children went to school, although every child had the right to go to its local neighbourhood school. Finally, for schools with a high proportion of Maori students, who were considered disadvantaged, and/or schools in areas of high unemployment, Picot advocated limited extra compensatory funding.

The ambiguities in Picot led to different interpretations which turned on the two most decisive issues in the debate on decentralization and markets. The first concerned the decentralized funding system. The bulk grant to be delivered to schools was divided between an operational grant for the day-to-day running of the school and a grant for teachers' salaries. The Picot model was some way away from the salary-funding model desired by proponents of marketization because it retained the idea of a nationally negotiated pay scale for teachers. Nevertheless, within this context it allowed room for manoeuvre to permit funds to be transferred between operational and salaries accounts: schools then would be free to trade-off computers against teachers, for example. However, the wording of this provision was quite ambiguous. Clearly, once it became possible for schools freely to transfer their funds from one account to the other, wide discrepancies between schools in staff–student ratios could arise and teachers' job security was threatened. Given that most of the members of each Board of

Trustees were parents, this recommendation opened the door for considerable conflict, instead of cooperation, between parents and teachers.

The second example of a significant ambiguity concerned the question of zoning. According to the Picot report, there were no good grounds for zoning: parents should be able, in principle, to send their children to the school of their choice. However, Picot also said that parents should have the absolute right to send their children to their local neighbourhood school. The problem is that it has been estimated that only 15 to 20 per cent of parents need to take their children away from a school before it becomes economically non-viable, so it is possible for a neighbourhood school to be closed down because of the exercise of consumer choice. Under these circumstances which principle will prevail, the right of a community to a neighbourhood school, or the dictates of the market?

The Labour government responded to the Picot report in its document *Tomorrow's Schools* (Lange 1988). For the most part it endorsed Picot's proposals, but during the course of developing the policies for their implementation, significant changes were made which produced a quite different model of devolution: one closer to the model of community participation endorsed by teachers. The government included several non-negotiable items in the charter objectives with respect to gender, ethnic and class equity, which it expected all schools to achieve. It limited the de-zoning and hence parental choice available. Maximum rolls were set for all schools, although these were based on a very liberal interpretation of the capacity of schools in order to encourage market competition. Zones were retained by schools where there was an excess of demand over capacity. Local students were guaranteed attendance through home zones while 'out-of-zone' enrolments were decided by ballot. While the state did not actively mediate parental choice by, for example, ensuring an even distribution of students across the range of prior achievements, the use of the ballot for surplus places obviated the possibility of social class or ethnic bias which might have occurred had schools been able to choose their students. As we shall see in the next chapter, there is some evidence that oversubscribed schools which use a ballot to determine their roll are less likely to be biased in the recruitment of students than schools which select their students.

Tomorrow's Schools retreated from a commitment to the devolution of funds relating to teachers' salaries and widened the criteria by which schools could qualify for compensatory funding to include schools with a high proportion of students from working class backgrounds. In addition, schools were not allowed to use fundraising income to augment staff salaries or staff positions. At the time this did not seem a significant point, but subsequent developments have made it so, as we shall see.

This model was far more acceptable to teachers and constituted an interesting compromise system that sought to satisfy national *and* local interests and needs. The danger in any move to devolution, as we noted previously, is that it can create the conditions by which the power of those with a direct interest in education (parents, teachers and students) is seriously weakened by a process of divide and rule. It is a means by which governments can devolve responsibility without devolving the necessary financial power to fulfil that responsibility. In this context, parents and teachers can be played off against one another and the state can blame schools in financial difficulty for their misfortunes because financial responsibility has been devolved to them.

In the event, the *Tomorrow's Schools* model was short lived, having only one year in operation. In 1990, the Labour government lost the election and the National party was returned to government. For the New Right, the *Tomorrow's Schools* policies represented a victory for the providers of education (teachers) and a retreat from the introduction of market principles in education. The Business Round Table found the National government by and large sympathetic to its views. The Business Round Table commissioned Stuart Sexton, an educational advisor to Margaret Thatcher's government, to write a report (the Sexton Report 1991) on New Zealand education. Many of his recommendations were taken up: the non-negotiable equity objectives in the school charter were no longer mandatory, schools were de-zoned to open up competition between them and the question of the devolved funding of teachers' salaries was reintroduced. For market proponents, the two key issues, which Sexton endorsed, were freedom of choice for parents and full autonomy for schools in the way they spent their funds. Without choice there is no market and without autonomy schools cannot engage in a full range of entrepreneurial activities such as expanding to meet demand or improving 'quality' by buying more 'expensive' teachers.

The incoming National government took a significant step down the road charted by Sexton in the 1991 Education Amendment Act, which set the rules for the operation of markets in New Zealand to this day. Home zones were abolished and enrolment schemes established for schools at serious risk of overcrowding. The details of enrolment schemes are currently left up to the discretion of individual oversubscribed schools, although they must not breach the requirements of the Race Relations Act (1971), the Human Rights Commission Act (1977) and the Bill of Rights Act (1990). The introduction of school-chosen enrolment schemes is significant because it may have a decisive impact on the theory and practice of education markets. This is because enrolment schemes allow oversubscribed schools to choose their students, thereby effectively insulating them from competition. Since there is no compulsion to take local students the stakes are high, because it is schools with high middle class intakes that are likely to be most oversubscribed. Assuming that such schools will see middle class students as most likely to succeed in exams it could be predicted that enrolment schemes will favour middle class students and exacerbate existing inequalities between schools. If so, the market proponents' assumption that there will be equality of choice within the market is cast into doubt and their critics' view that marketization is simply designed to increase the privilege of the already privileged is confirmed.

What was omitted from the policy was reference to the question of school autonomy over funding, which has been a source of conflict ever since. In the event, while schools can compete for students according to the rules described, they can only do so within the existing allocation of capacity; they cannot engage in the kind of entrepreneurial behaviour desired by the proponents of markets.

The overriding point to be made about the history of this struggle is that by and large the new system of schooling was imposed.[2] It had little popular support, but was driven by an ideological blueprint supported by the rather scant evidence in favour of markets we described in Chapter 1. New Zealanders had prided themselves on the egalitarian policies established by the first Labour government in the 1930s, and to many the introduction of markets in education broke faith with the myth that every child was entitled to a 'fair go'. However, true to the idea that New Zealand had become a social laboratory for the world, the fact that a relatively uniform market regime was established in education did allow for many of the claims made by market proponents to be tested. If you will, the New Zealand education system after 1991 constituted a natural experiment. It was our good fortune that we were given the opportunity to undertake the testing.

We now turn to an examination of the claims of the proponents and critics of the markets in education, starting with the two basic questions. Firstly, is there systematic social class inequality of choice within the market? And secondly, are schools rather than parents determining school intakes, by selecting students on the basis of social class and ethnicity?

four

Choice and power in the market

In this chapter we focus on the fundamental question of whether parents come as equals in their knowledge of the education market and in their ability to send their children to schools of their choice. If parents from differing social and ethnic backgrounds have that equality, then the basic pro-market assumptions about how markets should work will be confirmed. If, however, this assumption is not confirmed, then the view of market critics that education is a site of struggle over credentials is likely to be a more powerful predictor of educational outcomes.

How will parents act in education markets? Competing theoretical assumptions

Pro-market advocates tend to take a straightforward view of the key issues of choice, knowledge and the nature of education markets. They assume that parents will make choices which are in their children's best interests and that choice of schools will be the result of 'rational' cost–benefit analysis. Since market behaviour is fundamentally about economic calculations it is assumed that all parents will seek to send their children to schools which will be most successful in providing them with high level credentials. Of course, parents may have quite different assumptions as to what kind of school will best provide this service, which is why markets are supposed to encourage diversity. In making these choices parents will act logically by ranking a set of preferences against schools to see which one best fits their priorities. For example, preferences may be listed in order of priority by one family as: (i) high academic standards (ii) good discipline, and (iii) student happiness. The school which best fits this ranking is the school these parents will choose.

The knowledge parents need to make these choices is also considered relatively unproblematic and to be of the same order as the knowledge needed in any other market. Information about school performance from league tables and inspectors' reports coupled with that gained from school prospectuses is considered sufficient to enable parents to make informed choices. If parents initially do not have the necessary knowledge, then their interest in their children's educational progress will ensure that they will acquire it.

This view of knowledge cannot be divorced from the view of education markets that is taken by its advocates. It is assumed that there are no barriers to access across schools within the market, and this includes access to the knowledge required to make informed choices. The only barrier considered is that of the possible costs of travel, and this can be remedied by travel subsidies to those that cannot afford transport. In essence, then, markets are viewed as open and undifferentiated in the access they afford to parents.

The view taken by social conflict theorists of choice, knowledge and the nature of education markets is quite different. In Chapter 2 we noted that our own research and that of others had shown that the aims and significance of education are interpreted differently by working class and middle class students (Brown 1987; Lauder *et al.* 1992b). We coined the term *wisdom of the class* to describe the different frames of reference within which education is understood by different social class groups. The wisdom of the class refers to the rules, norms, tacit assumptions and horizons which govern the understanding of education of different social classes. These contrasting class wisdoms about the content and aims of education and hence about its meaning and significance have profound implications for the theories underpinning the marketization of education. For if different groups view the 'products', 'services' and signals of education markets in radically different ways, then it follows that these markets are not at all like those for, say, Coca-Cola or Pepsi. It also means that there is neither equality in the knowledge and expectations of parents, nor in the way that parents are responded to by schools.

Support for this view comes from the seminal work of Stephen Ball and his associates at King's College in London. In a key paper (Ball *et al.* 1997) they report that the reputations of schools in their study were exclusive to specific groups, *so* exclusive in fact that they comment, 'The point is that these reputations . . . are not even apparent to other "local choosers"' (p. 411).

The King's team also point to a second feature of education markets, namely that they are based on middle class consumption patterns and are, in that sense, 'rigged' in favour of them. Far from being undifferentiated, as market advocates assume, education markets are closely linked to families' lifestyles and thus differ according to class. The consumption process is informed by the social networks (the family, work, 'contacts'), the conception and use of social space and by the distribution of personal finance and 'knowing the system'.

Underpinning this claim is a wealth of detailed research on the contexts within which the different classes make educational 'choices'. Following Bourdieu's lead, they point out, for example, that working class ways of life remain organized around the practical business of getting by. Space and family organization are key elements in choice-making. As one of their interviewees put it:

> They catch the bus . . . there's a few children that go to the school, they live in the other road . . . in the morning, my parents . . . they take them because they have to go that way . . . I think you have to think of that now . . . where they go.
>
> (Ball *et al*. 1997: 412)

For their working class respondents, space, time and travel are closely tied to the choice of school. This is especially so for low income households. The fact that many of these families do not have readily accessible transport reinforces the emphasis on the local. The issue here, as these researchers emphasize, is not merely one of the limitations of time and space but, rather, that they are interwoven into a network of social obligations and reciprocal favours. Care givers, usually mothers, have to ensure that their children go to schools where they can be dropped off and picked up by relatives and neighbours when they, as is often the case, are unable to do so.

In contrast, for their middle class respondents, the interweaving of social networks and obligations is not so closely textured. They may have similar social obligations but their networks are more widely dispersed and they have another essential advantage: time horizons and 'the imagination of time'. According to the King's studies their middle class interviewees were more likely to imagine their children's futures in terms of the professions they took up (Ball *et al*. 1997: 412). At a most basic level these class differences will reflect material differences such as access to cars, telephones and flexibility in terms of paid work commitments.

The differences in the perception of education and the ability to access schools leads the King's team to the conjecture that choice of school is structured according to what they call *circuits*. In a neighbourhood, schools are divided according to their social class intake: Ball and colleagues hypothesize that high circuit schools will be those considered by professional middle class parents because they largely draw on a middle class intake. In contrast, low circuit schools, which have a majority of working class students, will be considered by working class parents. Parents may not articulate their preferences in terms of the social class composition of a circuit of schools; perhaps instead they may think in terms of 'reputation'. For example, those in the high circuit may be said to have good or excellent reputations for academic results whereas those in low circuits may have reputations for discipline, community participation and so on. In this way preferences and the opportunities that schools can offer are structured according to social class. Of course it is an open question – which we will test – as to whether parents' perceptions of the social class intake of a school are accurate.

In effect what this account does is to provide a way of hypothesizing how the wisdom of the professional middle class is *translated* into advantage within the market context. If as Brown (1997b) and the King's College team predict, market 'opportunity' structures will enhance the power of the middle class to gain an advantage for their children, we should expect to see the statistical expression of this advantage in the circuits of schooling theorized by Ball, Bowe and Gewirtz (1997).

This advantage will be reinforced by the ability of middle class parents to 'play the game' both to gain access to the schools of their choice and to ensure that as Lareau (1997) has shown, they achieve a customized education for their children. As we noted in Chapter 2, middle class parents have an underlying confidence that enables them to exploit the market to their own advantage; this is derived from their own cultural capital, success and familiarity with the conventions of middle class schooling.

Clearly the debate over education markets is based on quite different theories of choice, knowledge and the nature of education markets. In essence they constitute radically different views of the social world and the role of education within it. We will now turn to testing the theories in order to decide between them.

Testing the competing theories of educational choice

If markets are structured in the way hypothesized by social conflict theory it would be expected that the patterns of opportunity for access to middle class schools would be reflected in the patterns of choice and enrolment. We would expect that professional middle class parents would, by and large, choose high circuit schools, while white collar middle class parents would choose middle circuit schools and working class parents, low circuit schools. If this is not the case and there is a random distribution across the social class spectrum of parents' choices, then it follows that pro-market theories based on neo-classical economic assumptions will be confirmed.

In New Zealand, circuits may often be related to school type, in particular whether a school is single sex or co-educational. In this respect, it can be hypothesized that two key criteria for determining circuit will be school credential outcomes and the social class intake of the school. As we shall see, however, there may also be a significant gender dimension to choice with respect to single-sex schools, over and above that of class in our study, which we need to take into account.

The investigation of parental and school choice was undertaken in two of New Zealand's major cities, Green City and Central City. The details of the sample and methods used are in the Appendix. The school types included in the circuits are as follows:

High circuit

state:	1 co-educational
	1 single-sex boys'
	1 single-sex girls'
private:	3 single-sex boys'
	1 single-sex girls'
integrated:	2 single-sex boys'
	1 single-sex girls'

Middle circuit

state:	10 co-educational
	1 single-sex boys'
	1 single-sex girls'
integrated:	1 single-sex boys'
	1 single-sex girls'

Low circuit

state:	9 co-educational
integrated:	2 co-educational (Catholic)

We begin testing the competing theories of educational choice by documenting the process of educational decision making over time. There is a temporal and conceptual sequence that can be hypothesized in any process of parental choice of school. First, parents need information on the schools available in the market. Next, they have to select the schools they will seriously consider and gather more information about them if necessary. Third, they have to apply for a school or schools. If the preferred school has no enrolment scheme a single application may suffice. On the other hand, if the preferred school does have an enrolment scheme, a back-up application may be required. If the back-up school also has an enrolment scheme, a third application may be considered necessary, and so on. Fourth, places are offered. Where schools do not have an enrolment scheme, offers will be made to all applicants, but where an enrolment scheme is in place the choice process shifts to the school which has to select those to whom it will offer places. Finally the parents take up an offer and enrol their son or daughter. For some this will be a matter of taking the single place on offer, but for others there will be a choice to be made among alternative places offered. Conceptually, the sequence takes parents through a process from their ideal choice to the reality of which school gates the child enters at the beginning of the school year.

Class and circuits

Turning to the first step in this process, pro-market theories tend to assume that parents have widespread knowledge of the various schools that they could send their children to and, indeed, of the 'pecking order' of schools according to credential outcomes. In contrast, Ball, Bowe and Gewirtz (1997) found that working class parents had no knowledge of the upper circuit schools available to them. The question, then, is whether there is a significant social class difference in knowledge of the schools available to parents and, if so, the degree to which they consider these schools desirable for their own child. Our way of getting at this issue was to ask parents where they would really like their child to go to secondary school *assuming things like money and distance were no object*.

Table 4.1 shows that overall, 68 per cent of parents gave a high circuit school as their ideal, and that this percentage was approximately the same for all parents regardless of their socioeconomic status (SES) background. The differences between the SES groups are very small and not significant, which suggests that, by and large, parents across the board are aware that there is a hierarchy of schools. Clearly, then, in this particular sample there is considerable agreement as to what are considered the most and least 'desirable' schools across the SES groups. The finding of a hierarchy of schools appears to be at odds with that of the King's group and supports the assumption made by pro-market advocates that parents have widespread knowledge of which schools are perceived to be most 'desirable'. However, while they may have this information in the abstract, according to social conflict theory they may have neither the knowledge nor networks that enable them to convert this information into access to schools.

The crucial issue in deciding between theories of parental choice, therefore, turns on what parents consider to be *feasible* choices rather than their ideal choice. If the social conflict theory of schooling provides a more plausible account of how parents make choices, it follows that there should be systematic differences in the circuit of schools parents actually consider. We

Table 4.1 Circuit of school of ideal choice, by SES (per cent)

	High circuit	Middle circuit	Low circuit	(N)
High	69	25	5	111
Middle	66	30	4	113
Low	68	25	7	60
Total	68	27	5	284

(Chi-square = 1.55, df = 4, p = 0.818)

Table 4.2   Highest circuit of school considered, by SES (per cent)

	High circuit	Middle circuit	Low circuit	(N)
High	60	33	6	111
Middle	55	40	6	113
Low	38	47	15	60
Total	53	38	8	284

(Chi-square = 9.89, df = 4, p = 0.042)

look now at this issue. We asked parents which schools they had actually considered or would consider for their children. The responses were classified into school circuits, and the highest circuit considered was analysed by SES.

It can be seen from Table 4.2 that there are significant SES differences in the highest circuit of school parents reported had been or would be considered. Whereas 60 per cent of high SES parents named a high circuit school among those they had considered or would consider, only 6 per cent of them named only a school or schools in the low circuit. For low SES families, the difference is significantly less pronounced, with 38 per cent considering a high circuit school and 15 per cent a low circuit school.

While the shifts from Table 4.1 to Table 4.2 are in the same direction for all SES groups, there is a greater proportional shift for parents in the low SES group. Sixty per cent of the high SES families have considered or say they will consider a high circuit school. This is 87 per cent of the 69 per cent of high SES families whose school of ideal choice was a high circuit school. The equivalent figures for the middle and low SES families are 83 and 56 per cent.

If, as market proponents argue, all consumers have access to knowledge as information, why do parents from differing SES backgrounds activate this knowledge in differing ways? What initially appears so surprising about the changes between Tables 4.1 and 4.2 is that there is no time lapse or period of reflection to inform their judgements. There is a clear sense that while many parents (especially lower SES parents) are aware of the existence of high circuit schools, they do not consider access to such schools feasible. Already it appears as if the inequalities of the market have begun to structure parental aspiration and consideration of schools. This disjuncture between ideal school and the schools considered suggests that these data patterns are more consistent with social conflict theory than pro-market theory, at least in its 'pure' form. Pro-market theory would predict that both 'ideal' and 'considered' schools would be distributed randomly through the population, but the data show that schools considered are socially divided.

Table 4.3   Circuit of school preferred from those available, by SES (per cent)[1]

	High circuit	Middle circuit	Low circuit	(N)
High	59	34	7	642
Middle	42	45	13	684
Low	26	43	31	558
Total	43	41	16	1884

(Chi-square = 198.50, df = 4, p = 0.000)

The interviews were conducted prior to most parents' active engagement in making choices. Once the students were enrolled in the schools (approximately ten months later) we asked parents to tell us, retrospectively, about the choices that they had made. This enabled us to estimate the influence of engagement with the market over time.

Table 4.3 shows the results obtained to the question 'of the secondary schools available to you, which one did you most want your son/daughter to go to?' Clearly this is not the same question as the ideal choice question, which asked parents to ignore costs and travel considerations when selecting their school of first choice. It is more closely related to the question of which schools parents were considering.

The results show highly significant differences. High SES parents clearly prefer high circuit schools from those available to them, with almost 60 per cent choosing such schools and only 7 per cent preferring low circuit schools. Middle SES parents are almost equally split between high and middle circuit schools, with roughly 45 per cent preferring each type and 13 per cent preferring low circuit schools. As with the middle SES group, almost 45 per cent of low SES parents prefer middle circuit schools; but in contrast to the middle SES group, substantial numbers prefer schools in the low circuit.

When we compare these results with those from Table 4.2, it is clear that over time there have been changes in parental perception of schools between those they have considered and those they subsequently preferred. There has been little change in the preferences of high SES parents over time; in fact the percentages are remarkable for their consistency. However, there has been a significant drop in the number of middle and low SES parents who prefer high circuit schools, while the number who stated a preference for a low circuit school has doubled. In the intervening ten-month period, middle and low SES parents appear to have been systematically 'cooled out' in terms of the schools they once considered and now prefer. It is tempting to hypothesize that over this period the preferences of high SES parents have hardened in favour of schools that are likely to yield better

Table 4.4 Highest circuit of school applied for, by SES (per cent)

	High circuit	Middle circuit	Low circuit	(N)
High	63	31	6	645
Middle	44	44	12	681
Low	25	41	35	554
Total	44	39	17	1880

(Chi-square = 248.15, df = 4, p = 0.000)

exam results; while even if middle and low SES parents have the same motivation, they clearly do not think that such choices are either possible or preferable.

We should note that while conceptually there is a linear progression between ideal, considered and preferred, we asked the question about which school parents preferred after their child was attending a specific school. It is therefore possible that judgements about school of preference were coloured by the experience of gaining access to a school. But as we shall see the trends remain consistent between schools parents considered, preferred and then applied for.

Table 4.4 shows the highest circuit of school applied for, by SES. When we compare Table 4.4 with Table 4.3, we find that there are approximately as many parents who stated a preference for a school in a particular circuit as applied for a school in that circuit.

However, to apply is not necessarily to be accepted. Social conflict theory suggests that there may be a systematic bias in the ways in which oversub-scribed schools select students. Clearly, therefore, we need to investigate the process of selection by schools.

Do schools select students on the basis of SES?

Intriguingly it is at the point of school selection that social conflict theory and the logic of the market almost meet. The logic of the market suggests that schools will recruit the students who will increase their standing; hence, where possible, schools will recruit those most likely to enhance exam results. The twist that social conflict theory gives to this 'logic' is that it claims that it is those students from professional middle class back-grounds who are likely to constitute the best 'bet' in terms of producing the best exam results. It is worth noting here that pro-market advocates like Coleman have glossed over this point. Given these theoretical consider-ations the question is whether, on the basis of market 'logic' and social

Table 4.5 Percentage chance of being accepted for six selected schools, by SES (with Ns in brackets)

| | School | | | | | |
	A	B	C	D	E	F
High	75 (28)	75 (60)	91 (69)	70 (27)	85 (13)	87 (32)
Middle	61 (28)	74 (69)	83 (71)	86 (79)	93 (29)	95 (79)
Low	17 (12)	60 (20)	46 (28)	78 (37)	63 (8)	83 (58)
Total	59 (68)	73 (149)	80 (168)	81 (143)	86 (50)	89 (169)

conflict theory, schools with enrolment schemes do select on the basis of SES.

Most schools which are able to operate enrolment schemes are in the high circuit, so in our initial investigation of this question, for each of our SES groups we divided the number of acceptances for high circuit schools by the number of applications for high circuit schools. Whereas 88 per cent of the applications for high circuit schools from high SES students resulted in acceptances, 85 per cent and 72 per cent of applications from middle and low SES families were successful. So it does seem possible that selection by schools is based on SES. However, these percentages take no account of achievement or other variables which may be influential in the process of selection by schools and which are correlated with SES. We will return to consider the part played by SES after controlling for such variables later in this section.

To explore further the process of selection by schools we looked at patterns of acceptance in six schools drawn from both cities. The selected schools were those which (i) were state schools, (ii) attracted at least 50 applicants from our Smithfield sample and (iii) rejected the applications of at least 10 per cent of those applicants. These schools were selected because it would be difficult to argue a convincing case that it is appropriate for state schools to be selecting on the basis of SES, a sample of 50 plus was needed to give reasonably stable results, and schools rejecting at least 10 per cent of their applicants have the potential for discrimination. Table 4.5 shows the chance of being accepted for each of the schools, by SES.

Four of the schools are high circuit (A, B, C and E) and two are middle circuit schools (D and F). Four had home zones and interviewed out-of-zone applicants[2] (schools B, C, E and F), one had a home zone, accepted siblings and balloted extra places to out-of-zone applicants (school D), while one admitted siblings and selected all others on the basis of interview (school A). The six schools show markedly different patterns of acceptance. In schools A, C, E and to a lesser extent B and F, students from lower SES backgrounds appear to have a reduced chance of being accepted when compared with students from other backgrounds. School D is particularly interesting from a policy perspective because the use of the ballot for out-of-zone students has resulted in the most 'egalitarian' distribution.

However, it is difficult to interpret the figures in Table 4.5 in any detail because of the home zones. It would be possible for a school discriminating against low SES families to appear to treat low SES students equally or even favourably because a greater proportion of the within-zone students came from low SES backgrounds. For example, suppose a school accepted the applications of 80 per cent of both the low SES and high SES families who applied for it. Suppose further that this school operated a home zone and received 40 within-zone and ten out-of-zone applications from students from low SES families, and 20 within-zone and 30 out-of-zone applications from high SES families. The school could reject all ten out-of-zone low SES applications and accept two-thirds of the high SES out-of-zone applications in reaching the 80 per cent acceptance rates. The apparent even-handedness is illusory and the school is operating in a discriminatory fashion where it actually has a choice. Of course, a school might appear to be discriminating against low SES students even when it was not, if a large proportion of its within-zone applications were from high SES families.

As was pointed out above, there are other variables such as achievement which schools might be using to make their choices and which give the impression that SES is the crucial variable because of the correlation between these variables and SES. So we need to investigate the SES effect, net of other relevant variables. One obvious variable to control for is achievement.

Our results show that after controlling for achievement there is a highly significant relationship between SES and the probability of acceptance by a high circuit school.[3] We cannot claim that individual schools *intentionally* discriminate against lower SES students. However, in terms of the overall structure of the education system, the differences in selection between schools should be a cause for major concern. One of the primary reasons for

Table 4.6 Circuit of school attending, by SES (per cent)

	High circuit	Middle circuit	Low circuit	(N)
High	54	37	9	645
Middle	34	49	17	697
Low	18	43	39	570
Total	36	43	21	1912

(Chi-square = 263.83, df = 4, p = 0.000)

the removal of zoning, it was claimed, was to increase equality of access and opportunity for those students who have previously been disadvantaged by zoning policies that limited parental choice.

When we look at the final destination of students we can see the overall impact of the way opportunities are structured by the education market. Table 4.6 shows that while over half of high SES students attend high circuit schools, less than a fifth of low SES students attend such schools.

It is worth noting from Table 4.6 that, although the percentage of low SES students attending high circuit schools is considerably less than for high SES students, 18 per cent of low SES students do gain access to these schools. It could be claimed, therefore, that the current system at least provides low SES students with an opportunity to attend high circuit schools which they would not have had under a zoned system. If this claim were to have any plausibility it could be expected that the 18 per cent of students would mainly come from outside the catchment areas for those schools. All the high circuit schools in Green City operate enrolment schemes as they are oversubscribed, but they have prescribed geographic zones from which they automatically accept students. We have therefore been able to check how many of the low SES students from our cohort in these schools are from out of zone. We were able to trace 50 per cent of the Green City students (N = 56) of which 71 per cent were in zone for the high circuit school they attend, 18 per cent came from adjacent zones while 11 per cent travelled a considerable distance.[4] Because the Ns are relatively small these figures need to be interpreted with caution. However, the figures are consistent with the findings discussed in Chapter 6, which show that the further students travel from home to attend a school the higher their SES is likely to be. As such, the most likely interpretation of these figures is that the majority of low SES students in high SES schools are there because of the way the school zones have been drawn, rather than because of the workings of the education market.

Another way of looking at the opportunity structures of the education market is to look at the chances of students attending the high circuit school preferred by their parents (remembering that 'preference' follows a process of 'cooling out' identified earlier). Whereas 93 per cent of high SES parents who 'prefer' a high circuit school have their son or daughter attending one, the respective figures for the middle and low SES parents are 82 per cent and 69 per cent.[5,6]

The social conflict account of the marketization of education provides a far more plausible explanation and prediction of the consequences of the introduction of parental and school choice in education. Many working class parents have the information to identify the most 'desirable' schools, but there are clearly other factors involved which lead to the 'cooling out' of their aspirations for the school they want their child to attend. Here the explanations of social conflict theorists appear convincing.

Table 4.7 Percentage of parents who mention location or standards/exam results as reasons for choosing a school, by circuit of school

	Location	*Standards*
Circuit		
High	15	26
Middle	34	20
Low	51	11
Total	38	19

(Distance: Chi-square = 54.28, df = 2, p = 0.001)
(Standards: Chi-square = 9.10, df = 2, p = 0.001)
Note: These data are based on parents who had already decided on a school at the time of the interview.

Further support for social conflict explanations can be gained from Table 4.7. This shows two of the reasons offered when respondents were asked to say why they had decided on a particular school. The data suggest that for those in the middle and low SES groups the location of the school is of greater significance in school choice than standards, while for those in the high SES group, standards are more important than location. It would be incautious to read this table as implying that if parents were given the travel funds for their children to attend a more distant school the opportunity would be taken. If our theories regarding the way the market is structured are correct, then the provision of travel funds would make little difference.

Other factors also clearly make a difference. For example, if you want your son or daughter to attend a high circuit school you increase the chances of this actually happening by applying to more than one such school. The mean number of applications to high circuit schools from high, middle and low SES families who apply to at least one such school is 1.38, 1.21 and 1.14 respectively. This may be nothing more than a larger pro-portion of low SES families applying for only one high circuit school because of the distances involved in travel to other high circuit schools, it could, however, also be a matter of a lack of the knowledge of the rules of the game necessary to work out how to maximize one's chances of getting into a high circuit school.

In the next section we consider the relationship between ethnicity and school choice.

Ethnicity and choice

The question of ethnicity and education is highly significant in New Zealand. Maori are the *tangata whenua* (the people of the land) who have experienced colonialism over 150 years. The consequence, as in many other

Table 4.8 Circuit of school preferred from those available, by ethnicity (per cent)

	High circuit	Middle circuit	Low circuit	(N)
Maori	30	35	35	150
Pacific Island	41	19	40	106
Pakeha	42	44	14	1585
Other	61	29	11	119
Total	42	41	17	1960

(Chi-square = 106.78, df = 6, p < 0.000)

countries, has been that while their education outcomes have steadily improved over the past two decades, they are still underperforming relative to Pakeha or European students. Pacific Island families were attracted to New Zealand in the boom period of the 1950s and there has been steady immigration ever since. There are two ways in which the introduction of an education market was to address the failure of the educational system for Maori and Pacific Island students. Firstly, the bars of the 'iron cage of zoning' – which it was claimed was limiting the choice of these students by forcing them to remain in underperforming schools (Benton 1987) – were removed. Secondly, it was envisaged that as consumers Maori and Pacific Island students would have the power to influence school policy to be more responsive to their learning requirements, and this would ultimately encourage diversity of provision within the education market.

In this section, an exploratory analysis of ethnic choice patterns in terms of circuits enables us to examine two questions: do Maori and Pacific Island parents have different patterns of school choice from their Pakeha counterparts, and are they equally able to access their preferred schools?

The data patterns we report must be interpreted cautiously since the numbers of Maori and Pacific Island participants are small.

We begin, then, by revisiting the notion of circuits in relation to choice by investigating the responses to the parent questionnaire. Table 4.8 shows the responses (by ethnicity) to the question, 'Of the secondary schools available to you, which one did you most want your son/daughter to go to?' There are highly significant differences between the ethnic groups on this question, just as there were for the SES groups.

For Maori parents, choice is distributed fairly evenly across all circuits, although of all ethnic groups, they are the least likely to prefer high circuit schools. Pacific Island parents, in contrast, appear to be just as likely as Pakeha parents to prefer high circuit schools, but their preference is polarized between high and low circuit schools. Pacific Island parents are also

Table 4.9 Highest circuit of school applied for, by ethnicity (per cent)

	High circuit	Middle circuit	Low circuit	(N)
Maori	26	37	37	163
Pacific Island	36	20	44	99
Pakeha	45	41	14	1557
Other	58	29	13	112
Total	44	39	17	1931

(Chi-square = 120.87, df = 6, p < 0.000)

the most likely to prefer low circuit schools. Those coded as 'other' are most likely to prefer high circuit schools. These are predominantly Asian students.

Table 4.9 shows the ethnic differences in terms of highest circuit of school applied for. As was the case when we looked at the relationship between SES and school choice, parents who state a preference for a school in a particular circuit by and large apply for that school circuit. However, when we look at patterns of attendance a different picture emerges (Table 4.10).

We then investigated the question of whether schools select on the basis of ethnicity after taking account of achievement and SES, and found that they do.[7] So ethnicity is a factor, over and above achievement and SES, in determining the ability of parents and students to realize their choices in the education market place. Given these results the data patterns reported in Table 4.10 are not surprising.

Although at this stage of analysis our data do not allow us to examine the reasons why parents choose particular schools, research by Stuart Wells (1995) suggests that the 'rationale' for choices will differ within ethnic groups. Stuart Wells interviewed 37 African-American high school students

Table 4.10 Circuit of school attending, by ethnicity (per cent)

	High circuit	Middle circuit	Low circuit	(N)
Maori	16	40	44	169
Pacific Island	33	22	45	107
Pakeha	38	44	18	1596
Other	46	39	15	121
Total	36	42	22	1993

(Chi-square = 114.94, df = 6, p < 0.000)

and 34 of their parents and grandparents about their choice of school. She concludes:

> And while both race and class affect students' habitus, and therefore the way they perceive school choice opportunities, not all low-income minority students and parents will react the same way. Some will actively seek out schools that they believe will help them to attain higher status; others who fear competition or failure in a high-status school and those who have lost faith in the educational system will be most likely to choose not to choose.
>
> (Stuart Wells 1995: 33)

For groups which have traditionally been excluded from the benefits of the formal education system, such varied responses are not surprising; indeed, they have also been identified in the literature with respect to working class students (Brown 1987; Lauder *et al.* 1992b). Clearly, choice within the context of a system that has been exclusionary is likely to be highly problematic for those disadvantaged by it, and a uniform 'rational' response in the terms predicted by neo-classical economists is hardly to be expected.

However, the specific range of responses that excluded groups make will be determined by their history and culture. With this in mind, we revisit the sub-sample of Maori and Pakeha parents in one urban centre who were interviewed in detail about their process of school choice in 1993. Thirty-six Maori parents and 204 Pakeha parents were interviewed.

While the numbers are small, one result that emerged was that 22 per cent of Maori parents said they were considering sending their child to a church-related boarding school. Furthermore (in Pakeha terms), the majority of these were from lower SES backgrounds, although their 'status' may be assessed quite differently within the Maori community. In contrast, less than 2 per cent of Pakeha parents said they were considering boarding schools.

Our data suggest the possibility that these boarding schools (most of which are Maori in character) provide an important alternative to mainstream schooling for Maori families and are an indication of the desire by many Maori parents for an educational context which they believe is able to provide both academic achievement and a culturally appropriate environment. While many of these families had access to a local school which has a high percentage of Maori students and has made deliberate efforts to be bicultural, this school may not be perceived to be able to offer the same levels of achievement as a boarding school. Parental assessment of the benefits of these Maori boarding schools is consistent with Benton's analysis (1987). He notes that 'presence at a Maori boarding school was one of several factors isolated as having positive effects on achievement among secondary students in Waikato' (p. 45).

It is important to note, however, that the establishment of these schools pre-existed the current market context. At present there are no such alternatives available for the growing numbers of Pacific Island students in Aotearoa/New Zealand, and is difficult to see how the current market context can stimulate such initiatives.

Gender and choice

While the research on ethnicity and school choice has shown that ethnicity is an important factor in understanding the choices made by parents and the selection processes of schools, research also shows the importance of gender in educational decision making. David (1993, 1997), David *et al.* (1994), Newton (1994) and Watson (1997) suggest that gender may have an important role to play in school choice over and above social class, and it is to this issue which we now turn. In the light of these findings, we revisit our data to test whether the social conflict theory of school circuits holds true when the gender of the child is taken into account.

Gender and circuits

Table 4.11 shows the responses to the question: 'Of the secondary schools available to you, which one did you most want your son/daughter to go to?', classified by circuit for boys and girls in relation to their social class background. (The sample sizes vary in the following tables because not all

Table 4.11   Highest circuit of school preferred from those available, by gender and SES (per cent)

	High circuit	Middle circuit	Low circuit	(N)
Boys				
High	55	37	8	348
Middle	46	43	11	290
Low	26	43	32	298
Girls				
High	63	32	5	294
Middle	43	47	10	291
Low	27	42	31	260

(Gender: Chi-square = 4.70, df = 2, p = 0.095)

Table 4.12   Circuit of school attending, by gender and SES (per cent)

	High circuit	Middle circuit	Low circuit	(N)
Boys				
High	50	40	10	352
Middle	38	49	13	297
Low	17	44	39	305
Girls				
High	60	33	7	293
Middle	36	48	16	295
Low	19	40	41	265
Total	37	44	20	1807

(Gender: Chi-square = 3.62, df = 2, p = 0.163)

parents completed all questions.) It can be seen that the proportions of high, middle and low SES parents who prefer high, middle and low circuit schools for their sons and their daughters are not significantly different. As such, there are no gender-based differences in circuit of school preferred but the SES differences remain.

The same point applies with respect to school attended; again, there are no significant gender differences, as can be seen in Table 4.12.

Circuits and single-sex schools

While there are no differences on the basis of gender in the circuit of school preferred and attended, when we break down the circuits further into single-sex and coeducational schools, differences begin to emerge. An understanding of these differences is important because it could be argued that the reason more high SES parents prefer high circuit schools is because most high circuit schools are single sex. That is, it may be the single-sex character rather than the SES mix of the high circuit schools that attracts high SES parents. If it could be shown that the desire for a single-sex school was more important than the SES mix, then the notion of circuits of choice determined by SES may be weakened. It is to this issue that we now turn.

When asked which school parents would have preferred their child to go to, over 50 per cent of the cohort indicated their desire for a single-sex school. In Table 4.13 we examine more closely the ways in which the preference for single-sex schools was distributed by taking into account school circuit. There are 16 single-sex schools in the highest circuit, six in the middle circuit and none in the lowest circuit.

Table 4.13 Highest circuit of single-sex school preferred, by gender and SES (per cent)

	Boys		Girls		
	High circuit	*Middle circuit*	*High circuit*	*Middle circuit*	*(N)*
High	51	10	59	12	424
Middle	37	19	36	27	403
Low	23	28	20	27	273

Gender difference for high circuit schools (Chi-square = 1.75, df = 2, p = 0.418)
Gender difference for middle circuit schools (Chi-square = 5.15, df = 2, p = 0.076)
Boys N = 558, Girls N = 542

Table 4.13 shows that where high SES parents prefer single-sex schools, they are much more likely to prefer high circuit schools than middle circuit schools. Low SES parents who prefer single-sex schools, however, are fairly evenly divided across the two circuits. This demonstrates clearly that school circuit is not confounded by school type. Low SES parents, even where they have a preference for single-sex schools, still choose middle circuit single-sex schools more often than their high SES counterparts. Furthermore, very few high SES parents who prefer single-sex schools choose those from the middle circuit. This confirms the efficacy of the circuits of schooling theory and adds a further dimension, since it opens up the connection between school type and the SES mix of schools and the ways these interact to generate the hierarchy of circuits.

The question of the selectivity exercised by schools needs to be considered further in relation to school type. We have suggested that some high circuit schools appear to be exercising bias by selecting students from high SES backgrounds. It is worth noting that School A in Table 4.5 (which accepted the lowest proportion of low SES students) is a single-sex school. When we consider school type as well as SES mix, a further issue emerges. One of the key justifications for the removal of zoning was that parents would have access to greater diversity of provision: as the New Zealand Treasury (1987: 149) put it, 'Individual families would have as much choice as their location and inclination allowed.'

If low SES students are denied access to high circuit schools, and the majority of single-sex schools are in the high circuit, then these students are being denied access to schools of this *type*. This raises a question about the limited access low SES students have to what is, in principle, a strength of the education markets: a diversity of school types.

Reasons for choice of single-sex schools

The patterns presented in Table 4.13 suggest that choice of single-sex schools is governed by social class factors: that is, high SES parents are more likely than low SES parents to prefer single-sex schools. However, it does not follow that the reasons why parents choose single-sex schools can be explained exclusively in class terms. It has been argued that parental choice of school is likely to be influenced by the interrelationship between class and gender (David 1993; Watson 1997). More specifically, choice of school for girls is likely to be governed by different considerations to those often assumed by pro-market advocates (who look at the maximization of advantage in gaining credentials) and by social conflict theorists (who focus on the material and cultural bases of different classes).

One reason identified in the literature to explain these gendered differences in school choice could be that women take a dominant role in choosing schools for their children (David *et al.* 1994) and that they may take into account, therefore, factors which cut across class boundaries. For example, as we shall show in the next chapter, the question of male violence against girls was a consideration for some parents (and the girls themselves) in considering single-sex schools for their daughters. In the light of research by feminist educators identifying (among other things) the sex-based harassment girls are subjected to in co-educational schools, the decision to opt for single-sex schooling for their daughters may be seen as a responsible choice by parents. However, our data suggest that access to single-sex schooling is largely the privilege of the wealthy. Thus there appears to be an issue here concerning access to single-sex schools for low SES girls in particular. Quantitative analyses of the kind presented in this chapter do not allow us to address these distinctions in the reasons for choices, but qualitative research would alert us to the subtleties and complexities of the processes of school choice which are not accounted for in the economic framework of pro-market advocates. We take up these issues in more detail in the next chapter.

Overall these data patterns confirm the theory that the opportunity structures under choice regimes are consistent with the notion of circuits of schooling. While roughly half of our sample want to attend a single-sex school, there is a clear SES bias. The vast majority of high SES parents who preferred a single-sex school wanted to send their child to a high circuit single-sex school, whereas a small majority of low SES parents preferred middle circuit single-sex schools.

Conclusion

The promise held out by marketization was that all parents would be able to choose the school that they felt best suited their children. The reality is that across social groups, there are significant numbers of parents who cannot get their children into the school that they prefer. However, our data suggest that this experience of 'disappointment' is systematically structured according to class and ethnicity. In effect it is Maori and lower SES students who have the least chance of gaining entry either to the school preferred by their parents or the school(s) they have applied for.

Of all ethnic groups, Maori appear to have the least chance of gaining access to oversubscribed schools, even when SES and prior achievement are taken into account. It is, perhaps, because of the enduring bias against Maori in education (which now appears to have been extended to the new market system of choice and selection) that a proportion of Maori parents have sought an equally traditional response: to send their children to a Maori boarding school. In raising this possibility we should emphasize that our sample is small and, as such, we cannot confirm the extent of this response.

When we look at the data patterns we have identified we need to ask what effect the 'cooling out' process will have on working class and Maori parents and their children. It is hard to see how the original hypotheses of pro-market advocates as to the benefits of choice can apply when working class and Maori parents' ideal choices are so severely curtailed by the reality of the kinds of school they can access. In an important sense then, the judgement as to the success or failure of market policies in education not only rests on the high profile question of whether markets polarize student intakes but also on the qualitative impact that failure to realize choice has on parents' aspirations and attitudes in relation to their children's schooling.

If we are to understand more about the reasons why parents from different social class backgrounds make different kinds of choice in an education market, and how they respond to disappointment, we need to ask them. In the next chapter we focus our analysis on two families, looking in detail at the reasons for their choice of school for their daughters and the strategies they adopt to have them accepted. In this way we can also begin to unravel some of the complex dynamics of gender and class in an education market.

five

The hidden injuries of school choice

In this chapter we investigate the story behind the data patterns that we have identified in Chapter 4. To do so Sue Watson interviewed two families[1] from different ends of the social spectrum: the Hunts, a professional middle class family and the Allens, a working class family.

These families had indicated they wanted their daughters to attend the same high circuit state girls' secondary school, Sheppard High, in the following year. Both the families lived out of zone for the school, which was able to operate an enrolment scheme as it was oversubscribed. The families, therefore, had made a deliberate choice in favour of the school rather than to send their children to their local co-educational school. Families who wanted to send their daughters to a single-sex school were chosen in order to illuminate the dynamics of gender and class issues in an education market. As we shall see, however, their knowledge of the 'rules of the game' required to gain access to the school were vastly different, as was their ability to have their daughter accepted. In each family the parents and their daughter (who was 12 or 13 years old at the time) were interviewed.[2] By interviewing the girls as well as their parents, we introduce a further dimension to choice which we are not able to address in our other data sets, namely the influence of children and their peer groups on school choice.

The Hunt family

Sarah and Richard Hunt live in a highly priced suburb with their three children: Roger (17), Nicola (15) and Anna (12). They both come from professional backgrounds. Sarah's father is an accountant and her mother a primary school teacher; Richard's father is a church minister with a PhD in theology and his mother a skilled musician who taught from their home.

Both the Hunt parents attended elite single-sex state schools. Richard went on to study law at university and is now a partner in a relatively large urban legal practice employing about 50 people.

In contrast, Sarah did not go to university because her father was 'of the old school', believing that tertiary education was unnecessary for daughters. It was her father's idea that she become a dental nurse, which she agreed to because it was a ticket out of her home town, as the training she needed was not available there. After she met Richard, married and her first child was born, she gave up her job. But she did do some part time work which fitted into looking after her children. Although she wasn't entirely happy being at home, it wasn't acceptable among her friends to work when they had young children.

> *Sarah:* We thought they were terrible, like, how disgusting that people did that. I think deep down I envied them because I enjoyed being a mother and being at home but I actually enjoyed the time when I could go and do something for me and in a lot of ways I found it quite suffocating just to be somebody's wife or somebody's mother. Like I used to go to things with Richard and they'd say, 'Oh, you're Richard's wife', or at school, 'Oh, you're Roger's mother', and after a while it gets to be a little bit suffocating that – I'm Sarah, I'm not just Richard's wife or Roger's mother; you're those things as well. There's all sorts of pressures.

In 1989, Sarah began her three-year polytechnic training as a nurse, an ambition she had put on hold for many years.

> *Sarah:* I feel this is something I've done for me. I haven't got it as a result of being Richard's wife or somebody's mother. This is what I wanted to do and I've gone out and done it.

In order to do her training she saved money to help her through for two years prior to attending polytechnic. The demands of her training meant there were some changes at home.

> *Richard:* It changed our life. We all started doing things around the house that we'd never done before.

Despite being enrolled in a full time course, running the household was still seen as Sarah's responsibility, an attitude which Sarah has adopted in response to what she saw as a neglect in her own mother's life.

> *Sarah:* And I didn't like her teaching, I wanted her to be at home like other children's parents were at home. In those days not too many people's parents worked. I didn't like it when she worked. Not because I didn't want her to be an independent

person, but because I wanted her to be the same as my friends' parents.

Sarah saw the housework as her mother's responsibility; a role she also assumes but which has led to her having what she terms as 'unrealistically' high expectations of her own family and of the appearance of the house. Sarah's lack of opportunity in comparison to her brother, who was encouraged to go to university but didn't, has given her a determination to ensure that her daughters are not disadvantaged or limited by their gender. However, at the same time, her feelings of anger and frustration at her mother for prioritizing her paid work over the running of the household means that she expects her daughters not only to achieve academically and have a career, but to maintain high standards domestically.

Like her mother, the Hunt's 12-year-old daughter Anna sees caring for children as a woman's responsibility, and she sees doing paid work and having children as being mutually compatible.

Anna: Some people think that women should be like a maid, do all the work at home, but then some people think that they should do work, so it's basically pretty mixed.

Sue: What do you think you're going to do?

Anna: Well, I want to get married, I want to have kids and I just want to have a nice house and stuff.

Sue: Can you still do that even if you're a lawyer?

Anna: Yes, maybe. When I have kids I'll have to take leave.

MacDonald (1980: 18) expresses this dichotomy between academic achievement and family responsibility in the following way:

In the education of the middle-class girl, the situation is reversed. There is often a recognition of the desirability that women should achieve academically, in order to obtain some work fulfilment and career prospects; this is set against the likelihood that once married they will have much greater financial security and less need to work either for money or for fulfilment, given motherhood.

When asked to describe someone she admires, Anna describes her parents.

Anna: My mum and dad, both of them because my mum she was a dental nurse and then she got married and had us kids and now she's started work again. She went a couple of years ago and started training to be a nurse and now she works. I think it's pretty good that she still does most of the cooking for tea and prepares the lunches and cleans the house. Us kids also do some of that like we do vacuum cleaning. Dad's sort of like done his job. Ever since he got out of school he always trained to be a lawyer and like he goes to work really early and he works all day and he comes home about 6.30, it's quite a long day. He still has time for us and he's funny.

Anna admires her parents because they both work hard but she does not contest the division of labour within the family and accepts that she too, like her mother, will take leave from her job to look after her children.

Anna would like to be a lawyer, an idea she has got from her father and because she enjoys class discussions.

Anna: I sort of dominate a bit because if someone says something I don't agree with, I can't just sit there.

Anna's parents support her career aspirations, and Richard believes that the kinds of barriers to women's participation which Sarah experienced have largely disappeared. When asked if he thought it was harder for women than men to achieve a career, Richard Hunt replied:

Richard: I think it used to be. Times are changing. I think it's getting much more easy now. Back in the sixties, and to some extent the seventies, things like doctors and lawyers were traditionally male. I think if men want to keep their jobs, they're going to have to work a lot harder because women are more motivated.

Anna clearly demonstrates this motivation and she also believes that girls do better than boys at school.

Anna: Girls are probably more serious than boys but girls can also have fun as well. Like they can joke when it's time to joke but they're not like serious but they'll get their work done and still have time to joke and laugh. I think they're quite well organized and they use their time well.

The Hunts feel able to exercise choice with respect to their children's education and, given their financial circumstances, it is perhaps surprising that they have not chosen private education. Sarah said that they had considered a private girls' school for Anna but they were 'totally unimpressed' because they felt the subject choices were limited in the senior school.

Sarah: We felt once they got to sixth- and seventh-form level that the academic options were very narrow and much more towards the arts and not to sciences.

Sarah seems to be resisting the traditional view about subject choices for girls in which arts are given primacy over sciences. But her decision was also influenced by considerations of the 'type' of girls who she believes are produced by private schools, so that the perceived culture of the school was as important a deciding factor as purely educational considerations.

> *Sarah:*   We've got a few friends who have got children at that school and the type of child that they are or have turned into is not very appealing to the type of child that we want to produce as an end result.
>
> *Sue:*   What do you mean by that?
>
> *Sarah:*   Without sounding unkind, a lot of the children, there's a lot of competition with material things. To me it's not a big competition like we drive the latest car or have the latest clothing, I'm not into that. Although I like the kids to look nice. I just feel that there are more important things to concentrate your energies on. A lot of the girls are very cliquey whereas we haven't found that at all with Nicola, have we? I'm not saying it doesn't happen because I know it does from the things Nicola says: 'Oh, I'm glad I'm not in such and such a class because certain things happen.'

Sarah didn't feel comfortable with the socially competitive atmosphere she thinks is generated in such a setting even though it would seem that her children would be able to 'compete' in that environment. Sarah has an idea of what she would like her daughter to turn out like: that is, not materialistic or 'cliquey'. She appears to have a negative image of girls who go to private schools and is deliberately avoiding such an environment in order to prevent her daughters turning out this way.

Why, then, did the Hunts choose Sheppard High, a state, single-sex school for their daughter?

> *Richard:*   I think the courses, and the concept that we wanted a single-sex school.
>
> *Sue:*   Why?
>
> *Sarah:*   In my case, there was no choice. But having said that, when we looked at what the options were, we still felt, that whether it was a co-ed. school or single-sex, the main thing was the curriculum they offered. If you prioritize it, if you look at the curriculum then you look at the other features that you want, that's why we did it.

Taken out of context it might appear from this quote that Sarah is operating within a model of choice close to that of many pro-market theorists who assume that parents are primarily motivated by the pursuit of educational credentials. Sarah prioritized the curriculum, and other considerations were apparently secondary. However, the prioritizing was constructed within a broader value framework which had already rejected the 'end result' of the private school. At this point Richard stepped into the conversation to add a further twist to the process of making a choice.

Richard: I don't believe it, sorry. When you're at school, it's good not to be distracted, that influenced me.

Sarah: It may seem to some people that it's a narrow view but . . .

Richard: But you certainly don't have to worry about . . .

Sarah: But you see these days, it's certainly not like when we were at school. I mean these kids don't seem to have a problem relating with boys or the boys don't seem to have a problem relating to girls because they have a lot more things where they have things where the boys come to the girls' schools. They're always having dances, and they're always having lunch time things where the boys come over. It's not something silly like it was in our day. I mean if a boy came to our school, the poor boy was probably so embarrassed, the girls would go hysterical and cram into the windows, I mean, that sort of thing doesn't happen . . .

While Richard began by asserting that the curriculum as well as the single-sex character of the school were equally important, he went on to challenge Sarah's emphasis on the former and to say that, in fact, the single-sex character of the school was the most important deciding factor. Sarah then seemed to defend his view against a criticism that it might be seen as 'narrow'.

What this extract does indicate is the confusion in their own minds between what Lee and Marks (1992) describe as traditional and opportunity structures. By traditional structures, they refer to the ability of single-sex schools to offer a protective environment to girls, free from 'distraction'. Opportunity structures refer to the ability of the school to enable girls to achieve academically. The confusion which the Hunts express is an outworking of the contradictory nature of these two discourses in the schooling of girls. Lee and Marks (1992: 245) point out that while for boys, 'the traditional structure *is* an opportunity structure', this is not the case for girls. In a girls' school, the traditional structure is tuned to prepare girls for unequal status and power, whereas the opportunity structures provide girls with the potential for successful careers in the public sphere.

Connell *et al.* (1982: 137) make a similar observation of private, single-sex schools in Australia:

the [private] market provides a mechanism by which schools can change in response to changes in the ruling class . . . For one thing the pressures from the market are diverse and sometimes contradictory (when, for example, girls' schools are expected to provide both marriageable femininity and high powered academic competitors).

These changes in what Connell and his colleagues call the ruling class are aptly illustrated by the shift that has occurred in the one generation between Sarah and her daughter. While Sarah's father did not see it as necessary for her to attend university, Anna's father believes it is imperative for her to do so. However, rather than reject the discourse of femininity – which was seen as paramount to the ruling class a generation ago – a new discourse has been added, that of equal opportunity, while the contradictions between them remain unresolved.

Sarah's comments about the 'silly' behaviour of the girls in her school could be read as an argument in favour of co-educational schools since Sarah seems to be implying that such behaviour results from isolating girls and boys. However, she feels this can be overcome by ensuring that there is organized contact between boys' and girls' schools on a regular basis. Thus, while wanting to separate her daughters to ensure they are not 'distracted', the Hunts are equally keen to ensure they develop 'normal' socialization by maintaining some degree of contact with boys.

Anna presents a different view of distraction to that of her parents. While Sarah thinks the girls will be distracted by the boys in a co-educational school, Anna talked about the ways in which the boys actively work to distract the girls. It is not that the girls are being 'silly' around the boys, but that the boys annoy them.

Sue: What do you think about single-sex schools as opposed to co-ed.?

Anna: I like co-ed. schools but I think I could handle single-sex because sometimes the boys, you have to act like quite a rebel around them, sort of act quite cool around them otherwise they'll hassle you sometimes. And they sometimes annoy you when you're working.

Sue: Who do they hassle and pick on then?

Anna: Sometimes like if you're doing your work and they don't want to do it or something they sometimes hassle you for doing the work. Sometimes they say things like 'goody good' or something like that.

Sue: What do you do when they say that?

Anna: I just ignore them. It doesn't happen too often but it's just anyone that's working. Sometimes I think I would like a single-sex school 'cause you can make quite a lot of friends and you'd be able to get down and work and it'd be quite fun.

Sue: What do you mean by 'act a rebel'?

Anna: Sometimes you have to talk to them when you're not supposed to be talking. To impress them sort of.

From Anna's point of view the distraction that boys cause is different from that envisaged by her parents, where the girls will be attracted to and thereby distracted by the boys. One of the reasons Anna wants to go to Sheppard High, then, is because it offers a kind of sanctuary from the behaviour of the boys. She looks forward to the prospect of making friends and being able to work undisturbed. This would seem to be contrary to traditional discourses about femininity which position girls as being resistant to academic success. It is a point which Walkerdine (1984) also makes.

In choosing a school for Anna and her elder sister, Hillary High – a single-sex state boys' school – was the measure against which all other schools were assessed, since Richard is clear that he wants his daughters to have the same opportunities as his son.

Sue: What subjects would you like Anna to take at school?

Richard: We haven't really thought about that yet, have we? Nicola, we thought, would do better at languages than sciences although she's doing both. We wanted her really to have the same opportunities as Roger and we looked at Kauri College [a private school] and we rejected that and we came to the conclusion that Sheppard High was the female equivalent of Hillary High. That sounds stupid but that's proved to be the case . . .

Richard believes that equal opportunity in education is the key to success for women.

Richard: Education to me is the thing that women now have equal access to opportunity. The end result should be the same. If a woman has more of a career orientation then there's no reason why . . .

When asked why they chose to send Roger to Hillary High, a number of reasons emerge. It was clearly a well-thought-out decision. For Richard, the desire to find a school that was equivalent to his *alma mater* was a prime consideration, and he emphasized academic standards and discipline as being of key importance. However, as the following extract shows, he was also anxious to avoid the local co-educational college for which they were in zone. His knowledge of the unspoken rules by which entry is gained to

Hillary High for out-of-zone pupils is made explicit in the following extract.

Sue: Why did you send Roger to Hillary High?

Richard: It had some sort of academic attainment concept which Rimu didn't have a reputation for. It [Rimu] didn't have a uniform, didn't have any discipline that you hear about, didn't have a very good academic record, there was nothing going for it at all from my point of view.

Sue: Do you think that was influenced by the fact that you went to an elite single-sex school?

Richard: Absolutely, unashamedly. I went to see George [the principal] with fear and trepidation. Because we were out of zone, we had to think up an excuse. We fastened on Latin and discipline and academic achievement.

This quote clearly illustrates how the professional middle class have the confidence and the knowledge to gain access to the kinds of schools they want. However, as the following shows, there is a considerable degree of subtlety in how this is done.

Sue: Did you say Roger really wants to study Latin?

Richard: They didn't do it at Rimu, I mean, you've got to be intelligent about these things. George [the principal] knew where we were coming from. I'd talked about my [old] Grammar [school] with George, there was no secrecy about it. I told him what I thought and he seemed to take that all right.

As we shall see, in comparison with the working class parents in this study, Richard Hunt feels very 'at home' in the school contexts of his children and sees himself as an equal with the principals. He knows what the rules of the game are in getting his children into schools for which they are out of zone and feels confident and able to take part in this game and to 'win'. When the Hunts were re-contacted after the interview, Anna had been accepted for Sheppard High.

The Allen family

Rita and Bruce Allen own their own home in a working class area where they live with their daughter Patricia. Both Rita and Bruce have been married previously and have children from their first marriages, although they have all left school and no longer live with the Allens.

Rita was born in a small Pacific island nation and came to live in New

Zealand with her four sisters when she was 12. She went to the local co-educational high school and was put into a 'special' class because of her limited knowledge of English. At 15 she left school to work with her mother in the railway cafeteria and since then has always had unskilled or semi-skilled jobs. She now works full time in a small meat processing business as a meat packer.

> *Rita:* My mother was working at the railway station cafeteria so straight away I walked into a job you see, and I was actually working in the cafeteria but through school, the fourth form, I was actually working after school as well because I'm not from a wealthy family at all, but a go-ahead family with four girls and whatever. And, um, I wanted the things that my friends were having and things like that so I worked after school at the hospital, and I enjoyed it. Sometimes I never used to get home till about ten at night and things like that so homework lacked and things like that. After school I worked at the railway cafeteria with intentions in the new year of going for an apprenticeship in dressmaking and I never got there. You're working, you're earning big money, you're going out with girls you meet on the job. It was exciting, you're going out. I was enjoying life. Clean fun compared to now and I needed the money to carry on and I had a good job so I just worked there then, from that I think I worked as a shop assistant.

Rita has never had trouble finding a job but for most of her life she has had to work to survive financially. It is more important now than it ever was.

> *Rita:* I wouldn't dream of having a day off on our busiest days. I've got to be just about in hospital. So here I am, still uneducated and working hard.

Bruce's father was a driver and his mother worked in an unskilled paid job, as well as looking after the children because the family needed two incomes. He left college after 18 months to do an apprenticeship which he never completed, and from there he had a series of unskilled and semi-skilled jobs. His main interest was the guitar and he spent many years play-ing in bands. Bruce's lack of education has left him with a keen sense of inadequacy.

> *Bruce:* I always felt in my life that I had to be twice as good as some-one else so that I could be accepted . . . I was never qualified and even guitar-wise I felt that I had to be a lot better than that other person so they'd accept me as an equal.

Since his first marriage broke up, Bruce has completed his Royal College of Music exams and now works as an itinerant guitar teacher in several secondary schools. He and Rita are also in a band and play at functions in the local area. Bruce is dedicated to music and has high expectations for himself and the others he plays with. As well as playing, he enjoys teaching.

Bruce has three children from his previous marriage, all of whom attended the local schools in the working class area in which they lived. While Bruce was keen for them to be educated, it never occurred to him to send them anywhere other than the local schools. He blames his lack of involvement with their schooling and his marriage break-up for their lack of success.

Bruce: That's probably another reason why, with my kids in the previous marriage – that was the first thing in my mind was they're going to be educated. I had one of them to sixth or seventh form and Michelle was in the fifth form but then the marriage broke up and that's when the other kid, Peter –

Rita: – Peter, he finished his secondary schooling down here with us, but he didn't sit School C, he finished through the fifth form.

Rita also sent her only child, Shaun, to the local working class school but his education was also disrupted when her marriage broke up, and at 12 he was sent to live with his father in Auckland. With the benefit of hindsight, Rita recognizes her non-decisive stance in regard to Shaun's schooling.

Rita: And I think in those days my life was just so shallow you know, I mean, there's the school, you go to that school 'cause it's next door and of course his father was working right across the road in the butcher's shop and he [Shaun] was not going to go to another school except there. That was the only way he ever saw his father.

Shaun went to two colleges in Auckland but is now serving time in prison.

Rita: But he's an intelligent boy but he's never used it the right way. He was, I have to say, he's in the criminal world. But if you saw his background you could – I don't blame him.

Because the Allens are in effect on their second family cycle they have had a unique opportunity to reflect on their lives and their decisions in relation to their own and their children's education. This reflection has led them to make very different decisions with respect to Patricia's education. However, while they want to interact with the market in ways that will be advantageous to Patricia, they know they lack the resources of better off parents.

Rita: With the people I work for, they're all educational push for
their kids and they're doing very well and with her and I the
only females in the job, you talk, you know, like that. Their
daughter's at Kauri College [a private school]. We never
have that kind of money but that's the type of environment I
want, you know. I want Patricia to do well.

Just prior to Patricia starting school, Bruce was working as a caretaker at
a primary school in a middle class area. It was an unplanned series of events
that led the Allens to send Patricia out of their area for primary schooling:

Bruce: Actually, at that stage the roll was dropping, I was getting on
well with the principal and what have you, and they said
bring her up, no trouble at all.

Every day since, Bruce has driven Patricia to and from school, ten minutes drive away.

Bruce: She's at school where people have probably got a few more
dollars than what we've got and they're pretty pushy as parents. Oh, they hassle the teachers which I don't agree with
because I think teachers are qualified and they should know.
I mean, you might get the odd one who's slack but it's a go-
ahead thing. If we put her down the road here she'd still be
trying to know what a kettle looked like. It's not trying to be,
it's not racial, but um, so you know. How long have you been
there now? [to Patricia] Seven years. I take her there every
day, there and back, and it's going to pay off.

When asked if her life would have been different if she had gone to one of
the local schools, Patricia replied,

Patricia: I'd be dumber. The teaching isn't that good.

Rita has noticed the difference between the parent–teacher nights she
attended with her older children and those she has attended at Patricia's
school.

Rita: I think that with both of us, it's the fact that we both have
been married before, living and still living in the area and we
have kids that did go to school. I've got a son and he's got
three others that went to primary school here. I mean,
they're OK, they're doing OK, they're intelligent children
you know, but you can see the difference I s'pose in going to
their parent–teacher night to . . . [going to Patricia's parent–
teacher night].

As well as moving Patricia to a school in a middle class area – which may
be seen as almost serendipitous – Bruce has also taken an active interest in

her homework, something which he acknowledges he did not do for his other children. Patricia has always loved school, but there was one day when she didn't want to go because she couldn't understand her maths. Bruce sat down with her to 'nut out what they were doing', and Rita describes the result.

Rita: Her learning went zoom after the nights of him nutting it out with her.

The Allens confirm several aspects of Lareau's (1992: 208) description of working class parents.

I found working-class families had a pattern of separation between home and school. Parents turned over responsibility for education to higher-status teachers. Although they read to their children and helped their children with their school work from time to time, working-class parents reacted to school requests and rarely initiated contacts with teachers.

However, she goes on to say that working class fathers were 'almost entirely absent' from the processes of their children's education. While Bruce admits that this was the extent of his involvement with his first children's education, it is a stance which he has consciously and deliberately altered with Patricia.

It was Patricia who first proposed the idea of attending Sheppard High, an idea she picked up from one of her friends at primary school whose sister goes to the school. Rita and Bruce were happy with the suggestion since Bruce is teaching guitar at the local colleges and is 'not impressed with the standard of education'.

Bruce: I feel she's probably got more chance of learning if she's in town. The same people who are at Rifle River, who are not interested, they're filling in time aren't they, until they're 15 or 16 or till they can get the dole.

Rita: We didn't want Patricia in that kind of environment 'cause I think Patricia could be easily led as well. My son was.

Bruce: I want her to be given the opportunities and if she doesn't make the most of it then she's only got herself to blame.

While believing that the attitude of the students at the school has a major impact on achievement, they also assert that Patricia has a responsibility to make good use of the opportunities she is provided with.

Rita: I want Patricia in a sense to try and be one of the next generation that would not be unemployed, on the dole. I mean, who knows, she could probably throw this all off in our face and be a mother at 16 or 17. I hope not. I can say I hope not.

I want her to do something, do something with her life. Work in a career, whatever she chooses to do, you know. I want her to stay at school as long as it takes.

Bruce: I'd like her to get to university or something like that. That's what I've got in mind. I'd like her to do things like that.

There is an enormous weight of expectation and responsibility riding on Patricia. It is as if she is going to make up for the lack of opportunities and the mistakes of her parents and step-brothers and sisters, a responsibility which Patricia is well aware of.

Sue: What do you think your parents want you to do with your life?

Patricia: Don't throw it away but just do what I want to do but don't throw it away like my brother did. I wanna kill him. It's a waste of a life. But his daughter is beautiful. That's the best thing that came out of it . . .

Jones's (1990) research with a group of Pacific Island working class girls places Patricia's desire to achieve in a larger context. Jones found that, unlike the working class 'lads' in Willis's (1977) study, these girls developed a positive orientation towards schooling since they believed that qualifications provided the means of escaping from the 'occupational fates' of their mothers. She also noted that the girls considered domestic responsibilities to be an integral part of their future but that this would not alter their need also to be in paid work, since it is necessary for economic survival.

Patricia has two ambitions: to become a dance teacher, 'or the top designer in the world'. She has been dancing from a young age and takes classes in jazz, tap and ballet. She thinks that as well as dancing she will need to get School Certificate, finish school and maybe go on to polytechnic to 'widen her education'. Next year she would like to take Chinese because she has a Chinese friend who got her interested, and clothing because she likes sewing. While Patricia wants to go on to tertiary training she is unaware that in choosing a subject such as clothing she will be placed in a 'non-academic' stream at Sheppard High, and thus her chances of pursuing tertiary education are liable to be severely compromised (Middleton 1992). This total lack of familiarity of Patricia and her parents of the ways in which subjects, and the students who take them, are segregated means that they may make educational decisions which jeopardize their primary aim of upward mobility.

Patricia would also like to get married one day and have one or two children, but she is determined to continue in paid work, an example set by her dance teacher.

Sue: Is it possible to have children and work at the same time?

Patricia: Yes it is. It's not like in the old days where once you have kids, you gotta stay home, stay home with them, be with them for the rest of your life or something. I got all this from my dance teacher and she's done it about six times so . . .

She thus combines the dual expectations of taking primary responsibility for children with the need to be in paid employment by finding a career that enables her to do both and has the added advantage of involving dance, which she loves.

Patricia has a strong determination to succeed, and her desire to attend Sheppard High stems from this, but there is an extra dimension which the school can offer.

Sue: Why do you want to go to Sheppard High?

Patricia: I don't know, I just wanted to go there. I didn't want boys around 'cause of all the things they do to you. They become a pain, especially when they get older, ugh. I can work easier if the boys would just leave me alone. And if they're there, I just get weird and get all aggro, can't work. It just puts me off working. Plus when you get to an age, I thought, oh, I might get to this age so I thought oh, um, well I might be interested in boys and if they're at my school I'd get distracted and always get into trouble for not working and then not handing in my homework on time. But if they weren't at the school I'll get *all* my stuff done, I can do whatever I want.

Patricia's experience at primary school validates her desire to attend a single-sex school.

Sue: Who does get into trouble at school?

Patricia: Boys, boys, boys.

Sue: What sort of things do they do?

Patricia: Pull tricks on girls. Trip them over, um, all sorts of stuff. They do anything to get revenge or they make fun of people and stuff. Like people who are, like boys that aren't that popular – like the popular boys make fun of them and like tease them and stuff. They get into trouble . . .

Sue: What other things do they do to girls?

Patricia: They pull their hair and they vandalize the school sometimes, they flick pen.

Once a boy kicked Patricia in the head with a ball.

Patricia: I got so cross, he never did it again.

If necessary, the teacher may be called on to intervene, but this is a last resort. Patricia prefers to yell at them or say something back herself.

Mahony (1985) supports Patricia's description of the sexual harassment she is subjected to. She gives further examples of verbal 'put-downs' about academic ability and physical appearance directed at the girls by the boys. Jones (1985) describes the male violence which occurs in mixed secondary schools and which is similar to that which Patricia is already experiencing at primary level.

Bruce and Rita's reasons for wanting to send Patricia to Sheppard High stem from their desire to provide what they consider to be an appropriate learning context, one in which the students (and their parents) have a drive and willingness to learn.

> *Bruce:* I just want her to be around people that want to learn and it might rub off.

Bruce believes the students in the local colleges (as well as their parents) lack the necessary motivation or the knowledge of the system to enable them to achieve.

> *Bruce:* A lot of the Island people, they want them well educated and they don't know how to go about it. They say, 'You stay at school until you've got this, got that.' They're actually staying at school just filling in time, half of them. You know. It's good to know this side of life as well as what Patricia gets up there.

The educational environment at Sheppard High was Rita and Bruce's primary concern; the fact that the school is single-sex did not occur to them until they were contacted and asked to participate in the interview.

> *Sue:* Do you think there is something a single-sex school can offer that a co-ed. can't?

> *Bruce:* Put their mind on learning rather than worrying about what the other . . .

> *Rita:* Well, I think, now since you said that to me over the phone and why the interview, I thought, oh, I never thought about it that way. But why, is there a reason, and Patricia's was, she actually said to me. I said: 'why do you want to go to Sheppard High?' at one point, and she said, 'I don't want to go to the same school as the boys, they distract me.' She actually said that. Whether it's just out of the mouth of babes I don't know. But anyway, I just left that hanging. And I think too, I looked at it this way, that there's this sexist thing, male versus female. I can do anything you can do better type of

thing. You get that in a competitive type of – I don't know how to put that in words. You got that, but um, I think, distraction, yes she will be, she could be. But I never really thought that's because sending her to a single-sex school. Once again, we wanted her educated.

Bruce wants Patricia to be educated as a means of gaining independence, of being able to look after herself.

Bruce: The old attitude was, you're a girl, you're not meant to know anything. That's what I'm trying to make sure doesn't happen 'cause she's a girl and the old attitude, which I said before, when she gets to 21, 22, that she's going to be married with two or three kids; um, maybe that will happen, but if she's educated at the same time well maybe she can be independent, you know what I mean? Whereas, you're the breadwinner and you're just nothing 'cause you're a woman, that attitude. That's virtually the way I saw things.

Rita: Maybe we grew up . . . If she ends up at 22 with married, with kids or something like that, those kids are not there forever, are they? Maybe she can, I mean, that's what's happening in today's world, go back you know, or . . . But she's educated enough to do something, you know. These days, like I said, I don't know like, if my job went under at the moment, what the hell am I going to do? Even to go back on to a bar or something like that, I just about have to be qualified.

When the Allens were re-contacted after the interview, they had been informed that their application for Sheppard High had been unsuccessful. Rita did not know how out-of-zone students are selected and she did not ask to be placed on the waiting list. Their second choice of school is co-educational and near to their home, although they are not in the 'home zone' for this college. Bruce believes it is the best out of the three colleges available locally although it is by no means their first choice. They would prefer to send her to a co-educational college in a nearby middle class area but have heard that the zoning is very strict so they have not tried to apply. As Rita said, 'I thought, what chance have we got. So I didn't bother.'

Despite their best attempts, the selection processes of the school have worked against the Allen family. Unlike families such as the Hunts, they lack the knowledge of the system or the confidence to challenge it in ways that are advantageous for their daughter.

Conclusion

In presenting these interviews we have contrasted a professional middle class family, the Hunts, with a working class family, the Allens. This contrast highlights the way middle and working class families are positioned differently in relation to education markets. While for the Hunts, there were difficult choices to make between a private and an elite single-sex state school, both schools were in the same circuit of consideration and the Hunts had the resources to access either school.

The Allens differ from many working class parents, and indeed their earlier pattern, in that they wanted to send their daughter to Sheppard High. Patricia Allen carries her parents' hopes that she will go to university and do well. The choice of Sheppard High is clearly seen as a step in this direction since she will be with people who, as Bruce says, 'want to learn and it might rub off'. It is also a way of avoiding the distractions of boys. In a sense it is an attempt to lift Patricia out of a working class environment in which it is expected that girls will leave school early and marry. The problem for the Allens is that in contrast to the Hunts, they didn't have the knowledge of the unwritten rules governing entry to these 'elite' schools, or the confidence to bend the rules in their favour. Middle class readers who have been successful in the educational game may be surprised at the Allen's belief that gaining access to these schools is a matter of luck, because they take this 'insider information' for granted. But not everyone will. Our previous research (Lauder *et al.* 1992b) suggests that able working class students' careers are often serendipitous. The links between choice of school, curriculum options taken and subsequent career are simply not made in any way consistent with a pre-planned progression from education into a career. It is significant that the Allens did not ask for Patricia to be placed on the waiting list for Sheppard High. Nor did they seek to pursue the issue in any other way. In cases like the Allens it is unlikely that what pro-market choice theorists regard as the knowledge or information necessary to ensure that all will come to the market as equals can be as easily disseminated as they suggest.

While we have emphasized the social class differences between these families, we should also note that in terms of the education issues facing girls, they confronted similar problems. For both girls the distraction and threat of sexual harassment from boys was an issue. But while they resisted this kind of inequality, they also held aspirations for their daughters that they would be wives, mothers and have careers. Their choice of Sheppard High encompassed both the desire for 'equal opportunity' and access to educational achievement as well as the desire for appropriate socialization into femininity (Watson 1997).

These interviews have also raised the issue of access to diversity in the education market. While both families wanted to gain access to a single-sex environment for their daughters, their ability to do so was determined by their social class background. The problem is that education markets, subject to limited financing, will never be able to provide the variety of schools demanded. Consequently places are rationed according to social class, just as demand is determined by the social class intake of the school. The examples of the Hunts and Allens demonstrate the injustice involved in the promises offered by market systems of education.

six

Polarizing intakes: the impact of educational competition

In the previous chapters we established that choice in education markets is based on class, gender and ethnicity. But that analysis was a snapshot; what we need is a moving picture of the impact of markets on students and schools. Without a more dynamic and contextualized account, it could be claimed that the findings of the previous chapters are simply a 'one-off'. Pro-market advocates often claim that the kind of class-based findings of the previous chapter are to be expected because it takes time for 'market behaviour' to be adopted. They argue that as the reforms become 'bedded down', parents will acquire the information needed to compete in the education market. In this chapter we broaden the scope of our analysis to examine what happens to school intakes over time when they are directly affected by parental and school choice. Our data enable us to examine not only the effects of choices made by parents, but the ways in which schools themselves act to structure the education market.

The decisive test between the competing hypotheses of market competition is whether school intakes are polarized over time, over and above the polarization[1] we would predict from residential segregation. Market advocates – especially those with a concern for equity – usually predict that the iron cage of zoning, once lifted, will create more homogeneous intakes as working class students and those from ethnic groups that have 'underachieved' in education escape 'ghetto' schools for those that are more successful. Market critics, in contrast, would expect to see student intakes become increasingly polarized along social class lines. Our findings from the last two chapters suggest that the critics are likely to be right. Furthermore, since in New Zealand ethnicity is closely related to social class, we would also expect to see changes in the nature of schools' ethnic intakes.

An analysis of changes in student intakes enables us to examine the effects of choice in the education market and to address the question, in Chapter 7, of whether school performance is likely to improve or be adversely affected by the introduction of market competition. Market advocates argue that competition and choice will improve school performance for two reasons. Firstly, parents' increased ability to exercise choice will motivate them to become more involved in their children's education. Secondly, schools will be forced to raise their standards in order to compete for students. A further argument, of the kind advanced by Chubb and Moe, is that the localized management of schools in a market context is likely to be far more effective than under state bureaucratic control. The assumption here is that schools are indeed like businesses, and that if the management is sound the school will perform successfully. A significant omission from this perspective is any genuine consideration of the role of the students or the effects of student composition on a school's performance.

For market proponents, schools should be able to make a difference irrespective of the student composition of the school. In contrast, market critics see the student composition of a school as crucial to its exam success. As we saw in Chapter 2, the evidence from over 30 years of research has clearly established that the social class a child is born into is crucial to its education and life-chances. But there is also research to show that the social class mix of a school, as well as that of individual students, is important in determining student success.

Market critics point to a long line of research starting with Coleman and his colleagues (1966), which showed that the social class mix of a school had an impact on school performance after individual student backgrounds and prior achievement had been taken into account. This is known as the school mix effect. For example, the research has shown that when students from low social class backgrounds are grouped together in a school, individual students achieve less well than would be expected.

When this school mix effect is considered, the question of the polarization of school intakes assumes considerable significance. If the research by Coleman and others is correct, as school intakes become more polarized along social class lines, we would expect a decline in the performance of those schools which have suffered white middle class flight. The research reported in this chapter, therefore, sets the stage for tackling the crucial question of what happens to school performance in an education market.

Before we examine, in detail, the workings of one education market in New Zealand, we need a more complete conceptualization of how education markets are likely to work for without it we will not be able to explain the flows of students between schools.

The lived market

In Chapter 4 we suggested that, in contrast to the assumptions of pro-market advocates, education markets do not provide equality of access to all families. This is because middle class resources and networks enable them to access education markets in a way denied to working class families. We also established that popular schools, for whatever reasons, are more likely to accept white middle class students, even when those from working class or Maori families have the same level of achievement. But education markets, like many others, deviate from the ideal of perfectly competitive markets in other ways. Markets need to be studied in context because the outcomes generated by education markets will be determined both by the formal properties and informal arrangements of and within the market. The formal properties are typically established by legislation. Informal arrangements within a market are created by the actors, in this case schools, who will respond to competition by modifying it to their advantage. We call the outcomes of this combination of the formal and informal properties of a market the *lived* market.

As we saw in Chapter 3, political struggle at the national level gave a particular legal shape to the education market in New Zealand. But within this formal framework we would also expect to explain the flows of students according to the micropolitical interests of schools within any specific market. If this conjecture is correct then it raises serious questions about the effectiveness of such markets, as well as issues of fairness.

An additional factor which makes the workings of markets problematic is that specific markets will be influenced by the history of schools and by the sociogeography of the area (Bowe *et al.* 1992). The choices parents make will undoubtedly be constrained by the schools available and by their reputations. This may well cause unexpected fluctuations in 'demand' for a school. For example, if it is found that 'dope' is being smoked at an elite school this may temporarily damage its reputation, leading to a decline in demand. The problem for researchers is that generalizations about markets need to be made cautiously precisely because of the particular nature of specific education markets. This does not exclude the possibility of making generalizations; they need, however, to be made on the basis of multiple sources of evidence.

Testing the polarization thesis

In order to test the polarization thesis we have chosen to examine one market, that of Green City. Data were collected on new entrants to 11 state or integrated (Catholic) secondary schools between 1990, which was the last year of zoning, and 1995. State and integrated schools form over 90 per cent of Green City's secondary school provision. The schools in the sample included some from the inner city and some from a wedge of the city with both middle and working class suburbs. In contrast to many northern hemisphere cities, many of the elite single-sex schools are located in the city centre. Approximately 80 per cent of all students who lived in the centre of Green City attended the schools in our study, while for the suburban region, we had a higher coverage of about 90 per cent. The more comprehensive coverage in the suburbs usefully allowed us to track student enrolments, at or away from their local school: a key requirement for uncovering the overt and covert processes of an education market. Our general hypothesis was that we would expect to see a domino effect as the more middle class students in the study avoided the more socially and ethnically mixed local schools for those with a solid middle class intake. Notionally it was possible for students from the suburbs to attend an inner city school (and vice versa) without undue transport problems. If the market operated as pro-market theorists assume then we should see a two-way 'traffic' between city centre and suburban schools.

We selected four state co-educational schools in this suburban region in order to test our hypothesis. Weka College is in the suburbs and straddles a white middle class and a multi-ethnic working class area. Kea College, which is in relatively close proximity to Weka College, is in the working class area. Tui College is also in the working class area. Takahe College, in a largely middle class suburb, occupies a midpoint in the communications corridor to the central city. Sheppard College is the high SES school within the central city that featured in the previous chapter. In looking at the way schools have responded to the market, Sheppard provides an interesting point of contrast with our four case study schools. In theory, then, if our initial hypothesis concerning the idea of a domino effect in the flow of students from a predominantly working class suburb, through the middle class corridor to the high SES inner city schools is correct, it should be observed at work in the schools chosen for this case study. The sociogeography of this market is represented in Figure 6.1.

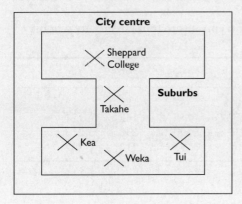

Figure 6.1 The Green City education market

The third-form intake of 11 Green City schools

Some overall characteristics of the students attending the 11 Green City schools are shown in Table 6.1.

Table 6.1 shows that the total number of students dropped steadily over the years with the third-form roll in 1995 being 76 per cent of the 1990 third-form roll. This drop reflected the national trend, although the Green City decrease was markedly greater than the national decrease (Ministry of Education 1991b, 1992, 1993, 1994 and 1995b). The socioeconomic background of students was almost constant at around three on a six-point scale; percentages of Maori and Pacific Island students remained stable at around 12 to 15 per cent for each group.

The general picture, then, is that the composition of the students was generally consistent from year to year, which makes it most likely that any compositional changes experienced by schools were primarily the result of between-school processes rather than underlying demographic shifts.

The overall picture presented in Table 6.1 does, however, obscure changes that occurred between schools in terms of the composition of their

Table 6.1 Basic descriptors of the third-form intake in 11 Green City schools 1990–5

	1990	1991	1992	1993	1994	1995
Total numbers	2448	2301	2059	1928	2033	1852
Mean SES*	3.08	3.06	3.12	3.08	3.00	3.12
Ethnicity						
Maori	13%	15%	15%	12%	15%	13%
Pacific Island	15%	13%	14%	13%	14%	12%
Pakeha	64%	66%	65%	68%	64%	67%
Other	8%	7%	7%	7%	7%	8%

* SES was based on an adaptation of the Elley and Irving scale where 1 was high and 7 was low

Table 6.2 Numbers of all third-form entrants to four Green City schools 1990–5

Year	1990	1991	1992	1993	1994	1995
Kea	200*	126	105	87	86	58
Tui	200	172	157	159	162	121
Weka	200	237	230	190	230	213
Takahe	200	220	209	195	213	202

* The actual rolls have been disguised.

third-form intakes. To demonstrate the effects of these changes, we have developed a sub-sample of four schools from the larger sample of 11. The four schools were located in a distinct geographical area, and thus we were able to track student movement in detail. Tables 6.2 to 19 look at the roll numbers, the SES mix and the ethnic composition of third-form intake (which is the first year of secondary school) across six years for these four schools.

Third-form intake of the sub-sample of four schools

In order to preserve confidentiality for the four schools the actual roll numbers have not been given on Table 6.2. Instead the roll for 1990 has been indexed to 200 for each school, with changes in subsequent years being reflected proportionally. The nominal figure of 200 for 1990 was not greatly different from the mean third-form roll of the four schools in that year.

The 1995 combined third-form roll of these four schools was 74 per cent of their combined third-form roll in 1990, which mirrors the overall decline in student numbers in the 11 schools. However, this decrease in student numbers was not spread evenly across the four schools. Kea's third-form roll fell dramatically, so that by 1995 it was not much more than a quarter of the 1990 roll. Tui College also showed a marked decline in the number of third-form entrants over this period with about a 40 per cent drop. The third-form rolls of Weka College and Takahe College stayed relatively constant over this time period.

When combined across all 11 schools, the mean SES of third-form entrants showed little change over time. However, Table 6.3 shows that when these SES data are examined in detail for each of the four schools in our sub-sample, clear patterns emerge.

Students attending Kea College clearly had the lowest mean SES of these four schools. Over the six-year period studied the mean SES of students at

Table 6.3   Mean SES* of all third-form entrants to four Green City schools 1990–5

	1990	1991	1992	1993	1994	1995
Kea	5.1	5.3	5.8	5.5	5.6	5.9
Tui	4.5	4.3	4.8	4.9	5.2	4.6
Weka	3.7	3.9	3.6	3.8	4.1	4.5
Takahe	3.2	3.2	3.1	3.1	3.1	3.2

* SES was based on an adaptation of the Elley and Irving scale where 1 was high and 7 was low.

Kea dropped markedly, reaching a low of 5.9 in 1995. It is clear that by 1995 this school was attended by students from very low SES homes. Tui College had students with a mean SES of about 4.5 to 5.0 throughout the six years, with no clear trend apparent. In 1990, the mean SES of students attending Weka College was closer to that of the highest ranking school (Takahe College) than to that of Tui. However, by 1995 the mean SES of students at Weka had dropped to equal that of Tui. The mean SES of students attending Takahe College was clearly higher than that of students attending the other three schools and showed no variation over the period.

Considered together, Tables 6.2 and 6.3 suggest that students from relatively high SES families bypassed Kea and Tui Colleges, thus decreasing their third-form rolls and lowering the SES mix of these schools over time. Furthermore, Kea College, which had the lowest mean SES in 1990, experienced the greatest decline in both mean SES and numbers of third-formers over the six-year period.

Table 6.1 indicated that across all 11 Smithfield schools in Green City there was no change in the ethnic mix from 1990–5. Tables 6.4 to 6.7, however, show some marked shifts in ethnic mix when the data are presented for the sub-sample of four schools.

Table 6.4 shows that in 1990, Kea College had a very high percentage of Pacific Island students, a sizable group of Maori students, but very few Pakeha or 'Other' students. As noted above, this school's third-form roll dropped dramatically with the removal of zoning. The ethnic composition of the smaller number of students enrolled in 1995 had changed since 1990. The percentage of Pacific Island students attending Kea College had increased greatly from 62 per cent to 80 per cent. At the same time there was a marked decrease in the percentages of Maori students attending this school.

As Table 6.5 shows, Tui College had sizable populations of Pakeha, Maori and Pacific Island students attending. After 1990 there was an increase in the percentage of Maori students attending, with no clear pattern emerging for Pakeha and Pacific Island students over time. Tui had a

Table 6.4 Percentages of all third-form entrants to Kea College in 1990–5, by ethnic background

	1990	1991	1992	1993	1994	1995
Maori	32	34	30	28	22	19
Pacific Island	62	62	64	69	71	80
Pakeha	7	3	5	4	6	0
Other	0	0	2	0	1	2

Table 6.5   Percentages of all third-form entrants to Tui College in 1990–5, by ethnic background

	1990	1991	1992	1993	1994	1995
Maori	33	42	36	47	49	42
Pacific Island	21	23	24	17	25	15
Pakeha	43	34	39	35	25	43
Other	3	1	2	1	0	1

Table 6.6   Percentages of all third-form entrants to Weka College in 1990–5, by ethnic background

	1990	1991	1992	1993	1994	1995
Maori	22	28	28	25	33	29
Pacific Island	22	24	31	29	28	27
Pakeha	53	43	38	42	31	35
Other	2	5	3	4	8	10

strong bicultural programme; it appears that with the abolition of zoning, Maori students moved to this school to participate in that programme, a trend which may partially account for the drop in the percentage of Maori students attending Kea.

Like Tui College, Weka College (Table 6.6) also had sizable populations of Pakeha, Pacific Islands and Maori students. However, the percentage of Pakeha students showed a major drop over the six-year period, with concomitant rises in the percentages of the other ethnic groups. In 1990, under zoning, approximately half of Weka's third-formers were Pakeha. By 1995, five years after the removal of zoning, the third-form roll was only about one-third Pakeha. The third-form intake to Weka was truly multicultural in 1995, with Maori, Pacific Island and Pakeha students in almost equal proportions.

Takahe College (Table 6.7) had predominantly Pakeha students throughout the six-year period, with the percentage of non-Pakeha students remaining stable over time. Clearly, then, Takahe was not affected by the demographic shifts experienced by the other three schools.

The overall picture presented by Tables 6.2 to 6.7 gives some sense of the dynamics that operate within a context of marketization and, in particular, of the differential impact of the removal of zoning on school intakes. Kea College, with the lowest mean SES and the highest percentage of non-Pakeha students, experienced the greatest drop in third-form intake and

Table 6.7   Percentages of all third-form entrants to Takahe College in 1990–5, by ethnic background

	1990	1991	1992	1993	1994	1995
Maori	6	10	10	7	8	10
Pacific Island	6	7	4	6	7	5
Pakeha	82	79	79	79	78	80
Other	7	5	7	7	7	6

also had a decrease in mean SES. In contrast, Takahe College experienced no change in either composition or roll numbers over time. Takahe was 'oversubscribed' and, as such, was able to operate an enrolment scheme after 1991.

Weka College is in an interesting position. While the number of students in the third-form intake has remained relatively stable over time, the ethnic mix and SES mix have undergone major changes. The decline in mean SES and the increase in the percentage of non-Pakeha students was attributable to two factors. Firstly, there was an increase in enrolments from lower SES, non-Pakeha students; secondly, Weka College experienced a decline in enrolments from higher SES and Pakeha students. Given the connection at Kea and Tui between student enrolments and both mean SES and ethnic mix, Weka College may soon experience a decline in student numbers as students exit or bypass the school in favour of one with a higher mean SES and a higher percentage of Pakeha students.

Clearly, then, there was considerable change in student enrolments in some schools over time. In the next section we track student enrolments in relation to residential address to see which students attended their local school and which students attended schools outside of their local area.

Enrolment patterns

Here we look at the overall pattern of student enrolments in the full dataset of 11 Green City schools.

On an area-by-area basis, the different schools were categorized as being either local, adjacent or distant. Schools were considered *local* when students lived within the original (1990) zone boundaries of the school. Schools which were clearly not the local school and for which travel was required were considered *adjacent*. To get to *distant* schools, students bypassed their local school and at least one other in a way that involved considerable travel.

The percentages of these students who attended local, adjacent or distant schools are given in Table 6.8.

Table 6.8   Percentages of third-form students attending schools which were local, adjacent or distant

	1990	1991	1992	1993	1994	1995
Local	76	69	71	71	66	65
Adjacent	14	20	20	18	22	25
Distant	10	11	9	11	12	10

The figures indicate that the majority of students attended their local school, although this percentage dropped from 76 per cent to 65 per cent over the years 1990–5. The percentage of students travelling to a distant school remained very stable at around 10 per cent, with a marked increase (from 14 per cent to 25 per cent) in those attending adjacent schools.

The flow that increased over the years was from local to adjacent schools. To consider this issue further, we explore in detail the ethnicity and socio-economic status of students who bypassed their local school.

Enrolment by ethnicity

An ethnic breakdown of attendance patterns is shown in Table 6.9.

In 1990, higher percentages of Maori and Pacific Island students attended local schools than the percentages for Pakeha students, with Pakeha students having the highest percentage attending distant schools. However, by 1995, a dramatic change had taken place. Pacific Island and Maori students bypassed their local schools in far greater numbers than did the Pakeha students (about a 20 per cent drop for Maori and Pacific Island students versus a 7 per cent drop for Pakeha students), so that by 1995, the percentage of Pacific Island and Maori students attending their local school was lower than that for Pakeha students. For Pakeha and Pacific Island students, the percentages attending distant schools showed little change over time, while for Maori students there appears to be an increase by 1995. However, the greatest movement of Maori and Pacific Island students was to adjacent schools. By 1995, these groups had higher percentages of students at adjacent schools than did Pakeha students. The students from other ethnic backgrounds (largely Asian) showed a movement from local to adjacent schools that was greater than that of Pakeha students, but less than that of the two Polynesian groups.

These figures would seem to indicate an increase in the number of Pacific Island and Maori students attending adjacent schools since the removal of zoning. However, once the SES background of these students is considered in detail, a different picture emerges.

Table 6.9 Percentage of all third-form students by ethnicity and locality of school

	1990	1991	1992	1993	1994	1995
Maori						
Local	79	70	73	69	66	61
Adjacent	15	25	22	25	28	29
Distant	6	5	5	6	7	10
Pacific Island						
Local	83	72	65	67	62	62
Adjacent	13	22	31	28	33	32
Distant	5	6	4	5	5	6
Pakeha						
Local	74	68	71	72	67	67
Adjacent	13	18	18	16	18	22
Distant	13	14	11	12	15	11
Other						
Local	76	68	75	69	62	65
Adjacent	16	27	19	17	30	29
Distant	8	5	7	14	9	6

Enrolment by socioeconomic status

Table 6.10 shows that students who attended distant schools consistently came from higher SES homes than those attending local or adjacent schools. However, with the exception of 1990, students attending adjacent schools came from lower mean SES homes than those attending local schools.

Taking the figures at face value, it appears that de-zoning increased the number of lower SES students attending an adjacent school. If this were the case then this would provide some support for pro-market advocates because it would appear that at least some choices, even if only to the adjacent school, were being made. However, these figures are complicated by two factors. The first is that zones will encompass a diversity of neighbourhoods; they may encompass what may generally be thought to be a working class area, but even within that there will be neighbourhoods, for example, where more families have someone in work than others. The second is that zones are not drawn equidistantly between schools, and it may be that an adjacent school is in fact closer to some homes than the 'local' school. In this case what appears to be the exercise of choice may be no more than an expression of convenience. One way of examining this issue is to see

Table 6.10 Mean SES* of all third-form students by locality of school

	1990	1991	1992	1993	1994	1995
Local	3.09	2.96	3.14	2.99	3.00	2.90
Adjacent	3.01	3.11	3.21	3.20	3.12	3.10
Distant	2.52	2.42	2.39	2.51	2.35	2.59

* SES was based on an adaptation of the Elley and Irving scale where 1 was high and 7 was low.

whether there are ethnic or SES differences 'in the propensity to pursue enrolment options within the same attendance area' (Maddaus 1990: 284). In other words, we wanted to ask who in a given neighbourhood, rather than zone, is more likely to go to the local rather than an adjacent school.

Our data allow us to take neighbourhood characteristics into account to monitor trends closely both within and between suburbs. In order to focus on enrolment processes for a given residential area, we compared the student's SES to the mean SES of the neighbourhood the student lived in to give a measure we termed 'relative SES'. A positive relative SES indicates that the student is of higher SES than typical for the neighbourhood in which he or she lives; a negative relative SES indicates that the student is of lower SES than typical for the neighbourhood. When calculating relative SES the mean SES of each neighbourhood was computed on a year-by-year basis to ensure the greatest possible accuracy.

Table 6.11 shows the mean relative SES of students attending local, adjacent and distant schools. It can be seen that the relative SES of students attending local schools was consistently lower than that of students attending adjacent or distant schools. This indicates that local schools were consistently populated by students whose families had lower SES than others in their neighbourhoods. In contrast, students who attended adjacent or distant schools were from families who had relatively high SES in comparison with their neighbourhoods.

The clear pattern in Table 6.10, of students from distant schools having

Table 6.11 Mean relative SES* of all third-form students by locality of school

	1990	1991	1992	1993	1994	1995
Local	−0.08	−0.10	−0.14	−0.12	−0.15	−0.12
Adjacent	0.16	0.13	0.35	0.25	0.30	0.24
Distant	0.35	0.40	0.33	0.35	0.33	0.17

* Relative SES refers to a student's own SES subtracted from that student's neighbourhood SES.

a higher mean SES than those attending adjacent schools, was true in Table 6.11 for only 1990 and 1991 when relative SES of students is compared. From 1992–5, the mean relative SES of the two groups was roughly equal. There was an increase in relative mean SES from 1992 to 1995 compared to 1990 and 1991 for students attending adjacent schools. Therefore, in contrast to the picture presented in Table 4.10, it was the relatively well-off students who attended adjacent schools after 1991, while those relatively worse-off were most likely to go to their local school.

It appears, then, that de-zoning has not increased the likelihood that students who are relatively worse-off (in comparison with their neighbourhood) will attend non-local schools.

Enrolment by ethnicity and socioeconomic status

The method of using a student's own SES compared with the neighbourhood SES can also be applied to examine the SES dimension of ethnic attendance patterns.

Table 6.12 indicates that for all ethnic groups, those with the lowest relative SES were most likely to attend their local school.

For Maori students, there was a trend for the relative SES of students attending distant schools to be a little higher than for those attending adjacent schools, although for distant schools the number of students on

Table 6.12 Mean relative SES* of all third-form students by ethnicity and locality of school

	1990	1991	1992	1993	1994	1995
Maori						
Local	−0.64	−0.95	−0.87	−0.99	−0.69	−0.77
Adjacent	0.40	−0.31	−0.08	0.09	0.28	0.30
Distant	0.45	−0.13[†]	−0.12[†]	0.20[†]	1.00	0.43
Pacific Island						
Local	−0.60	−0.60	−0.72	−0.70	−1.02	−1.00
Adjacent	−0.42	−0.10	0.30	0.09	0.12	0.24
Distant	0.41[†]	0.07[†]	0.58[†]	0.08[†]	−0.39[†]	−0.71[†]
Pakeha						
Local	0.20	0.14	0.13	0.10	0.13	0.06
Adjacent	0.24	0.30	0.45	0.33	0.47	0.29
Distant	0.43	0.43	0.37	0.36	0.32	0.18

* Relative SES refers to a student's own SES subtracted from that student's neighbourhood SES.
† Indicates 16 or fewer cases.

which the figures are based is sometimes small. This pattern is not evident in the Pakeha and Pacific Island figures, where half the figures favour adjacent schools and half distant ones in each case. Clearly though, for all three ethnic groups, it was the relatively advantaged who were able to attend non-local schools.

Enrolment profile of the sub-sample of four schools in 1994

In this section we return to the sub-sample of four Green City schools in order to examine student enrolments in greater detail. In the previous section, we presented an analysis across six years of school intake data. In this section we focus on just one year, 1994. We examine in detail the composition of the third-form intake at the sub-sample of four schools.

There are two reasons for exploring the third-form intake of 1994 in greater detail. Firstly, as the tables in the previous section show, at that time, four years after the removal of zoning, it is clear that the pattern of relatively advantaged students moving away from their local school was confirmed. Secondly, we were able to track student enrolment in detail in 1994 since this was the year that the Smithfield students (who we could track on an individual basis) entered secondary school. By focusing on one area in Green City which was serviced by four schools, we could therefore track the impact of the general trend identified in the previous section, on the lived reality of the market.

It should be noted that although acceptably high percentages of the third-form intake in three colleges were part of the Smithfield cohort (66 per cent for Tui, 68 per cent for Takahe and 74 per cent for Weka), only 40 per cent of the Kea College intake were in the Smithfield cohort in 1994.

Smithfield students who bypassed their local school

Table 6.13 Percentages of 1994 Smithfield third-formers bypassing their local school area, by family SES

	Local school bypassed			
	Kea	*Tui*	*Weka*	*Takahe*
High	*	80	73	20
Middle	79	76	63	20
Low	58	35	39	15

* There were only five students from high SES families who lived in the Kea locality, so these figures were omitted from the table.

Table 6.14 Percentages of Smithfield 1994 third-formers bypassing their local school, by ethnicity

	Local school bypassed			
	Kea	*Tui*	*Weka*	*Takahe*
Maori	79	30	27	0
Pacific Island	53	25	50	10
Pakeha	69	61	61	20

Table 6.13 shows that while 80 per cent of high SES students who lived in the catchment area for Tui College bypassed the school, only 35 per cent of students from low SES backgrounds did so. For all four schools, a clear pattern emerged, with students from low SES backgrounds being less likely to bypass their locality for another school than those from higher SES backgrounds. This confirms the general trend shown in Tables 6.8 to 6.12, that it was the relatively advantaged who bypassed their local school. The low percentage of students from any SES group who bypassed Takahe College would seem to indicate that it was a popular school.

The ethnic backgrounds of students who bypassed their local school area are examined more closely in Table 6.14.

Very high percentages of all ethnic groups bypassed Kea College, with Maori students being the most likely to move. Pakeha students were markedly more likely to bypass Tui than were Maori or Pacific Island students. Sixty-one per cent of Pakeha students and 50 per cent of Pacific Island students bypassed Weka College, although the number of Pacific Island students involved was small. Relatively few students bypassed Takahe College, but of those who did, most were Pakeha. Figures have not been presented by school for students whose ethnicity was coded as 'Other' as there were less than 10 such students in three of the four school areas. However, overall a high 63 per cent of 'Other' students bypassed their local area.

Taken together, Tables 6.13 and 6.14 show the impact of student ethnicity and SES on enrolment. Pakeha students and those from high SES backgrounds were most likely to bypass their local school. Furthermore, the mean SES and the ethnic mix of the school was also related to student enrolment. Schools with the lowest mean SES and the lowest percentage of Pakeha students were most likely to be bypassed by students from their local catchment area.

Enrolment of Smithfield students by school circuit

In Chapter 4 we introduced the notion of 'circuits' as a method of dividing schools according to their popularity within the education market.

Table 6.15   Percentage of Smithfield 1994 students who bypassed their local low circuit school and moved to higher circuit schools, by SES

	To middle circuit	To high circuit	Total
High	30	35	65
Middle	13	35	48
Low	8	7	15

High circuit schools all operated enrolment schemes, had a high mean SES and, with one exception, were single sex in character. These schools had relatively high numbers of students who travelled long distances to attend them. Low circuit schools often had declining student numbers, had a low mean SES and were all co-educational. Middle circuit schools had a mean SES between that of the high and low circuit schools, and while one or two operated enrolment schemes, they had relatively few students travelling long distances to attend them. They comprised both single-sex and co-educational schools.

In Chapter 4, we used the notion of circuits to track patterns of student enrolment across 23 secondary schools in two cities. That report showed that Pakeha students and students from higher SES families were most likely to attend higher circuit schools.

In this chapter, we use the notion of circuits to explore enrolment patterns of a smaller sample of Smithfield students from the four schools in our sub-sample. Table 6.15 shows the percentages of these students who lived in the catchment area for a low circuit school but who bypassed their local school in favour of a higher circuit school.

Table 6.15 shows that 30 per cent of the high SES students who lived in the catchment areas of the low circuit schools (Kea, Tui or Weka) moved to the adjacent middle circuit school (Takahe) and another 35 per cent of these high SES students moved to a high circuit school in the central city. In total, then, 65 per cent of high SES students bypassed their local low circuit school and moved to one which was higher circuit. Of students from middle SES families, a total of 48 per cent bypassed their local low circuit school to attend a higher circuit school, while only 15 per cent of students from low SES families moved to a higher circuit school. This pattern makes it very clear that family SES had a major impact on the likelihood of students from the locality of a low circuit school moving to a middle or high circuit school.

While 50 per cent of Pakeha students and 42 per cent of 'Other' students bypassed their local low circuit school to attend a higher circuit school, only 8 per cent of Maori and Pacific Island students did so.

Together, Tables 6.15 and 6.16 show that comparatively few Smithfield students from Maori or Pacific Island families or from families with low SES backgrounds bypassed their local low circuit school in favour of a

Table 6.16   Percentage of Smithfield 1994 students who bypassed their local low circuit school and moved to higher circuit schools, by ethnicity

	To middle circuit	To high circuit	Total
Maori	3	5	8
Pacific Island	2	6	8
Pakeha	21	29	50
Other	21	21	42

higher circuit school. In the previous two chapters we considered the extent to which this was a matter of student choice or of selection by the higher circuit schools themselves.

Bypassing local schools – effects on composition of schools

In order to see the effect which student enrolment had on the SES composition of the schools, we need to compare the SES composition of students attending each school with the SES composition of those who live in the catchment area of the school. In this analysis, the term 'catchment areas' refers to the school zones operating in 1990. The mean SES of all third-form students living in the catchment area around each school is contrasted in Table 6.17 with the mean SES of each school's third-form intake.

Table 6.17 shows that while the mean SES of third-formers attending Kea College in 1994 was 5.6, the mean SES of all third-formers who lived in the catchment area surrounding the school was higher at 5.0. Tui College and Weka College also had a lower mean SES for students attending their schools than the mean SES of students living in the catchment areas of those schools. In contrast, the mean SES of students attending Takahe College exactly reflected the SES of students who lived in the locality.

Table 6.17   Mean SES* in 1994 of all third-form students attending the four schools and of all students living in the school catchment area

	School	Catchment area
Kea	5.6	5.0
Tui	5.2	4.1
Weka	4.1	3.1
Takahe	3.1	3.1

* SES was based on an adaptation of the Elley and Irving scale where 1 was high and 7 was low.

Table 6.18   Ethnic background (per cent) of all 1994 third-form students attending the four schools and of all students living in the school catchment area

	Kea College	Area	Tui College	Area	Weka College	Area	Takahe College	Area
Maori	22	29	49	44	33	16	8	8
Pacific Island	71	57	25	13	28	10	7	7
Pakeha	6	8	25	41	31	69	78	78

Hence, students bypassing their local school had the effect of lowering the mean school SES at Kea, Tui and Weka, while the mean school SES of Takahe was not affected. The reasons for this will be discussed shortly because they touch on the politics of the lived market. However, the general point is that the data show that markets exacerbate residential segregation.

The effect of students bypassing their local schools on the ethnic composition of the schools is shown in Table 6.18.

Once again, students bypassing the local school had the greatest effect on Weka College, where the percentages of Maori and Pacific Island students attending the school were double that in the school catchment area (33 cf. 16 per cent for Maori and 28 cf. 10 per cent for Pacific Islanders). At the same time the percentage of Pakeha students attending the school was less than half that of Pakeha students in the catchment area (31 cf. 69 per cent). Kea College had an increase in the percentage of Pacific Island students and a small decrease in percentages of Maori students. Tui College showed a marked drop in the percentage of Pakeha students, a doubling in the percentage of Pacific Island students, and a slight increase in the percentage of Maori students. Students who bypassed their local school had no effect at all on the ethnic composition of Takahe.

Having seen that movement away from the local schools is related to the SES and ethnicity of students, we now examine in detail the effects of this movement on the enrolment numbers at the four schools. With the exception of one low SES suburb that was divided into catchment areas for two schools, the catchment areas of the four schools under discussion are distinct geographical areas divided by natural features, (such as rivers or hills) or other features (such as major roads or industrial areas). The catchment areas of the four schools were close enough that students could move easily from one to another. Each of these four school catchment areas is on a public transport route to the central city, although travel to or from the city would be in excess of half an hour in each direction. Given that theoretically there was free movement between the four schools and the

Table 6.19 Numbers of Smithfield 1994 third-formers who attended local schools or moved to another school

	Numbers attending from other areas	Numbers leaving for other schools	Net gain or loss
Kea	2	72	−70
Tui	20	47	−27
Weka	68	73	−5
Takahe	41	29	+12

central city schools, we now examine the extent of the movement between them.

The four schools show markedly different patterns in Table 6.19. Kea College gained only two students from another catchment area, but lost 72 students who lived in its locality but moved to other schools. Tui College gained 20 students and lost 47. Weka College gained almost as many students as it lost. Takahe College gained more students than it lost.

Figure 6.2 presents diagrammatically the general patterns of movement that actually occurred. This figure omits cases where only one to three students moved from one school to another.

Figure 6.2 gives the detail of student movement between schools. For example, very large numbers of students (48 to 53) moved *to* Weka College from Kea's catchment area and *from* Weka's catchment area to central city schools. Smaller numbers (11 to 18) moved to Weka from Tui, with moderate numbers (21 to 26) moving from Weka to Takahe.

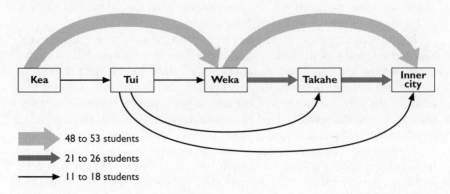

Figure 6.2 Numbers of Smithfield students from each school's catchment area who attended another school in 1994

Overall, the flow of students shown in Figure 6.2 is clearly unidirectional, with the flow going in the direction Kea, Tui, Weka, Takahe and to the central city, so confirming our original hypothesis. No students from the central city moved to any of these four suburban schools; and the few movements against the flow between the four schools involved only one to three students in each case. There is an exact match between the direction of flow of students and both mean SES of schools and percentages of Pakeha students. Kea College, for which the flow was outward, had a mean SES of 5.6 and only 6 per cent Pakeha students. The central city schools with an inward flow of students had a mean SES of 2.9, and 77 per cent of their third-form intakes were Pakeha. The mean SES and the percentages of Pakeha students for the other three schools fell between these two extremes in the same order as the flow shown on Figure 6.2: for example, Tui College (which had the second smallest inflow of students) had the second lowest mean SES and the second lowest percentage of Pakeha students.

It is clear from this figure and from our results that there are three polarizing consequences produced by the introduction of education markets:

1 Students from high SES backgrounds have the greatest opportunity to avoid working class schools, and most take it.
2 In terms of the relative opportunities of different SES groups within a neighbourhood to exercise choice, students with the highest SES backgrounds in a neighbourhood are most likely to exercise choice.
3 The exit from working class schools induces a spiral of decline. Consequently, the impact of exit from local schools is not felt equally under conditions of increased competition brought about by the removal of zoning. Schools in working class areas with high percentages of non-Pakeha students fare worst, while schools that are able to operate an enrolment scheme effectively insulate themselves from the effects of the market.

We now need to look beneath the figures to understand how schools responded to the market through the formal and informal techniques they adopted for survival. In other words we shall look at how the *lived market* operated in Green City.

The response to market competition

To understand how schools responded to the market we interviewed the principals of three of our four suburban schools at the end of 1993. As a point of contrast we also interviewed the principal of one of the inner city's elite single-sex schools, Sheppard High. From these interviews we can begin to classify the kinds of responses schools make. These are:

1 overt responses in terms of marketing;
2 non-responses or avoiding decisions which schools judge their local market would find unacceptable;
3 political responses which seek to change the rules or terms on which schools compete;
4 networked responses which involve collusion or 'cooperation'.

Together these responses comprise the *lived market* which has a direct effect on whether and how schools survive in a competitive context and how student flows are determined. However, in the three schools most threatened by the introduction of competition these responses were weighed against what was seen, in their professional judgement, as educationally desirable. The tension between market image and educational vision was ever present (Bowe *et al.* 1992). The lived market is not value free in the way it is structured, as other commentators (Ball 1990; Grace 1995) have noted.

The 'marketing response' was most evident in the working class schools. Faced with a dramatic spiral of decline the principal of Kea College commented:

> The fact of the matter is that we have to target everyone who comes.
> (Principal, Kea College)

A strong drive was being made to increase the roll and to set up a publicity committee to coordinate marketing activities. Initially, the strategy was one of damage control through some highly visible means. These included a new discipline system to reduce parental fears of violence and unruliness at the school, the introduction of an attractive yet inexpensive new uniform and improving promotional resources and activities.

> There are things which can be done which probably needed changing anyway but they are always good shots to gain publicity and turn things around. I mean the discipline system, even though it is less rigorous than before in that you fire kids out less easily, the parents see you being firm and addressing what they see as a discipline problem. You can always change the uniform, that goes down well . . . [and] change the prospectus and do some promotional things in [the local shopping centre].
> (Principal, Kea College)

These kinds of activities were not enough, however. The school also needed to turn around its academic vision and performance:

> I've told the Board and the teachers that we have played all our cheap, easy cards now, the only thing which can make a difference is what happens in the classrooms.
> (Principal, Kea College)

As a result some new initiatives were developed. The major innovation was to respond to the low levels of prior achievement of students entering the school by retaining them for an extra year in the junior school before they reached the examination-oriented senior classes. By retaining students for an extra year the school hoped to increase the size of its roll by an entire year group and also meet worthwhile educational aims. These aims included ethnic language programmes in which students would take two hours per week in their own ethnic language and a life skills programme.

Another innovation was to employ management consultants. This was not only for the merits of their advice. Showing the school to be 'progressive' in using TQM management consultants was a useful publicity device and offered the possibility of bringing in resources from a variety of interested corporate and government sources:

> We came across this programme which in philosophy is stuff all different from what we are doing anyway. We've got the inside track and a lot of help from a number of consultants associated with the school so we decided that we would try and make that a part of the reforms we put in place because we can significantly improve staff and student practice. I'm not at all worried about the fact that it is a bandwagon at the moment, it's likely to be a bandwagon that can push quite a lot of training and resources our way.
>
> (Principal, Kea College)

Kea College's attempts to increase its intake were not without problems. Staff were facing increasing demands at a time when their numbers were being severely cut. The context in which this occurred put substantially greater daily demands on teaching than in most schools, so that the marketing exercise came as an ill-afforded cost. There were no spare resources, and the strain told:

> Most of the teachers are on side although I guess there must be some that are not comfortable. I mean the system is set up to make them work a lot harder. We are at the bottom of the heap, we have to put in extra hours in order to get kids here. That's what we want to do in order to preserve jobs. Some [staff] I think are uncomfortable with it [marketing efforts], I expect a backlash at some stage.
>
> (Principal, Kea College)

At Weka College the principal had to handle a decline in the numbers of Pakeha students and an increase in the number of Pacific Island students. Weka had prided itself on being a socially balanced comprehensive school which taught in mixed ability classes. Now with the changes wrought by the market, the school was faced with a series of moral and educational dilemmas.

The principal of Weka College had little doubt that the white flight following the increased Maori and Pacific Island Polynesian enrolments has both racial and socioeconomic dimensions. According to the principal, racism played a part in this white flight, so that if he was to keep an ethnically well balanced school,

> We need to be able to demonstrate that we are not going to be overrun by 'blacks' . . .
>
> (Principal, Weka College)

Related to this were fears about the academic standard of the school and its mixed ability approach:

> [There] is a perception abroad in the community that we don't stretch and extend the top academic group and that they should probably go elsewhere, and that's probably true because it takes an awful lot of specialized effort to bring up the bottom group. Parents of what they think are reasonably academic kids . . . see their kids as being sacrificed to less able kids who take more attention and are more likely to be disruptive and more demanding of teachers' time.
>
> (Principal, Weka College)

Given its situation, marketing for Weka College might be seen as a matter of attracting the kinds of white, able, middle class students the school needed to signal its quality to the Pakeha community and prevent further white flight. Yet marketing to this audience presented major ethical dilemmas for the school:

> I suppose the question really is, are we going to drastically change our approach, try and get rid of our [former Kea College zone] clientele and market ourselves as a middle class school, or do we say we are a state school and educate everyone who comes through the door? . . . So we are in the situation . . . do we compromise our basic principles for the sake of marketing ourselves [with the Pakeha community] or do we say well, we are educationalists and we are going to do what is best for our total clientele and if some people suffer and want to go elsewhere, well, tough?
>
> (Principal, Weka College)

One solution to Weka's problems was to stream the school. This was seen as being likely to increase middle class Pakeha enrolments, but such a move would have gone against the ethical and educational values the school has followed since inception. Furthermore, given the current context it would segregate the school on an ethnic basis:

> Weka College was premised on the fact that we would be a non-streamed school, there is a strong commitment to that among the staff but whether it will stand up to the pressures I don't know . . . If we

broad-banded or streamed we would end up pretty much with a school
that had three or four Pakeha upper stream classes. The proportion of
Pakeha kids in the bottom stream classes would be very small . . .

(Principal, Weka College)

Weka was clearly caught between making decisions which were antithet-
ical to its educational philosophy and attracting middle class Pakeha students, and so sought a political solution to escape the dilemma. This
entailed getting the maximum roll reduced in order to impose an enrolment
scheme that would enable the school to choose its students. They would
then be able to reduce the non-Pakeha enrolments from Kea College's
former zone and retain the closer, predominantly Pakeha students. However, the principal found that this strategy was unlikely to work:

The unofficial word I've had from the Ministry yesterday is that they
wouldn't see much mileage in this – they are totally committed to non-
zoning and if a school goes to the wall, well, tough bikky.

(Principal, Weka College)

During 1993 the school was still 'trying to become proactive in taking
control' of its market position by attempting to get the roll reduced on the
grounds of inadequate space in specialist areas of the school, but again with
little luck.

At the top of the local hierarchy, Takahe College stood to grow rapidly in
size. Positioned in the gap between the central city and suburban schools it
drew on an essentially middle class intake, which was reflected in its exam
results. The likely increase in the size of the school was a concern to the
school's principal in two respects:

The Board and I had discussed the whole question of the size of the
school and I put the view very strongly to the Board that I was sick of
big schools, that I did not think they did as good a job as smaller
schools and, other things being equal, it's better to have a smaller school
than a larger school. Secondly, that the Board had a social responsibility to Weka, Tui and Kea Colleges and that they ought not to be
making this school a big school at the risk of perhaps closing other
schools.

(Principal, Takahe College)

The principal gave several grounds for being concerned about this situation and the lack of resources, skills and knowledge to cope:

We were suddenly in the position of having absolutely no control over
who came here and people came to the school with a range of educational problems for which we had no solutions because we had no special or discretionary staffing to deal with them . . . As for us thinking

that we could educate the kids from that area better than the teachers at Tui College can, that is a ludicrous notion!

(Principal, Takahe College)

The principal thought the popularity of his school, as against other schools in the area, could be based on an element of racism:

> I seriously wonder how much of the decisions people make about schools is actually related to their perception of the race situation at a particular school. And sadly some people do have some justification, or some way to justify the view that schools which have too large a proportion of this group or that might be unsafe for their children . . . I reckon, and I suppose this could be taken as a totally racist statement, that given the state of play of Maori education, Maori SES, Pacific Island education, Pacific Island SES, once you get past a school balance which is 70 per cent European, 30 per cent Polynesian, you start to run into difficulties. That is a 'rule of thumb' thing but I reckon that is the case, both at the school and the parent choice level.

(Principal, Takahe College)

In 1991, intensified exit from the former zones of Weka, Tui and Kea Colleges increased Takahe College's intake by 10 per cent. Prompt action was therefore taken. This centred around getting the maximum roll of the school reduced by the Ministry of Education so that the school could apply for overcrowding status and develop an enrolment scheme. Here, Takahe College was very successful because of the national standing and charisma of its principal and Board who negotiated with the Ministry and lobbied the local MP:

> We were originally told that this school with all its facilities could house 1800 students if we really had to. That was a crazy notion. They graciously then allowed us to have 1400 and then when we had a seizure over that they said well 1200 . . . And then [the Board] argued very strongly for the lowest number the Ministry might agree to which was 1050 . . . That indicated we were prepared to take an increase, because you know, the government view was that parents ought to have a choice of school, so we were saying, 'OK, let's take another 40 or so'. But the Ministry said no, 1200, so we had another stand-off. Then [the local MP] intervened on our behalf so we were offered 1080, and we figured that's as low as they would go at the moment, so that's our maximum roll and that's more than enough.

(Principal, Takahe College)

Takahe College's action was extremely successful by any measure. By 1992 the school was clearly likely to exceed its new maximum roll, so that it was able to impose a zone-based enrolment scheme with few out-of-zone places. This was a crucial step to retain the stability of the school, and it even increased enrolments from families who would otherwise have bypassed the school:

> Since it has become known that we have an enrolment scheme and that it's hard to get into this school, it's interesting to notice how many people are now trying to get into this school from other schools . . . So it's a fascinating exercise in community psychology. Maybe there is some truth in the notion that where something is seen to be a scarce commodity people want it.

(Principal, Takahe College)

Takahe College has few marketing problems. Since imposing a zone, its exclusivity has intensified and its reputation consolidated. It has reinforced its dominant position in the local hierarchy and has become more competitive with the high SES schools in the city centre. The main requirement now is to sustain its competitiveness with the higher SES schools, something that has prompted renewed emphasis on academic acceleration and general excellence. In particular, the school has some streamed junior classes although it is unlikely that it could move to mixed ability groupings (even if it thought it educationally desirable to do so) because of the fear of exit by middle class students to the central city schools. It is a case where an educational decision to stream or teach in mixed ability classes is simply banished from the agenda by market forces. It also casts the spotlight of reality on the optimistic claims of writers like Chubb and Moe (1990) and Coleman (1992) who saw markets creating greater autonomy for school management. Cases like this illustrate the potential confusion between educational vision and image (Bowe *et al.* 1992).

Within certain communities, of which Takahe College may be an example, educational vision is linked to rhetoric about educational standards and the role of practices like streaming in maintaining 'standards'. If the school seeks to maintain a reasonable proportion of middle class students, it clearly needs to model its practice according to rhetoric. We stress that this kind of potential dilemma for educators is contingent on the views of the local community. In another school in our sample, which draws on a large lower middle class/upper working class intake, the introduction of mixed ability teaching was well received because parents perceived it to offer greater opportunities for their children because banding was considered elitist.

We should contrast the problems that an education market posed for these schools with the experience of one of the central city's elite high schools, Sheppard High.

Sheppard High is a long-established and prestigious state school with a high SES and mainly Pakeha intake. Many of its students come from the middle class areas surrounding the school, while almost a third of the intake

travel considerable distances to attend. These distant students have a relatively high SES compared to the residential areas in which they live. For this
school, at the upper end of Green City's education market, little has
changed under the de-zoning reforms. Oversubscription is the norm:

> We are in a position where we get more children than we can take, so
> whatever our enrolment policy is of the day or any directive from on
> high, we always have more than enough.
>
> (Principal, Sheppard High)

However, the school was trying not to grow for two reasons. Firstly, it
already had a space shortage and secondly, there would be little advantage
in further growth, even if space were available:

> Once you are much bigger than we are you would need a different
> administrative structure. We would spoil ourselves. We would lose the
> personal relationships you can have under a certain size. We need to
> keep the school person-centred . . .
>
> (Principal, Sheppard High)

Given this situation, the maximum roll provided to the school by the
Ministry in 1990 was considered to be too large and, like Takahe College,
the school fought successfully to get it reduced. None the less, the school
still had to increase its intake in 1991:

> We were given a very high roll and were very angry about that and
> negotiated it down a bit but even so, because zoning of any kind was
> abolished . . . we have a rather big bulge of fourth-formers going
> through which of course makes it difficult in planning your school.
>
> (Principal, Sheppard High)

Following the 1991 Act, the school was able to take more control. It put
its own enrolment scheme in place under the overcrowding provision and
managed its intake down to a more sustainable level. The school decided to
largely retain its former zoning arrangements; in-zone students were given
priority regardless of their characteristics, while out-of-zone students were
enrolled, when space was available, at the principal's discretion. These
enrolments were apparently selected on the basis of whether applicants'
subject choices could be accommodated by the school. Overall, then, Sheppard High was largely unaffected by the market:

> We still offer the same thing, we still get kids wanting to do the same
> things, we still get more than we can take, our geographical zone is [the
> same].
>
> (Principal, Sheppard High)

The principal noted the irony of parental 'choice' in a situation where
popular schools are oversubscribed:

You don't really get any choice because we cannot accommodate. Last year we turned away about 150 [third-form enrolments]. It goes right against the party policy because of the constraints we are under.

(Principal, Sheppard High)

Given the situation where the school has far more enrolments than it could accept, marketing activities were unnecessary:

I do not spend a single cent on publicity. I have the plainest, simplest prospectus. I do not do anything public at all except have an open night and it is so packed you can't fit into the hall. I say quite publicly that our advertising is what goes out of the school gate and that's where it stops . . . I don't have to market the school, the product is there, people know it's there, marketing is a non-issue.

(Principal, Sheppard High)

Conclusion

All the marketing in the world has not helped Kea College. As the principal of Weka noted of the marketing response in general:

The evidence from a place like [School XX], they spent literally thousands of dollars on promoting it, their magazine and prospectus and so on would be too good for Eton. They were on the radio last year. It has not made one whit of difference. The kids are still going off to [schools with better reputations]. People just don't believe you, it's a waste of time.

(Principal, Weka College)

Tui College, whose principal we did not interview at this time, was successful in creating a niche as a school which was culturally safe for Maori because it attracted Maori students from Kea. But it could not avoid entering a spiral of decline, largely because the school was bypassed by a significant proportion of girls. If Weka College was unsuccessful in its attempts to alter the terms of the education market in a way consistent with its professional philosophy, Takahe College's success led to a quite different experience. Takahe's political ability to change the terms of the competition in its favour had some ironic consequences. On the one hand, this action averted the threat of middle class flight to the central city while, on the other, it held the line for the schools in the adjacent working class suburb. In essence, it probably preserved one of the schools from extinction. But in the act of preserving its middle class roll, it potentially tied its own hands with respect to the issue of streaming versus mixed ability teaching. Market structures impose limits to action which may never be observed.

In successfully introducing an enrolment scheme, Takahe College raises a further element in the study of schools in a competitive context which needs attention in subsequent studies: namely, the notion of networking between organizations which are ostensibly in competition (Nohria and Eccles 1992). We have no information on whether Takahe College's intention to introduce an enrolment scheme and its likely impact was known to the adjoining schools, but clearly, in some respects, it was to their advantage. Certainly the lived education market is far more complex than its advocates have recognized.

Lastly, the case study of Sheppard High shows that high SES schools have been insulated from the reforms: in effect they enjoy close to a monopoly position. The school was forced to grow in 1991 as a result of the balloting system but then, because it has always been oversubscribed, it was able to reimpose a zone. This has allowed it to stabilize its roll and ensure a favourable intake by restricting in-zone enrolments to high status residential areas and selecting out-of-zone enrolments. Whereas all the other schools have been forced to engage with the market in one way or another, at Sheppard High, the impact of de-zoning has been largely a non-issue.

The overall impact of the introduction of the education market was to force the least able schools to compete while the strongest schools were effectively insulated from the market. The worst aspect of competition was the rate of change that schools had to endure. For schools like Kea, Tui and Weka were not only threatened with a spiral of decline, they also had to cope with ethnically changing intakes which would have required different kinds of cultural understandings and possibly teaching styles.

In theoretical terms, we have raised further reasons as to why education markets are unlikely to work in the way predicted by economic models. Clearly, some of these schools operated politically to insulate themselves from market competition and, while we have no direct evidence from this study, it is likely that various kinds of collusion took place between schools to ensure their survival. Certainly other principals in Green City have confirmed to us that collusive practices in recruiting students operate.

The key question now is whether the impact the market had on these schools affected their performance and, if so, whether it raised their game as pro-market advocates would expect, or whether the combination of polarization and stress which the working class schools experienced would impact negatively upon them.

seven

The impact of markets on school performance

In previous chapters we considered two of the major issues at the heart of the debate over markets: the issue of choice and the issue of polarization. We now turn to the third major issue, the issue of effectiveness. If some groups within society are less able than others to exercise choice in a market system and this leads to the polarization of schools on ethnic and social class lines as we have argued, what then are the consequences for the effectiveness of schools?

To set the scene for what follows we need to explain some of the terms we will use frequently. Imagine a set of schools which have exactly the same average or mean scores on some outcome measure. Imagine further that the students within each school differ from each other and they differ to the same degree as the students in any other school. In this situation the variation that exists between the students has nothing to do with the school attended because each school has the same mean score; in fact it has to do with differences between the individuals within the schools. In the jargon of statistics we would say that, in this case, the variance is between individuals and not between schools. Now imagine a different situation in which we have a set of schools which have different mean scores on some outcome measure. Imagine further that the students within each school perform at exactly the same level as each other on this outcome measure. In this situation the variation which exists between the students has everything to do with the school attended because within each school there are no differences between individuals. We would say that the variance is between schools and not between individuals. Neither of these situations is very likely. In a real situation we would expect that there would be both variation between individuals and variation between schools. That is, in the jargon, we would say that part of the total variance is between individuals and part is between schools. Research on school effectiveness attempts to identify the percentage of the total variance which is between individuals and the percentage which is between schools; it then tries to identify variables which can account for each kind of variance.

Some variables which may be related to variance between individuals and variance between schools are known as individual-level variables. Students may have differences on a range of abilities, achievements and characteristics which are related to performance. Variables such as prior achievement, aptitude, attendance, gender, ethnicity, SES and so on will, to different degrees, be related to performance. These are called individual-level variables because they are variables individuals would take with them if they changed schools. These individual-level variables will help account for the variance between individuals, and they may also help account for the variance between schools. Clearly, if schools differ in terms of the individual characteristics of their students, and these differences are related to performance, then we would expect differences in the outcomes between schools.

However, there is a second set of variables which can be used to account for the differences between schools: these are known as school-level variables, so called because they involve characteristics of the school which students would not take with them if they transferred to another school. So, for example, if school size was related to outcomes then we would expect differences between schools to be at least partly accounted for by school size; a student transferring from one school to another would swap one school size effect for another.

Critics of markets would claim that, as a consequence of the polarization of schools, outcome differences between schools will be exacerbated under market conditions and that a substantial percentage of the total variance will be between schools. They would also claim that, while individual-level variables may account for part of the between-school variance, they will leave a substantial part to be explained by school-level variables. In addition they would claim that the school-level variables explaining most of this remaining variance will be variables over which schools have little or no control – such as the average SES of the students in the school or the stability of the school roll – rather than variables related to policy and practice, for which they could be held accountable.[1]

In order to investigate outcome differences between the schools in our project we undertook two separate studies of school effectiveness in an effort to untangle school effects from individual differences and then to attempt to account for any school effects identified. The first of these studies investigated outcomes at the end of Year 10 after the students had almost completed two years of their secondary education. It involved 19 of the 23 Smithfield schools. Data were gathered on two outcome measures developed specifically for the project; two others were adapted by permission from tests developed by the New Zealand Council for Educational

Research (Hughes *et al.* 1997). The second study investigated outcomes in all 23 Smithfield schools on the School Certificate examinations which are taken at the end of Year 11 after three years secondary education (Hughes *et al.* 1999). We will refer to these studies as the 'Year 10 skills study' and the 'Year 11 School Certificate study'.

In the past, school effectiveness studies have been handicapped by the lack of appropriate statistical models required to deal adequately with the hierarchical structure of school organization (Raudenbush and Willms 1991). Schools are organized hierarchically: individual pupils belong to classes and the classes in turn belong to schools. In New Zealand the hierarchy stops at the school level, but in other countries there may be higher levels such as local education authorities in Britain or school districts in the United States. Students within a class have a degree of similarity not shared by students in other classes, classes within a school have a degree of similarity not shared by classes in other schools and so on. Put more generally, we can say that units grouped together at any level have a degree of similarity not shared by units in other groups at that level (Hutchison 1993).

Recently, statisticians have developed procedures which recognize the fact that schools are organized hierarchically. These powerful new statistical techniques, which are known collectively as multilevel modelling or multilevel regression (Paterson 1991), enable us to separate out the variability in outcomes between schools that is attributable to variables at each of the different levels in the hierarchy. So they allow us to answer questions such as: to what extent are the differences in outcomes between schools a function of individual differences in prior achievement rather than, for example, differences in the socioeconomic mix of the schools? One version of multilevel modelling is Hierarchical Linear Modelling (HLM), which is the procedure we have used in our studies (Bryk *et al.* 1996).

HLM allows us to divide the total variance on our outcome measures into two parts, the part that is between individuals (Level 1) and the part that is between schools (Level 2). If 80 per cent of the variance in a School Certificate subject is between individuals and 20 per cent is between schools, then we can say that 80 per cent of the variance is Level 1 variance and 20 per cent is Level 2 variance.

We then attempt to account for the variance at each level. Accounting for the variance at Level 2 is crucial for understanding school effectiveness. We need to know how much of a school's apparent performance is really due to the school and how much to individual differences. Then we need to look to see which school-level variables are important in explaining the school's performance: those over which it has policy and management control or those over which it does not.

To account for the Level 1 variance we use a set of individual-level or Level 1 independent variables such as socioeconomic status, prior achievement, gender, self concept, attendance and the like. These variables are then analysed using HLM to produce an equation which shows the relationships between them and the outcome measure and to identify the percentage of the Level 1 variance we can account for with these variables. So, for example, we might find that 70 per cent of the Level 1 variance in geography can be accounted for by prior achievement, SES and ethnicity.

To account for the Level 2 variance we use two sets of independent variables. First, we use the Level 1 variables used to explain the individual-level variance. If the intakes to secondary schools differ on a range of Level 1 variables then we might expect these differences to account for at least part of the between-school variance. For example, if the sample of schools we are studying contains some schools which have a majority of their students with high prior achievement, high SES and dominant ethnic status, while other schools in the sample have many students with lower prior achievement, lower SES and minority ethnic status, we would expect at least some of the differences between the schools to be related to these individual differences between their pupils. Second, we use a set of school-level or Level 2 independent variables. These school-level variables are of two kinds. First, there are Level 1 variables aggregated to the school level, such as the mean socioeconomic status of the school or the percentage of the school cohort who are Maori. These variables are known as 'mix variables' or 'contextual variables'. Then there are other variables which do not involve aggregating Level 1 variables to the school level, such as the size of the school or the stability of the school roll. So, for example, we might find that 50 per cent of the Level 2 variance can be accounted for by Level 1 variables and 30 per cent by Level 2 variables. If the significant Level 2 variables include, for example, mean SES, then SES has a second effect on outcomes which is additional to its effect at the individual level.

The data collection and variables

In order to explain the two HLM studies undertaken as part of the Smithfield Project it is necessary to explain the data collection and variables investigated in some detail at this point.

The Smithfield data were gathered over the period 1992 to 1997 and include outcome measures, individual-level (Level 1) variables and school-level (Level 2) variables. We detail the methods of data collection and their timing, concentrating on aspects relevant to the two HLM studies, describe the variables used in the studies and give them the variable names we will use throughout this chapter. We begin with the independent variables which are almost identical in each study and so are discussed together.

Independent variables

1992

The Smithfield Project began in 1992 when we selected our target secondary schools. Twenty-two secondary schools in two urban centres plus one rural secondary school were selected to cover a wide range of school types. We then identified the main primary and intermediate schools which fed students into these secondary schools. Next, we approached the parents of Year 7 students within these feeder schools, invited them to be part of the project and asked them to complete a consent form and brief questionnaire. Of relevance to the HLM analyses, the questionnaire gathered information on the socioeconomic status and ethnic background of each family and the number of parents/caregivers in the home. We identified the student's gender from the school records and, of course, we knew whether the student was attending a full primary or an intermediate school.

In recent educational research in New Zealand, SES has usually been established using the Elley/Irving scales (for example Elley and Irving 1985). To use the Elley/Irving scales, the occupation of the person to be rated is ascertained and looked up in a list of occupations. Beside each occupation is a numerical SES value for the occupation derived from an equal weighting of the educational attainments and remuneration levels of the people in that occupation as determined from census data. Typically, a snapshot of a single parent or caregiver has been taken by asking for his/her current occupation and using this to establish the SES of the family.

Clearly, occupations are not completely stable and people move from one occupation to another over time, have periods of redundancy, are promoted within a firm, leave a paid position to buy a business, and the like. For our primary measure of SES for the Smithfield sample we wanted an index which took this into account and which counted the occupations of both parents/caregivers (where they were present in the home). The questionnaire asked each parent/caregiver in our study to state the three jobs he/she had spent the longest time in and how long had been spent in each one. Each of these jobs was rated using the most recent Elley/Irving scale (Irving 1991a) and weighted proportionately by the number of years that job had been performed. The resulting figures were averaged in two-parent/caregiver families (see Waslander *et al.* 1994 for further details). This approach allowed us to give each family an SES score, even in cases where one or both parents/caregivers were unwaged at the time of filling in the questionnaire, and allowed us to take a more complete account of each family's cultural capital and experience in the labour market. As used at Level 1 the scale ranged from 1 (unskilled) to 6 (professional) and had the variable name SES.

The questionnaire also asked the families to respond to an open-ended question in which they described their family's cultural background. To provide the Level 1 ethnic variables used in the analyses undertaken in these studies the data were coded into the four categories described below and treated as dummy variables (see Hughes *et al.* (1996a) for further details).

1 Maori – this included those who identified as (i) Maori only or (ii) as Maori/something else with Maori first. Variable name, MAORI. Coded 1 for Maori and 0 for any other ethnic group.
2 Pacific Island Polynesian – this included those who identified as (i) Pacific Island Polynesian only, (ii) any specific Polynesian ethnic or cultural background (for example Tongan, Nuiean, Samoan) or combination thereof, or (iii) Pacific Island Polynesian/something else with Pacific Island Polynesian first. Variable name PACIFIC. Coded 1 for Pacific and 0 for any other ethnic group.
3 Pakeha/European – this included those who identified as (i) Pakeha or European only, (ii) any specific ethnic or cultural background within the British Isles, White Commonwealth or Eastern and Western Europe, (iii) New Zealanders or Kiwis, or (iv) Pakeha, European, etc./something else with Pakeha first. Variable name PAKEHA. Coded 1 for Pakeha and 0 for any other ethnic group.
4 Other – this included those describing themselves as (i) Asian only, any specific Asian ethnic or cultural background (for example Indian, Cambodian, Chinese, Vietnamese, Taiwanese) or combination thereof or anything else not elsewhere included. Variable name OTHER. Coded 1 for Other and 0 for any other ethnic group.

In the Year 11 School Certificate study we included a Level 1 variable called FAMSTR which was not included in the Year 10 skills study. This indicated whether the family had one or two parents/caregivers present and was coded 1 for dual-parent families and 0 for one-parent families.

Student gender was given the Level 1 variable name GENDER and was coded 1 for boys and 0 for girls.

The Level 1 variable PTYPE indicated whether the primary school attended in 1992 was an intermediate school (in which case it was coded 1) or a full primary school (in which case it was coded 0).

1993

At the beginning of 1993 we gathered information on reading comprehension, reading vocabulary, listening comprehension and mathematics as measured using the Progressive Achievement Tests (PAT) published by the New Zealand Council for Educational Research (Elley and Reid 1971; Reid and Elley 1991; Reid 1993). These nationally standardized tests are almost universally used in New Zealand primary schools as part of their regular testing programme.[2] At Level 1 the variable name was MPAT; at Level 2, where we found the mean score for the Smithfield students in each school, it was MPATMIX.

We also produced some measures specifically for the project which were administered for us by the classroom teachers in the feeder schools during the first term of 1993 when the Smithfield students were in Year 8.

We felt it was important to complement the PAT tests with measures which were less tied to particular curricula or school programmes; we wanted to use tests which could be considered to be further towards the generality end of Anastasi's Continuum of Experiential Specificity (Anastasi 1988), and so we produced a Verbal Analogies test and a Number Series test. The Verbal Analogies test was used as an outcome measure in the Year 10 skills study and is discussed in detail when the outcome measures are considered below. The Number Series test (for example, 'Which pair of numbers comes next in the following series: 3, 5, 9, 15, 23, ?, ?') comprised 15 questions selected from a pool of 18 after trialling and item analysis.[3] At Level 1 the variable name was MAPTITUDE; at Level 2, where we found the mean score for the Smithfield students in each school, it was MAPTITUDEMIX.

We also felt it was important to measure student self concept, so we developed our own Self Concept scale. This was also used as an outcome measure in the Year 10 skills study and is discussed in detail below. At Level 1 the variable name was SELFC; at Level 2, where we again found the mean score for the Smithfield students in each school, it was SELFCMIX.

1994

In 1994 the Smithfield students entered secondary school. In April of that year we recontacted the Smithfield cohort by mail and asked the parents to fill out a questionnaire which included a question asking which of the schools available to them they had most wanted their son or daughter to attend. Students were coded 1 if they were attending the high school most wanted and 0 if they were not, to form the Level 1 variable CHOICE. This variable was included to see if the 'disappointment' of not attending a first-choice school impacted on students' performance.

While we had identified the main feeder schools for our selected high schools, the Smithfield students did not make up 100 per cent of each school's third-form intake. We wanted information on the composition of the complete third-form intake, including both Smithfield and non-Smithfield students, in each of the Smithfield secondary schools. To get this 'composition data' we gathered information on reading comprehension, socioeconomic status and ethnicity. To measure reading comprehension we gathered scores on the PAT: Reading Comprehension Test (Reid and Elley 1991) as administered by the schools. The mean PAT: Reading Comprehension score for all Year 9 students in each school was the Level 2 variable READINGMIX.

In addition, we used the school records to gather information on the SES and ethnicity of all the students in the Smithfield secondary schools' intakes. The mean SES was used as a Level 2 variable with the variable name SESMIX. The percentage of the Year 9 intake who were of Maori, Pacific Islands, Pakeha or Other ethnicity formed the Level 2 variables MAORIMIX, PACIFICMIX, PAKEHAMIX and OTHERMIX.

1995

During 1995, observations were carried out in classrooms in each of the Smithfield schools during lessons in the core subjects (mathematics, English, social studies and science). In each school, we observed two Year 10 classes carefully selected so that, as far as possible, they matched across schools on SESMIX, READINGMIX and ethnic composition. The two classes were each observed for two periods in each subject, giving approximately 16 hours of observation in each school. Each lesson was also recorded on audio tape.

Three Level 2 variables were obtained from these observations and recordings. Each 50-minute observation session was divided into 200 intervals and the class members were systematically observed one after the other. The number of intervals in which the observed student was predominantly on task was divided by the total number of intervals to give the Level 2 variable ONTASK.

Following the lessons, the number of positive teacher comments for good behaviour and the number of negative teacher comments for poor behaviour were coded from the audio tapes to give the Level 2 variables POSCOM and NEGCOM.

1996

At the beginning of 1996 a third questionnaire was sent to the entire cohort. Among other things, this questionnaire asked the parents to indicate the number of times they had contacted the school their son or daughter was attending to discuss their child's academic progress during 1994 and 1995. This gave us the Level 1 variable CONTACT which ranged from 0 to 11, with 11 meaning that the parents had contacted the school 11 or more times.

We also gathered information on the attendance of the Smithfield students in 1994 and 1995 to create the Level 1 variable ATTNCE and the Level 2 variable ATTNCEMIX by calculating the mean attendance of the Smithfield students in each school. These two variables were used in the Year 10 skills study only.

We were particularly interested to see whether roll instability, as caused by spirals of decline, would have an impact on school performance. The

Directory of Primary, Secondary and Tertiary Institutions (Ministry of Education 1996) was used to establish the 1995 roll in each school which formed the Level 2 variable SCHSIZE. The 1995 and 1991 directories (Ministry of Education 1991a, 1995a) were consulted and the 1994 roll for each school was divided by the 1990 roll to create the Level 2 variable STABILITY. Schools with values below 1.00 had falling rolls and those with values above 1.00 had rising rolls. The Level 2 variable RETENTION was created by dividing the total school roll in 1995 by the number of students entering the school in 1994. We were interested in this variable because we knew that some working class schools had high levels of turnover or turbulence and we wanted to see whether this had a significant impact on school performance. At Kea College, the poorest school in our study, 30 per cent of students who entered the school in Form 3 had left the school two years later. This phenomenon appears to be common among the socially excluded in Western societies and is a cause of major concern in the United States (General Accounting Office 1994). Under these circumstances, we conjectured that market processes simply compound the instabilities of schools which already have highly unstable student populations.

The Level 2 variable SCHTYPE indicated single-sex and co-educational schools, with single-sex schools coded 1 and coeducational schools 0.

1997

Information was gathered on the attendance of the Smithfield students during 1996 to produce the variables ATTNCE96 and ATTNCE96MIX, which were the attendance variables used in the Year 11 School Certificate study.

The outcome measures

The outcome measures are quite different in each study and are discussed separately.

The Year 10 skills study

The Year 10 skills study concentrated on the year prior to the students' first major public examination, School Certificate, which is the equivalent of GCSEs in England and Wales. We decided to look at outcome measures which might enable us to judge how well schools were preparing students for their future educational careers. Therefore we tested 'cognitive skills' and 'affective traits' which might be predicted to enhance later learning at school. Students with good verbal reasoning abilities, good vocabularies, good study skills and positive self concepts might be predicted to be able to profit more from their secondary school studies than those with less of these attributes, and they were the outcome variables we selected to study.

The Verbal Reasoning or Analogies test comprised 21 four-option multiple choice items of the type 'Hand is to arm as foot is to . . .' selected from a pool of 26 items following trialling and item analysis.[4]

The Study Skills test was made up of items from the Progressive Achievement Tests of Study Skills (Reid *et al.* 1978). These included questions which tested how well students could:

- use a table of contents from a book;
- skim a text and extract information from it;
- read a multiple line graph;
- read a bar graph and an associated table;
- use a dictionary.

The Vocabulary test comprised 55 items and was adapted from the Progressive Achievement Tests of Reading (Reid and Elley 1991). Students selected from five options the word which was closest in meaning to an underlined word in a given sentence.

The Self Concept scale was developed specifically for use in the project. The final scale was a set of 30 bipolar descriptors (for example, I hate school/I love school) between which were five small circles arranged in a horizontal line. The students had to fill in the circle which best indicated what they thought they were like in relation to the bipolar descriptors. The final scale was selected from 35 descriptors following trialling and factor analysis. As with the Verbal Analogies test, the Self Concept scale was read to the students (see Waslander *et al.* 1994 for further details).

The Year 11 School Certificate study[5]

At School Certificate no subject is compulsory, hence the number of candidates in each of the aproximately 30 subjects varies enormously. In 1996 there were almost 64,000 candidates: there were some 47,000 sitting English, 44,000 mathematics and 38,000 science (New Zealand Qualifications Authority 1996). The next most popular subject was geography (15,000). Once the number of candidates sitting a particular subject drops much below half the total number of candidates, the number of candidates taking that subject in some of our smaller schools falls to the point where undertaking an analysis for that subject is pointless. So we limited our attention to English, mathematics and science, where the numbers were high enough to justify the analyses.

Table 7.1 shows a summary of the independent variables at Level 1 and Level 2 and outcome variables in the two studies.

Table 7.1 Summary of the Level 1, Level 2 and outcome variables in the two studies

Level 1 variables	Level 2 variables	Study skills outcomes	School Certificate outcomes
SES	MPATMIX	Self Concept	English
MAORI	MAPTITUDEMIX	Study Skills	mathematics
PACIFIC	SELFCMIX	Verbal Analogies	science
PAKEHA	READINGMIX	Vocabulary	
OTHER	SESMIX		
FAMSTR*	MAORIMIX		
GENDER	PACIFICMIX		
PTYPE	PAKEHAMIX		
MPAT	OTHERMIX		
MAPTITUDE	ONTASK		
SELFC	POSCOM		
CHOICE	NEGCOM		
CONTACT	ATTNCEMIX†		
ATTNCE†	SCHSIZE		
ATTNCE96*	STABILITY		
	RETENTION		
	SCHTYPE		
	ATTNCE96MIX*		

* This variable was used in the Year 11 School Certificate study only.
† This variable was used in the Year 10 skills study only.

Results

We began our HLM analyses by calculating the total variance, the variance that was between individuals and the variance that was between schools for each outcome measure. We then calculated the percentage of the total variance that was between individuals and between schools. These values may be seen in Table 7.2, which also indicates whether the schools differed significantly on each outcome measure.

While the variances are different from outcome to outcome there is a marked degree of similarity between the outcomes in terms of the percentage of the total variance between schools, with the clear exception of Self Concept, where the differences between the schools are not significant and almost all the variance is between individuals. For all other outcomes the schools differ significantly, and the percentage of the variance between schools ranges from 11.9 for Verbal Analogies to 20.9 for School Certificate mathematics, with a median of 16.4 per cent.

Table 7.2 Partitioning the variance

	Study Skills	Vocabulary	Verbal Analogies	Self Concept	English	Maths	Science
Total variance	99.9	101.0	37.8	77.7	293.6	411.0	288.3
Level 2 variance	16.8	14.6	4.5	0.7	48.1	86.0	47.3
Level 1 variance	83.1	86.4	33.3	77.1	245.6	325.0	241.0
% Level 2 variance	16.8	14.5	11.9	0.8	16.4	20.9	16.4
% Level 1 variance	83.2	85.5	88.1	99.2	83.6	79.1	83.6
Significance	<0.000	<0.000	<0.000	ns	<0.000	<0.000	<0.000

Table 7.3 Summaries of the Level 1 and Level 2 analyses

	Study Skills	Vocabulary	Verbal Analogies	Self Concept	English	Maths	Science
% of Level 1 variance accounted for by Level 1 independent variables	56.1	67.0	45.0	9.4	47.6	43.9	50.6
% of Level 2 variance accounted for by Level 1 independent variables	40.5	50.8	22.9	–	45.1	53.9	57.0
% of Level 2 variance accounted for by Level 2 independent variables	49.2	42.6	73.6	–	39.9	31.7	30.1
Total % of Level 2 variance accounted for	89.7	93.4	96.5	–	85.0	85.5	87.1

Next we investigated our Level 1 independent variables in an attempt to account for the Level 1 and Level 2 variance on our outcome measures, following which we investigated our Level 2 independent variables in an attempt to account for the remaining Level 2 variance. The results of these calculations may be seen in Table 7.3. Again, there are marked similarities between the outcome measures with the exception of Self Concept. Because the differences between the schools on Self Concept were not significant Self Concept has not been analysed at Level 2, and under 10 per cent of the Level 1 variance has been accounted for. The two variables which were significantly related to Self Concept were SELFC and ATTNCE.

The other variables have between 43.9 and 67.0 per cent of the Level 1 variance accounted for by Level 1 variables, with the median value being 49.2 per cent. The Level 1 independent variables account for between 22.9 and 57.0 per cent of the Level 2 variance, with the median being 48.0 per cent. The Level 2 independent variables account for between 30.1 and 73.6 per cent of the Level 2 variance, with the median being 41.3 per cent.

Table 7.4 summarizes the Level 1 and Level 2 independent variables, which are significantly related to the various outcomes in the two studies with significance levels codified.

The Level 1 independent variables significantly related to the outcomes were as follows: MPAT was significantly related to every outcome measure. Attendance at schools in the form of ATTNCE or ATTNCE96, depending on the study in question, was significantly related to every outcome except Verbal Analogies and Vocabulary. MAPTITUDE was significantly related to Study Skills, Verbal Analogies and science, while SES was significantly related to Verbal Analogies and the three School Certificate subjects. SELFC was significantly related to English and mathematics. Girls outperformed boys in English, giving a significant effect for GENDER; Maori students performed significantly worse than other ethnic groups in science, giving a significant effect for MAORI.

The Level 2 independent variables which were significantly related to the outcome measures included several mix variables. Mean prior achievement in the form of MPATMIX was significantly related to all three outcomes in the Year 10 skills study and to School Certificate science; READINGMIX was significantly related to School Certificate English and mathematics. Socioeconomic mix as measured by SESMIX was a significant predictor of Verbal Analogies and School Certificate English and science, while ethnic mix was related to outcomes in Vocabulary and School Certificate English. In Vocabulary, schools with a smaller percentage of Pacific Island students had higher scores; in School Certificate English, schools with fewer Maori students had higher scores. MAPTITUDEMIX was significantly related to School Certificate science and SELFCMIX to School Certificate mathematics.

Table 7.4 Level 1 and Level 2 independent variables significantly related to outcomes

	Study Skills	Vocabulary	Verbal Analogies	English	Maths	Science
Level 1 variables	MPAT‡ ATTNCE* MAPTITUDE‡	MPAT‡	MPAT‡ SES* MAPTITUDE‡	MPAT‡ ATTNCE96‡ SES‡ SELFC‡ −GENDER‡	MPAT‡ ATTNCE96‡ SES‡ SELFC*	MPAT‡ ATTNCE96‡ SES‡ MAPTITUDE‡ −MAORI†
Level 2 mix variables	MPATMIX‡	MPATMIX‡ −PACIFICMIX†	MPATMIX‡ SESMIX*	SESMIX† −MAORIMIX† READINGMIX†	READINGMIX† SELFCMIX*	MPATMIX† SESMIX† MAPTITUDEMIX*
Level 2 non-mix variables	STABILITY‡	STABILITY*		STABILITY*	STABILITY* −POSCOM*	−POSCOM†

* $p < 0.05$
† $p < 0.01$
‡ $p < 0.001$

Two non-mix Level 2 variables were also related to outcomes. For Study Skills, Vocabulary, School Certificate English and School Certificate mathematics, STABILITY was a significant predictor of outcomes, and POSCOM was negatively related to School Certificate mathematics and science.

Discussion

Our results suggest that, depending on the School Certificate subject studied, about 16 to 21 per cent of the total variance in English, mathematics and science is between-school variance (Level 2 variance), with the remaining 84 to 79 per cent being variance between individuals (Level 1 variance). When we analysed Study Skills, Vocabulary and Verbal Analogies, the Level 2 variance was typically a little less, ranging from about 12 per cent to about 17 per cent. These differences between schools are all highly significant. To the extent that differences between schools are associated with school-level independent variables we would expect effects to be cumulative, and so the differences between the two studies are minimal given that the 'skills' study measured outcomes at the end of Year 10 and School Certificate was administered one year later. There are reasonably substantial differences between our schools on all six cognitive outcome measures.[6]

However, when we analysed our affective outcome the results were quite different. On Self Concept less than 1 per cent of the total variance was between schools. Studies using educational self concept measures similar to our own have suggested that schools can make a difference to self concept (Mortimore et al. 1988), but in our study the differences between schools were not significant. It is not clear how this result should be interpreted. It might be that working class schools are working hard to maintain the educational self concepts of their students despite the fact that their performance on cognitive tests is below that of students from other schools. From this point of view the lack of significant differences between schools is a plus for working class schools whose efforts enable them to maintain the self concepts of their students despite their lower academic achievement. Alternatively, it might be that students make judgements about their performances which are highly contextualized and use their school peers as the reference group, rather than comparing themselves to their high achieving peers at other schools. If this is the case, working class schools cannot claim any credit for the insignificant between-school differences on self concept, just as they cannot be blamed for the effects of contextual variables such as mean SES or mean prior achievement.

After controlling for our Level 1 independent variables we were able to account for about 56 per cent of the individual-level variance in Study Skills, 67 per cent in Vocabulary, 45 per cent in Verbal Analogies, 48 per cent in School Certificate English, 44 per cent in School Certificate mathematics and 51 per cent in School Certificate science. Again, Self Concept was quite different, with only 9.4 per cent of the variance accounted for despite the fact that SELFC was an independent variable in the analyses. So, with the exception of Self Concept we were able to account for approximately half the variance between individuals using the Level 1 independent variables we investigated. The most important variables were prior achievement (MPAT), level of school attendance (ATTNCE and ATTNCE96), socioeconomic status (SES) and aptitude (MAPTITUDE), although self concept (SELFC), ethnicity (MAORI) and gender (GENDER) were also significant variables in some analyses.

These Level 1 independent variables also accounted for roughly half the Level 2 variance on outcomes except for Verbal Analogies, where they accounted for 23 per cent. The other figures were 41 per cent and 51 per cent for Study Skills and Vocabulary, and 45 per cent, 54 per cent and 57 per cent for School Certificate English, mathematics and science. Clearly, if only about half the between-school variance can be accounted for by Level 1 independent variables a substantial percentage of the between-school variance is potentially able to be explained by Level 2 variables.

What we found was that the Level 2 independent variables we investigated accounted for roughly half the variance in our Year 10 skills study and roughly one-third in our Year 11 School Certificate study. The actual figures for Study Skills, Vocabulary and Verbal Analogies were 49 per cent, 43 per cent and 74 per cent, while for School Certificate English, mathematics and science they were 40 per cent, 32 per cent and 30 per cent. The Level 2 variables which were important in accounting for the differences between schools included a set of context variables, most notably mean prior achievement in the school (MPATMIX and READINGMIX) and mean socioeconomic status in the school (SESMIX). Also significant on occasions were the percentage of the school roll which was of ethnic minority status (MAORIMIX and PACIFICMIX, both negatively related), the mean aptitude in the school (MAPTITUDEMIX) and mean self concept in the school (SELFCMIX). In addition, two non-mix variables, the stability of the school roll between 1990 and 1994 (STABILITY) and the number of positive teacher comments (POSCOM, negatively related) were also related to outcomes.

To sum up, our studies suggest that while most of the overall variance in secondary school outcomes in the cognitive domain is between individuals rather than between schools, the between-school variance is reasonably substantial and ranges from about 12 per cent to about 21 per cent, depending on the outcome being studied. Roughly half this variance can be accounted for in terms of the individual-level differences of the intakes to the various schools on a range of variables such as prior achievement, attendance, SES and self concept, acting at the individual level. However, importantly, around 30 to 50 per cent of the between-school variance is related to school-level variables. Some of these variables are mix variables so that when individual variables are aggregated to the school level they account for additional variance. The mean SES of the students in the school, their mean prior achievement scores and the like are related to performance over and above the relationships found at the individual level. Schools with larger proportions of students with high initial achievement, larger proportions of students with high socioeconomic status, fewer ethnic minority students, stable rolls and the like are at an advantage, and students will perform better in them than they will in schools with the opposite mix of students.[7]

Other non-mix variables, such as the stability of the school roll, are also related to achievement. If it is assumed that these independent variables are causal – and we will discuss this further below – the conclusion that must follow is that it does make a difference which schools students attend.

Taken together, the Level 1 and Level 2 variables in our studies account for between 85 and 95 per cent of the between-school variance in the different outcomes. Even if all the remaining variance could be accounted for by school-level variables having to do with school policy and practice, these variables would be much less important than the contextual variables identified as significantly related to outcomes in our studies.[8] However, we believe there are good reasons why we cannot attribute the remaining variance to school management or policy, as if it were independent of school mix. In related research Martin Thrupp (1999) undertook a qualitative study of the impact of social class mix on four of the schools in our sample. One was working class and three were middle class. He found that social class mix was likely to have three kinds of effects on schools. Firstly, there was a peer group effect. Attitudes and aspirations of middle class students were likely to 'rub off' on working class students in middle class schools. Secondly, different kinds of curriculum programmes, aims and modes of teaching were undertaken in working and middle class schools. In the working class school, senior students were more likely to take preparatory vocational courses, study skills were emphasized as a preparation for future academic programmes and classes were more likely to be characterized by lower academic difficulty and lower student engagement. Thrupp (1997: 64) has this to say about what is at the heart of these differences:

> These differences in response suggest that teachers in the middle class schools and Tui College (the working class school) had different sets of curriculum priorities and goals. Central to this were their differing emphases on 'content' and 'skills' which they tended to pit against each other. While the teachers at the middle class schools usually felt that teaching curriculum content was important, teachers at Tui College typically argued that if students had the literacy/study skills needed to

access information, they could pick the content up 'any time'. So while the general assumption at the middle class schools was that students were already reasonably literate and needed knowledge and ideas for examinations, at Tui College the possession of such skills was not usually assumed and with justification; instead it was often believed curriculum content would fall into place if students could get these 'basic skills'.

Thrupp also identifies the likely impact of school mix on management. At Tui College the senior management team spent far more time on guidance, discipline and crisis management. More time was also spent on maintaining staff morale in the light of a decline in roll than at the middle class schools. In effect what Thrupp is arguing is that school mix cannot be separated from school policies and management. The nature and dynamics of the student intakes framed what was possible and what was not.

It is significant that Thrupp completed his study before we were able to analyse the data reported in this chapter for it might have been suggested that had we published these findings, they might have unduly influenced his research. As it stands, the two studies provide powerful support for one another.

The view that school mix has an impact on the life of the school over and above the influence it has on the attitudes and performance of peers is reinforced by Ho and Willms (1996). Their study was primarily focused on the relationship between aspects of parental involvement in schools and children's achievement. They conclude:

> Our analysis shows that children's academic achievement and the extent to which parents are involved in schools also depend on the intake characteristics of schools. Children scored significantly higher in both mathematics and reading if they attended a high SES school, irrespective of their own family backgrounds . . . Similarly, irrespective of their own SES, parents were more likely to volunteer or attend PTO meetings if their children attended high rather than low SES schools . . . The results also suggest that the effects of school participation were moderately related to the relationship between reading achievement and SES. Volunteering perhaps not only improves the quality of schooling but also reduces inequality between social-class groups.
>
> (Ho and Willms 1996: 138–9)

We have quoted at length because their conclusions are significant in the light of the claims made by pro-market advocates like Coleman that parental choice would also encourage parental interest and participation in their children's education. These findings, coupled to Thrupp's and our own, provide a strong counter-argument, that the crucial factor at the school level is the mix of the students.

The policy implications of these findings are probably more far-reaching than the discussion has so far suggested. This is because students' scores on measures of achievement and aptitude are undoubtedly affected by previous schooling. If there are school effects of the magnitude we have found in our studies, then some of the individual-level differences which are useful in accounting for between-school effects are actually school effects. We must assume that these effects start to operate at pre-school level and accumulate over the years of schooling. We are not in a position to quantify these effects but it is obvious that they are there: an inference supported by Sammons (1995).

Students arrive at pre-school with certain skills and characteristics which are important for pre-school outcomes. However, the (pre-)school effect influences these outcomes. An argument might be mounted that school effects are likely to be greater at pre-school level than at other levels within the system because of the enormous importance of the pre-school years for future achievement and the fact that pre-school education is not compulsory, and some children do not even get any while others get only a limited amount of it. Barney (1975) has documented the unequal access to pre-school education which occurs as a function of socioeconomic status and ethnicity. However, for the purposes of the argument we can assume that pre-school effect is the same as we found at high school level.

Students then enter primary school, where their performances on the outcomes of pre-school are related to primary school outcomes both at Level 1 and Level 2. The outcomes of primary school are therefore a function of two school effects: the direct primary school effect and the indirect pre-school effect operating to the extent that relevant Level 1 variables are related to between-school differences. When the students move on to intermediate school the outcomes are subject to three school effects: the direct intermediate school effect, the indirect primary school effect and the indirect pre-school effect. By the time students get to School Certificate there are four school effects: pre-school, primary school, intermediate school and secondary school.

Taken together these school effects would sum to considerably more than the 8 per cent figure we found for the direct secondary school effect, unless there is no correlation between the school effects for the different school levels. That is, to the extent that attendance at 'good' schools and 'poor' schools is not random across the different levels of the school system, the effects would be additive at least in part. Based on the results reported in Chapters 4, 5 and 6, we would argue that attendance is not random in this sense. Students living in working class areas with large proportions of ethnic minorities will go to schools with 'less favourable' Level 2 characteristics at each stage of their schooling than students in more affluent areas. In our view, failure to appreciate the additive nature of school effects is a serious oversight. If our argument is correct then it points to policy solutions which take into account the entire educational career of a student. In turn this suggests that the focus in raising standards and achieving greater equality of opportunity cannot be just related to individual school performance and accountability. Rather, policies need to be established which take account of students' educational histories.

Despite its mathematical sophistication we must not lose sight of the fact that HLM is a correlational procedure and the analyses we have carried out do not, of themselves, indicate the causal relationships among the variables. It might be argued, for example, that 'failing' schools cause falling rolls. The fall in the roll follows the school's failure to perform but does not cause it. On this view, if the school would only 'pull its socks up' and perform better the deserting students would return and the roll would rise. However, it might, in contrast, be argued that schools with large proportions of the 'wrong' kinds of students (working class, ethnic minority, etc.) lose students despite the fact that they are well run schools, and that this loss of students causes additional problems for these schools which impact on outcomes. On this scenario it is easy to see how a school's roll might dive through no fault on the part of the school and stabilize at a point which is inimical to positive outcomes. The evidence from Chapter 6 would support this interpretation, for it is clear that from a social conflict perspective that it is quite 'rational' for parents with the appropriate cultural and material capital to choose schools which have students with higher prior attainment and higher social class backgrounds. On such data and argument we rest our case for a causal relationship between the Level 2 variables we have found to be significant and the educational outcomes.[9]

eight

Conclusion

In the first two chapters of this book we outlined some of the major competing predictions in the debate over marketization in education. We are now in a position to say how these predictions have fared within the particular education market we have studied in New Zealand. Three major issues lay at the heart of the debate: choice, polarization and school effectiveness.

As regards choice, proponents of marketization predicted that parents and caregivers from any ethnic or social class background would have an equal opportunity to exercise choice. In contrast, critics of marketization have argued that those already endowed with cultural and material capital would simply shore up their existing advantages by being given greater ability to exercise choice in education. The work of Willms and Echols (1992) provides additional empirical support for the latter view. However, when confronted with evidence of gross inequalities in terms of the ability to exercise choice, proponents of marketization have a fallback position. They argue that while working class and disempowered ethnic groups may not have the same range of choices with respect to schools (compared to their middle class counterparts), competition between schools in the 'working class' segment of the market would nevertheless raise standards and help to meet 'consumer' interests and demands.

In *general* terms our study has found that the trends predicted by critics of marketization are confirmed. Students from professional and managerial middle class backgrounds are able to exercise greater choice and are more likely to travel greater distances to enter schools with high SES mixes. Furthermore, it appears that the choice to travel away from local, working class schools is more likely to be made by those from the upper end of each social class group. The effect of this movement has been to exacerbate the polarization in school intakes that already existed on the basis of residential segregation.

The consequences of the polarization we have identified impacts on schools in two ways. Firstly, schools with a high proportion of students with low prior achievement and which are solidly working class or have a high concentration of Maori or Pacific Island students, are likely to perform less well than schools with a more balanced student mix. The important point here is that the reason for their poorer performance is largely due to the school mix effect, a factor over which these schools have very little control. In addition, the instability of the school roll these working class schools experience and which is caused by a 'spiral of decline' also imposes an additional penalty on school performance. The evidence we have presented suggests that spirals of decline are caused by middle class 'white flight' and in some cases 'brown flight' as relatively advantaged students exit their local working class schools. The consequence is that the recent history of working class schools has been one of stress and change triggered by the market. In contrast, the elite schools have remained virtually untouched.

The response to these variations in school effectiveness in much of the contemporary policy focus is on holding schools more 'accountable'. It is clear from our research that this is a bogus exercise unless the sociogeography and history of a school within the stratified market is analysed. Even so, there are aspects of a school's market behaviour that will have an effect on its perceived academic performance that we have not been able to consider. For example, Coleman and Hoffer (1987) consider the point that private schools have greater freedom to remove students at risk of failing and 'to expel them without due process' (p. 97). They find that 'In the Catholic sector, the other private sector and the high performance private sector, the likelihood of transferring to a public sector school increases sharply for students whose high school grades are low' (p. 108).

The clear inference is that these students are 'inconvenient' in a competitive market.

Inevitably this kind of strategy must find its way into the state sector. State schools must behave increasingly like private schools if they are to thrive, and this is especially the case where league tables are used as a market signal for school performance. We could expect, therefore, that high performing schools in terms of external exam results would seek to 'offload' their at-risk students to other schools or simply not enter them for public exams. We have anecdotal evidence that this was occurring in the market we studied, but much stronger empirical evidence comes from England, where Levačić, Hardman and Woods (1998) report that the numbers of poorer students (as measured by their entitlement to free school meals) declined in the grant-maintained schools in their study. Grant-maintained schools have control of admissions and are usually elite schools. Similarly Tomlinson (1997, 1998) has shown how a school in London which was closed down on the grounds that it was failing was taking at-risk students offloaded from other schools in the neighbourhood and thereby providing an education to those who were not considered 'desirable' by other schools.

Underlying these strategies is a profound question about whether schools in a state-created market for education can operate as a public service in which the needs of all children are addressed, irrespective of their exam potential.[1] The logical consequence of a market is that these 'at risk' students will be herded into special schools which cater for low performing and/or disruptive students. The implications of this deliberate rejection by some schools have, to our knowledge, simply not been considered by policy makers.

Within these overall trends some complex issues emerge which suggest the proponents of marketization have at least some points that critics need to address. For a start, it seems clear that students from professional and managerial middle class backgrounds were exercising choice before de-zoning was introduced: zones had not prevented middle class flight. This finding is consistent with McCulloch's (1991) study of zoning in Auckland, where he established that the professional middle class used zoning to exclude working class students from their schools. It seems the professional middle class will achieve the advantage they seek in spite of (in our case) or because of (in McCulloch's case) zoning. In this they are aided by the construction of the formal rules of the market which allow high SES schools to select their students. In essence, this insulates high SES schools from competition and raises the question of whether they are selecting 'able' out-of-zone students. Our data suggest that some of these high SES schools may be using social class and ethnicity as a proxy for ability and as the basis on which to select students.

If the present market structure appears to provide additional means for those from middle class backgrounds to gain further advantage in the competition for credentials, what of those ethnic groups which have been systematically disempowered by the previous bureaucratic system of education? Recall that for two supporters of choice, Coleman and Benton, it was hoped that the introduction of a market system of education would free these ethnic groups from the 'iron cage' of zoning and hence educational 'failure'. Here the evidence is mixed.

Our data have shown that an assumption by some critics of competition – that the removal of zoning would create a market divided into an 'alert' and actively choosing white professional middle class and an 'inert' ethnically mixed working class – is false. While the evidence suggests that working class parents either do not have the choice in practice, or do not choose to send their children to the elite middle class schools, many seem to make choices within available working class schools. Moreover, competition does appear to have begun to produce schools with niche markets which may address the needs, for example, of Maori. In our sample, Tui College's bicultural development had clearly attracted Maori students. However, it had done so, in part, at the cost of Kea College, which entered a spiral of decline. Since Kea College had many Maori students the question of whether Maori interests overall have been well served by marketization is a moot point. What can be said about this issue is that supporters of marketization who seek to equalize the life-chances of ethnic groups like Maori have tended to take a rather static view of the effects of choice and competition in a market system. Tui may have attracted Maori boys but the school itself was still suffering from a declining roll.

The fundamental problem with education markets is that they are designed so that some schools will fail. In allowing some schools to fail, policy makers are also allowing the students in these schools to fail. While the threat of failure may spur some schools to greater heights, if the possible cost of this policy is sacrificing the education of the students in the failing schools, then, in our view, the policy is morally unacceptable.

If it is accepted that our findings produce a fairly clear picture which, with some caveats, suggests that neither efficiency or equity are well served by education markets, then pro-market advocates can react in two ways. They can suggest that the New Zealand markets we have studied are specific in their effects and may have little application to the education market outcomes elsewhere in the world. They may also argue that the market we studied was not a 'true' market and that if perfect market conditions had been more closely approximated, the inequalities we have identified would not exist. Our response addresses both arguments.

We have identified four mechanisms operating within the market which militate against the achievement of a 'perfectly competitive' market and which we believe will operate in any market where there is open enrolment and where popular schools can decide which students to admit. These are, firstly, that choice in education markets is determined by social class, ethnicity and gender. Secondly, individuals do not have equal ability to compete in the education market. Thirdly, where schools are oversubscribed they will, by and large, choose those students who will enhance the schools' exam reputation. And, while we have not been able to demonstrate it in this study, there is clearly a market logic to 'offload' students who are at risk of failing. Schools will also use whatever means at their disposal, whether it be by lobbying or collusion, to insulate themselves from the 'rigours' of the market.

Finally, in response to our research, pro-market advocates may argue that the class- and ethnicity-based inequalities we have identified are temporary and that over time, as market behaviour becomes embedded, all will be equally able to exercise choice. We believe this is an *ad hoc* defence of the market position. We have shown that high SES parents are three times more likely to get their children into high circuit schools than their low SES counterparts, and that behind these figures is a process of 'cooling out' working class parents. While we know there was no significant educational impact on students who did not get their first choice of school, it may well have a long-term impact on the collective wisdom of the class. Working class parents who do not 'actively' choose a school may do so on the basis of what they have learnt from the experience of their class, rather than from apathy, puzzlement or lack of interest. But perhaps the more important point here is that it assumes a naive view of education. For what lies behind this claim is the view that working class parents are, by and large, 'slower learners' in adapting to market rules. But the evidence presented in this book would lead us to dispute what is a pervasive liberal assumption about the behaviour of working class parents in competing on equal terms in education. Our findings are consistent with the view that education is a site of struggle for credential advantage; the issue, therefore, is not whether all would eventually come to the market as equals but why professional middle class parents would allow and indeed contribute to such an equality. The tactics used by professional middle class parents and schools that we have documented clearly show that education markets serve to exacerbate the exclusion of working class and Maori students.

But would a market which more closely approximated 'perfectly competitive' conditions obviate these mechanisms of exclusion and advantage? Suppose, for example, that the condition of allowing schools complete freedom over their budgets, which New Right policy makers in New Zealand have been pushing for, was met. Would that make a difference? Would, for example, Sheppard High, which performs so well on raw examination results, expand to include more students? The principal said she did not want to increase the number of students at the school – from her perspective, rightly so. If the apparently successful schools expanded while others closed down, all that would happen is that the problems associated with the schools closing down would be exported to the 'successful' schools. But what about the case of the working class school, Tui College, which did adopt appropriate market behaviour by creating a niche for itself? Clearly, as Thrupp (1999) has shown, the social class and ethnic mix of the school had a profound impact on within-school processes.

The fundamental problem is that the premise of pro-market advocates is flawed. School organization, management and market sanctions and incentives are not the key factors in school success: the prior achievement, social class, ethnic and gender intake and mix of a school are crucial to its success in raw examination results. In this respect social conflict theory is a more powerful predictor of the outcomes of education markets. When we consider the triumphalism of market proponents that we documented in Chapter 1, it is clear that the world is a far more complex place than they envisaged. In many ways it is extraordinary to witness such a bout of revolutionary certainty at the end of the twentieth century when the experience of the last hundred years ought to have extinguished such hubris.

Open enrolment markets do not achieve the goals that have been set for them by their advocates; in this sense they quite simply don't work. Moreover, the evidence we have presented suggests that they will exacerbate the unacceptable polarization between rich and poor in countries like the United States, Britain and New Zealand. If education is to be the source of competitive economic advantage in the twenty-first century then we need to ensure that the rules of educational competition within nations are fair. It is an issue from which governments of both New Right and Modernizer persuasion have retreated. Equality of opportunity has been replaced by the more slippery concept of fairness (Brown *et al*. 1997). The question is what kind of education system will work by providing greater equality of opportunity and overall higher standards?

Towards a fairer and more effective system of education

Any education system which is to remain a national system must satisfy certain basic criteria: fair competition for credentials; equality of resourcing across all schools with the exception of disadvantaged schools for which compensatory funding is needed in order to help ensure a fair competition for credentials; and equality of choice in the subjects offered. Against these considerations and in the light of the development of a greater awareness of individual and group identities and interests in today's society, we need a school system which balances national with individual and group interests. Markets do not take account of the national interest because their underlying principle – that the wealth and wishes of parents should determine educational careers – clashes with the meritocratic principle. Nor, as we have seen, do they take into account the interests of key groups in society: in the case of New Zealand, the indigenous Maori population.

Given these considerations, the evidence that we have marshalled in the previous chapters points in two directions. Since the school mix or composition of the student body is such a key factor in school performance, it is important that schools have student intakes which are as well balanced on variables such as prior achievement and social class as is possible. The best way of balancing individual and national interests is by community-mediated choice within a comprehensive system. Under such a system parents would be able to list a set of school preferences but the community, as expressed through the local state, would have a mandate to reconcile parents' preferences in order to achieve well balanced school intakes. This seems to us the most direct way of improving school performance across the board while ensuring equality of opportunity. If this is politically difficult in an age of individualism, then the fall-back position is one in which parents have the right to send their child to their local school. Here 'local' would be defined in such a way as to capture as broad a social and ethnic range of students as is possible. Where there is spare capacity, applicants for schools would be balloted. Neither of these proposals necessarily take account of the gender issues raised in this book. Here the question of diversity of provision is crucial, and it is clear working class girls should have the choice of being able to attend well balanced single-sex schools.

A further issue, which we raised in the last chapter, concerns the cumulative effect of schooling on student performance. Schools cannot be seen as individual 'cost centres' which are judged according to doubtful performance criteria, such as raw exam results. Rather, from the perspective of a student's educational career we need to see schools as part of a coherent strategy which integrates pre-, primary and secondary schools in such a way as to achieve the best balance according to social class and prior achievement mixes. In this respect community-mediated choice needs to be extended to all forms of pre-school and compulsory education.

While we see the principle of state-mediated choice within a comprehensive system of education as the key to a fair and effective system of education, we recognize that for some groups, such as Maori, there are other considerations that need to be taken into account. Maori have underperformed educationally because of a well documented history of colonialism and attendant racism (intended or unintended), and some evidence for this has been given in this book. The lesson that we have learnt in Aotearoa/New Zealand is that if there is only one system of education in a pluralist society, it will inevitably be assimilationist. It is far better to enable and resource the different ethnic groups in society to work through their problems instead of the state attempting to intervene on their behalf. Where states have sought to act on behalf of 'Others' they have failed, and New Zealand is a glaring example of this. Different ethnic groups should be given control of their schooling according to their own cultural predispositions and assumptions. Edward Said once said that it is not what people know but who they are that counts. In our view the two must go hand in hand: *we learn in the secure knowledge of who we are.* Culturally autonomous schooling creates an appropriate learning context for these students, and frees them from the racist and assimilationist environment in 'mainstream' schools. This concept of 'self-determination', as it has been termed in New Zealand, is a different principle for creating greater equity and effectiveness to that of balancing school mix. Nevertheless, it has a clearly identifiable rationale; in New Zealand it has caused a resurgence of Maori development.

There is no reason why the two principles of social integration and cultural autonomy and determination cannot co-exist. The majority of students in the foreseeable future will attend comprehensive schools, yet Maori immersion schools provide an important alternative to the mainstream.

Schools cannot be divorced from the wider public and political context of which they are a part. The overwhelming evidence from studies such as ours, as well as the tradition of origins and destinations studies (Halsey *et al*. 1980) is that schools cannot compensate for society. Therefore, the most effective way of raising educational performance is by reducing poverty and social exclusion and by promoting systems of education which are fair and effective. The evidence presented in this book is not conclusive and should not be read as 'proof' that market systems of the kind we have investigated cannot work. However, we do believe that the evidence presented provides a powerful case that education markets trade-off the futures of young working class students to the advantage of those more privileged. We believe there are better ways of achieving a diverse and equitable system of educational provision.

Appendix

An outline of the research programme

The Educational Performance and Opportunities research programme, which later became known as the Smithfield Project, was initiated in 1992 under contract to the Ministry of Education. The central focus of the project was the impact of government reforms on certain aspects of the education of a cohort of 3300 students as they moved from Form 2 (Year 7) at primary school in 1992 to Form 5 (Year 11) at secondary school in 1996. We will refer to this cohort as the *Smithfield sample*.

However, in addition to this central focus, the enrolment patterns at 11 schools in one city were studied over the years 1990–5. The reforms brought in by the Labour government, which instigated *Tomorrow's Schools*, were operating by 1991. When the National party assumed the Treasury benches following the 1990 general election, further changes to the legislation were enacted to take effect from 1992. So, by the time the Smithfield Project got off the ground the reforms were fully in place. We collected retrospective enrolment data on the 11 schools so that we could document the changes taking place from 1990 (which was the final year before the implementation of the reforms) to 1995 (when they had been fully in place for four years). We will refer to this sample as the *composition sample*. During the period November 1992 to February 1993 interviews were carried out with a selected sample of the principals of these 11 schools to discuss the impact of de-zoning on the schools and the marketing activities undertaken by them.

Our Smithfield sample was too large for us to carry out labour-intensive data collection procedures such as interviews with the complete group, so we selected a sub-sample to interview by telephone about their choice of secondary school. This sample will be referred to as the *telephone sample*.

Each of these samples will be dealt with in turn to explain what was done. More detailed descriptions may be found in the various Smithfield reports. The data for the Smithfield sample were gathered over the period 1992–7, and the discussion is broken down by year.

 The Smithfield sample

1992

We began by selecting a set of target secondary schools. In all, 23 secondary schools were selected for the study although not all of them have been involved in every stage of the project for a variety of reasons. For example, when we undertook our initial study of school effectiveness, one school misadministered the outcome measures and another was unable to provide us with the attendance data we needed; both schools were dropped from this study. We chose 11 schools in an urban centre we call Green City and the same number in a second urban centre we call Central City. The final school was a state co-educational school in a rural area we call Fieldtown. In marked contrast to the urban schools in the study, Fieldtown's intake is drawn from very small provincial towns and farming areas.

A number of considerations were taken into account when the target secondary schools were selected. In order to observe the actual workings of an education market we chose neighbouring urban secondary schools in each urban centre although we also selected some schools which were relatively isolated geographically. To find out whether market policies have a different impact on different schools, we selected schools covering a wide range of school types. Thus included in the study are private, state and integrated schools, single-sex and co-ed. schools, and schools with a broad range of socioeconomic and ethnic compositions. The target schools in the two urban centres were chosen to complement each other, so that the two urban centres together provide the full range of schools.

In all, we selected the following types of schools (with Ns in brackets):

- single-sex boys' (4), single-sex girls' (3), co-educational (16);
- state (19), integrated (3), private (1);
- predominantly (i.e. 80 per cent or more) Pakeha (10), predominantly (i.e. 60 per cent or more) Maori and Pacific Island Polynesian (3), mixed (10);
- higher SES (i.e. 3.6 and higher) (8), middle SES (8), lower SES (i.e. 2.6 and lower) (7).

We then identified the primary and intermediate schools which fed students into our target secondary schools.

In general, it was relatively easy to identify the main feeder schools in the urban areas by simply selecting all the full primary and intermediate schools in the areas surrounding the secondary schools. There were exceptions, however. For example, the private school in the sample has a preparatory school feeding into the secondary department, but additional pupils begin attending in Year 9. Such pupils came from a wide range of schools and could not be specifically targeted, although some of them were in the feeder schools we selected. To focus our energies we decided not to contact feeder schools with fewer than 50 students in the entire school. This led to a total of 77 primary schools, 60 full primary and 17 intermediate schools that both were identified as feeder schools into our target secondary schools and agreed to take part in the study.[1] The rural target school had 12 full primary feeder schools, none of which was very large, and all took part in the study.

Next we approached the parents of Year 7 students within the feeder primary and intermediate schools and sought their involvement in the study.

In the urban centres an explanatory letter, consent form and initial questionnaire were distributed to parents by the schools and collected in through the schools during October to November 1992. We used a number of strategies to maximize the response rates for this initial contact. For example, the material sent out was gender specific and personalized and was translated into a number of Pacific and Asian languages. A second wave of consent forms was sent out during March 1993 to parents who had not responded originally. This increased our response rate by an additional 4 per cent.

About a year after the urban cohort was contacted, parents of students in the rural feeder schools were approached in much the same way. However, no second wave of consent forms was sent out because of time constraints.

Response rates

Table A1 Response rates by centre

Response rates	Total % (N)	Green City % (N)	Central City % (N)	Fieldtown % (N)
Year 7 rolls	(4394)	(2100)	(2073)	(221)
First wave				
Reply consent form	78 (3435)	80 (1687)	77 (1603)	66 (145)
Consent	71 (3140)	73 (1539)	71 (1463)	62 (138)
Second wave				
Reply consent form	5 (237)	4 (89)	7 (148)	
Consent	4 (180)	3 (62)	6 (118)	
Total reply consent form	84 (3672)	85 (1776)	84 (1751)	66 (145)
Total consent	76 (3320)	76 (1601)	76 (1581)	62 (138)

Table A1 shows the response rates that we obtained. The response rate for the rural cohort is clearly below that of both the urban centres, even when allowance is made for the fact that no second wave of consent forms could be sent out. The overall reply rate of 84 per cent stands up quite well when compared to other studies. Nash, Harker and Charters (1990a), for example, report a response rate of 82 per cent after researchers visited people at their homes, a practice which tends to lead to higher response rates than sending out written material. About 8 per cent of urban parents who were approached explicitly said that they did not want to take part in the project, so that overall 76 per cent of the students who were targeted make up the Smithfield sample.

Questionnaire data

The initial questionnaire included a question on family ethnic background, as well as questions on employment status and work histories for both parents/caregivers which we used to measure socioeconomic status.

Ethnic background

In the questionnaire we asked about ethnic background in an open-ended way so that parents could define their own 'ethnic background' as they pleased. The question was:

> People living in New Zealand see their cultural backgrounds in a variety of ways. For example some people regards themselves as Europeans, Maori or Tongans, others as New Zealanders of Samoan or Chinese or Dutch descent and others see themselves as from a mixture of cultures such as Pakeha/Maori, Anglo/Irish or Fijian/Indian/Scottish. How would you describe your family's cultural background?

Not surprisingly, there was a wide range of answers; some people gave us their ancestry for many generations while others simply put 'Kiwi' or 'New Zealander'. For analytic purposes, where we wanted to look at some general patterns these responses have been reduced to four categories. For comparisons with other studies, we essentially follow the standard procedure that is used in the Census and elsewhere, in which priority is given to, first, indigenous Maori and, second, to any minority status.

Maori
Includes those who either

- identify as Maori (only);
- identify as Maori/Pakeha (Maori first, Pakeha second);
- identify as Maori/Pacific Island Polynesian (Maori first, Pacific Island Polynesian second).

Pacific Island Polynesian
Includes those who either

- identify as Pacific Island Polynesian (only);
- identify as any specific ethnic or cultural background such as Cook Islander, Fijian, Nuiean, Tokelauan, Tongan, Pitcairn Islander or Samoan;
- identify as any combination of the ethnic or cultural backgrounds mentioned above;
- identify as Pacific Island Polynesian/Pakeha (Pacific Island Polynesian first, Pakeha second);
- identify as Pacific Island Polynesian/Maori (Pacific Island Polynesian first, Maori second).

Pakeha/European
Includes those who either

- identify as Pakeha/European (only);
- identify as any specific ethnic or cultural background within the British Isles, Eire, the White Commonwealth, Eastern and Western Europe;
- identify as Kiwis;
- identify as New Zealanders;[2]
- identify as Pakeha/Maori (Pakeha first, Maori second).

Other
Includes those who either

- identify as Asian (only);
- identify as any specific ethnic or cultural background such as Indian, Cambodian, Chinese, Indonesian, Japanese, Laotian, Malaysian, Philippino, Taiwanese, Vietnamese, Fijian Indian, Bangladeshi, Pakistani, Sri Lankan;
- identify as any combination of the ethnic or cultural backgrounds mentioned above;
- identify as anything else that has not yet been mentioned.

Table A2   Ethnic composition of the Smithfield cohort compared with the ethnic composition of New Zealand as a whole (per cent)

	Smithfield	*Census 1991*
Maori	11	13
Pacific Island Polynesian	7	5
Pakeha/European	75	79
Other	7	3

Applying this coding scheme to the responses given by the parents of our cohort gives the figures in Table A2 which also provides comparative data from the 1991 census.

Socioeconomic status

As the Smithfield Project is a New Zealand study, we wanted to use a measure of either social class or socioeconomic status that was specifically based on the New Zealand social structure. The only existing scale which met this criterion was the Elley and Irving index (Irving and Elley 1977; Elley and Irving 1985). The Elley and Irving index is occupation based and should be seen as measuring SES rather than social class.

We did not want to obviate the possibility of using other scales in the future, such as new scales which may be developed for New Zealand or scales for the purpose of international comparative research. All occupations were therefore coded into the New Zealand version of the 5-digit ISCO codes (NZSCO90), which is also used by the Census. These codes have been recoded into scores on the Elley and Irving scale.

The Elley and Irving index is an occupational-based scale and was derived from Census data. Using 3-digit NZSCO-codes, the median income and educational levels were computed per occupational group and then combined with equal weighting.

The occupational ratings were divided into six categories so that the actual scale has a range from 1 to 6, with 1 referring to occupations with the highest income and educational levels. In the past, different versions have been developed for males and females although the version we used (Irving 1991a), which was produced by the Ministry of Education in 1991, does not have different codes for males and females. James Irving, who provided us with the scale, has informed us that there were very few differences between males and females on this scale.

The most commonly used method to indicate SES is based on the current occupation of the main, and mostly male, breadwinner in the household. This approach has come under wide criticism as such a measure is severely limited with growing numbers of women in paid employment. We therefore decided on a family-based indicator for SES. Hence in cases where two parents or caregivers are in paid employment, we averaged their scores. For solo parents and families with occupational data available for only one parent or caregiver, the job information of that parent was used to gauge the family SES.

In the economic recession of the 1990s New Zealand faced considerable unemployment, underemployment, sub-employment and short-term contracts, so that analysis based on the current job might be seriously flawed. To obtain more reliable occupational data, we opted for a work history approach whereby parents/caregivers were asked to give us both the nature and the length of the three paid jobs they had held for the longest time. Any temporary 'aberration' in a job career can then be counteracted by the other information available.

For each of the parents/caregivers a 'history-based' measure of occupational ranking was derived. All the jobs that were stated were first coded into the Elley and Irving scale, then each jobscore was multiplied by the number of years the job had been performed, added up per individual and divided by the total number of years accounted for by the respective jobs. In other words, the jobs were proportionally weighted by the number of years they had been performed. These individual scores were then used as a basis for the indicator of SES at the family level, as described above.

This approach allowed us to attach a score for SES to families in cases where the parent(s)/caregiver(s) did not have paid employment at the time of the questionnaire. In those cases SES was based on the information we had referring to the past. This approach does not exclude job information on people, mainly women, who were in paid employment in the past but at the time of the questionnaire were full-time homemakers.

The socioeconomic composition of the Smithfield cohort is very similar to the SES composition of other New Zealand studies, such as the studies conducted by Nash, Harker and Charters (1990a, 1990b) and Lauder and Hughes (1990a, 1990b). Comparisons between our data and data available from earlier censuses as reported by Elley and Irving (Irving and Elley 1977; Elley and Irving 1985) are shown in Table A3. Figures for the Smithfield cohort include both the urban and the rural cohorts.

The table shows that parents in the Smithfield sample tend to come from somewhat higher SES backgrounds than the national average when compared with the Census data. It must be kept in mind, however, that the sample information is much more recent, so that changes in the New Zealand workforce may account for some of the differences.

Table A3 SES comparisons for men and women (per cent)

	Men		Women	
	Smithfield	Census	Smithfield	Census
1	11	7	4	2
2	17	11	15	6
3	21	23	28	24
4	31	33	27	35
5	17	17	17	21
6	5	9	10	12

Note: Data for men are from the 1981 Census and data for women are from the 1971 census.

Gender

Over the whole Smithfield sample 52.7 per cent were boys and 47.3 per cent were girls. Nationally the ratio of boys to girls at this year-level is 52:48 (Ministry of Education 1992). The very slight overrepresentation of boys in the cohort will be due to the fact that we have four single-sex boys' secondary schools in the study but only three single-sex girls' secondary schools.

1993

Test data

During the latter part of the project we were primarily concerned with the impact of choice regimes on school effectiveness. To measure a school's effectiveness, it is necessary to have information on relevant characteristics of the students who enter that school. This applies to the socioeconomic and ethnic background of the students and their gender, but it also applies to achievement, aptitude and affective measures. Only by analysing these so-called presage variables in combination with data collected during secondary schooling is it possible to identify school effects.

Achievement tests

Towards the end of 1992 the feeder primary and intermediate schools for the target secondary schools were asked which standardized tests they would administer at the beginning of 1993 to their Year 8 students. The vast majority of schools were planning to use PAT: Reading (Reid and Elley 1991), Listening Comprehension (Elley and Reid 1971) and Mathematics (Reid 1993), but few schools intended using the other standardized achievement tests available for use in New Zealand schools. Because we could not afford to fill in the missing data on these latter tests, we decided to collect information on the four tests which were most widely used: PAT: Reading Comprehension (PATRC), Reading Vocabulary (PATRV), Listening Comprehension (PATLC) and Mathematics (PATM). Where necessary we filled in missing data by carrying out the testing ourselves.

Aptitude tests

Following Anastasi (1988) we do not find it helpful to classify tests strictly into achievement and aptitude categories, but we do recognize that there are differences in the kinds of background experiences necessary for successful performance on various tests. According to this view, achievement tests are typically tied to a specific school curriculum that must have been learnt, whereas aptitude tests require less specific experiences. The distinction between achievement and aptitude tests is thus a difference in degree of specificity rather than a difference in kind.

We felt it was important to complement the achievement tests with measures less tied to particular curricula or programmes, hence we considered the possible use of TOSCA, the acronym for the Test of Scholastic Abilities (Reid *et al.* 1981). However, about half of the feeder schools did not administer TOSCA as part of their regular testing programme and the cost of filling in the missing scores was prohibitive, so we decided to produce our own aptitude measures.

Our search for possible alternatives to TOSCA began by looking at an unpublished test battery developed by Brian Keeling at the University of Canterbury about 25 years ago. This battery contained verbal analogies, vocabulary and arithmetic tests. The vocabulary test was discarded because it overlapped too much with the PAT: Reading Vocabulary test but the verbal analogies test appeared worthy of further consideration. These items were of the kind: 'hand is to foot as arm is to . . .'.

We began by attempting to modify the verbal analogies questions in an effort to make them more suitable for the ethnically diverse students in the sample. In doing so we came to realize that the vocabulary used to frame the questions was rather difficult for primary school students. This seemed undesirable given that we already had a vocabulary test and wanted to produce a test which was as free as possible from the influences of school curricula. Accordingly we began rewriting the items, sometimes modifying Brian Keeling's original item but often writing a completely new one, making sure that the vocabulary was kept as simple as possible. We wanted the difficulty of an item to be a matter of understanding the relationships in the analogy rather than knowing the vocabulary. Altogether we generated 26 five-choice items for trialling. The items were read to the students to avoid the possibility of students with weak reading skills not being able to read some of the words, even though the words were commonly used.

The arithmetic test had various items of a traditional arithmetic and algebraic type, but also number series items. The arithmetic items were considered to be inappropriate because they overlapped too much with the PAT: Mathematics test, but the number series items seemed ideally suited to our purposes. These items were of the type: 'Which pair of numbers comes next in the following series: 3, 5, 9, 15, 23, ?, ?'

Because number series items are largely free of the mathematics taught in schools, we considered them to be much more curriculum-free than the PAT: Mathematics items. From the 20 original number series items, 18 were selected unchanged for trialling.

Self concept

In addition to achievement and aptitude tests we considered it important
also to have an affective measure, and decided to use a self-concept scale.
We began by studying published self-concept scales which we found unsat-
isfactory for a variety of reasons, not least of which was cost. We therefore
designed a scale of our own and constructed a set of 35 bipolar descriptors
(such as 'I hate school/I love school'). The students were asked to indicate
what they were like on a five-point scale by filling in one of five circles
between the bipolar descriptors. To avoid response bias, half the items had
positive descriptors on the left and negative descriptors on the right, while
the other half were the other way around. Most of the descriptors were
clearly about school, some were more general (for example 'I'm an
unhappy person/I'm a happy person'), but none was about family relationships, religion and the like, as was the case with many published scales. As
for the analogies test, the items on the self-concept scale were read to the
students.

The Self Concept scale (SELFC), Verbal Analogies test (VA) and the
Number Series test (NS) were trialled at the end of 1992 on the entire
second form of an intermediate school which was not taking part in the
project (N = 147) . The results were then used in item analyses of various
kinds to make decisions about which items to keep in their original form,
which to modify slightly and which to exclude, how much time to allow for
the number series items and so on.

Answers given on the SELFC items were scored from one to five (with
five indicating a positive self concept) and added to provide a total. Correlations between items and total scores were computed, and a principal
component factor analysis was also done. The 30 selected items all have
item/total correlations and factor loadings of at least 0.39.

Conventional item analyses were carried out for the VA and NS tests,
using the top and bottom 27 per cents, to generate difficulty and discrimination indices.

For Verbal Analogies, five items with poor discrimination indices and
high difficulty were dropped. Most items had one distracter which was not
working satisfactorily, and we decided to drop the poorest distracter in
each item. The 21 remaining items, which had difficulty indices ranging
from 25 to 90 (median = 53) and discrimination indices between 0.20 and
0.88 (median = 0.55), were ordered according to difficulty to form the final
test.

An analysis of the words used in the final 21 items was undertaken using
the Wright list of the 10,000 most common words in English prose (Wright
1965). In the Wright list, the most common thousand words have a rating
of 1, the next most common thousand words have a rating of 2, and so on.
Of the 147 words used to frame the verbal analogies items 6 were missing

from the list (rimu, Alsatian, Friday, Wednesday, Monday and, inexplicably, pet). Of the remaining 141 words, 64 per cent were at Level 1, 21 per cent at Level 2, 1 per cent at each of Levels 3 and 4, 5 per cent each at Levels 5 and 6 and 1 per cent beyond Level 6.

For Number Series, three items with discrimination indices lower than 0.30 were discarded, and the remaining 15 items were ordered according to difficulty. The final selection of items had discrimination indices between 0.33 and 0.97 (median = 0.52) and difficulties ranging from 20 to 61 (median = 42).

The SELFC, VA and NS tests were put into a single booklet and known collectively as the Smithfield tests.

Data collection

During 1993, while the Smithfield sample students were in Year 8, PAT test data were collected for all students in the cohort. We also asked the schools to administer the Smithfield tests, which were sent to schools in the first week of March 1993 and collected at the end of the first term. The Smithfield tests for the rural schools, which joined the project later than the urban ones, were done between August and October 1993.

A split-half reliability coefficient, corrected using the Spearman-Brown formula, was computed for a sampling fraction of 5 per cent of the cohort. After students with missing data on any item were excluded, a total of 143 scripts remained. A corrected coefficient of 0.92 was obtained.

Reliabilities for both the Verbal Analogies and Number Series tests were calculated using a random sample of 120 scripts from one urban centre. The split-half reliability for the VA, corrected using the Spearman-Brown formula, was 0.76, which is on the low side for a test with 21 items. The same reliability coefficient for the NS was 0.85, which is very good for a test with 15 items.

Missing data

Data were missing mainly because students did not attend school on the days the testing was done, although in some cases schools had not administered all the PAT tests they had said they would and had not advised us so that we could not fill in the missing data. We decided to 'impute' data in cases where scores were missing on the achievement and/or aptitude tests. We used regression analyses to estimate the missing data. We incorporated SES, ethnic background, gender and all available test scores in all the models to make the estimates more accurate.

1994

Context measures

School effectiveness research studies are basically designed to assess schools to find out what proportion of the total variance is between individuals and between schools. The between-school variance is then analysed to find out how much of it can be accounted for by the individual characteristics of the students attending the schools (acting at both the individual level and the school level) and other school-level variables related to school characteristics such as school size and school policy and practice. We were concerned to measure some of these school-level variables to include in our analyses of school effectiveness.

While we had identified the main feeder primary schools for our selected high schools, the Smithfield sample students did not make up 100 per cent of each school's third-form intake. Indeed, in some schools the Smithfield students made up fewer than 50 per cent of the total third-form roll as a consequence of parents not replying to the initial questionnaire or declining to take part in the study, families moving into the district after the initial questionnaire had gone out, the school drawing its students from a wide geographical area, a number of very small schools feeding some pupils into the school, and such like.

We wanted information on the composition of the complete third-form intake, including both Smithfield and non-Smithfield students, in each of the secondary schools. To get this 'contextual data' we gathered information on the PAT: Reading Comprehension Test (Reid and Elley 1991), socioeconomic status and ethnicity for the entire third-form intake in each of the target secondary schools in 1994. These data were gathered from school records solely to provide school-level measures and were not recorded in the data base for individual students.

Questionnaire

In April 1994 we recontacted the Smithfield sample in the two urban centres by mail and asked parents to fill out a questionnaire which included four questions relating to school choice.

1 Of the schools available to you, which one did you most want your son/daughter to go to?
2 Please write down the names of any secondary schools that you applied to for your son/daughter.
3 Which of these schools was s/he accepted for?
4 Which school is s/he going to this year?

At the end of June the combined response rate to this questionnaire for Green City and Central City was approximately 60 per cent. The highest response rates were for high SES Pakeha families and the lowest were for Maori, Pacific Island and low SES families. It was decided to conduct follow-up telephone interviews with those parents who had not responded to the original questionnaire. In Green City, two Samoan interviewers and one Maori interviewer were employed to conduct the interviews with Pacific Island and Maori families. One Pakeha interviewer was also employed to interview Pakeha parents and those whose ethnicity was coded as 'other'. In Central City, one Pakeha interviewer was employed to interview Pakeha parents and a small number of Maori and Pacific Island parents.

The aim was to raise each ethnic and SES group's response rate to at least 60 per cent. Where the response rate was already over 60 per cent no phone interviews were done with that group. The interviews took an average of ten minutes each. A total of 99 were completed in Green City and 70 in Central City. As a result of the follow-up phone interviews the total response rate was raised to 74 per cent in Green City and 72 per cent in Central City. However, the response rates for low SES Maori, Pacific Island and 'Other' families remain below 60 per cent because we were unable to contact sufficient parents in these groups to get the response rate up. These families had no phone, had given a phone number in the initial questionnaire in 1992 which had changed or been disconnected or had not consented to being contacted by phone on the initial consent form.

1995

Classroom observations

As part of our data collection in 1995, in classrooms in the sample schools we gathered data on a number of variables which we planned to use in our analyses of school effectiveness. In each school, we observed two fourth-form classes for two periods in each of their core subjects (mathematics, English, social studies and science), giving approximately 16 hours of observation in each school.

To allow us to make meaningful comparisons between schools in terms of the data generated by the observations, we needed to minimize the impact resulting from differences in the composition of the student population in our target schools. We therefore selected classes on the basis of the context data gathered in 1994. To do this, the target schools provided class lists for all of their fourth-form core subject classes. From these lists, the mean SES, the mean PAT: Reading Comprehension score and the ethnic composition of the total fourth-form sample and each class within the sample were calculated. Then, the two classes within each school which most closely matched the mean statistics for the total sample were selected for observation. Once classes were selected, a letter explaining the purpose and process of the observations was sent to the subject teachers involved asking their permission to undertake the observations and guaranteeing the confidentiality of the recorded data. If requested, a meeting was held with staff to answer any questions and address any concerns they might have had. Teachers were asked to continue with their normal teaching activities while their classes were being observed.

An observation instrument was developed to measure the extent to which a number of teacher and student behaviours that have been linked to student learning could be found in the classes in our target schools. In developing the instrument we reviewed a number of articles, including several that summarized the literature in this area (Purkey and Smith 1983; Rosenshine 1983; Brophy and Good 1986; Teddlie et al. 1989). The observation instrument was based on the findings of this research and included a number of student and teacher variables. In addition to the observational data, teacher comments were recorded on audio tape and coded after the observations.

Of relevance to the analyses presented in this book are (i) the total number of intervals students were engaged in on-task behaviour (which was coded during the observations), (ii) the number of positive teacher comments for good behaviour, and (iii) the number of negative teacher comments for poor behaviour (both of which were coded from the tape recordings after the observations were completed). Research has shown that teachers in effective schools give praise freely and apply discipline infrequently. An example of a teacher comment which would count as positive on our schedule is publicly praising a student for paying attention during class while an example of a negative comment is admonishing a pupil for talking during silent reading.

The off-task student observational data were collected by a 'predominant activity' time sampling procedure (Tyler 1979). According to this procedure, an observer judges whether or not pre-defined behaviours were the predominant behaviours of the subject or subjects during a pre-determined interval of time. Any data generated during an interval is recorded during the following interval. In accordance with this procedure, in our study, the observer received pre-recorded signals from an audio cassette player via earphones. At the start of the lesson the observer selected the first pupil for observation and set the cassette player in motion to record teacher comments. The observations were divided into one-minute intervals which were further segmented as follows:

Seconds Activity
5   Observe student A
5   If student A is 'off-task', record on sheet
        Select student B for observation
5   Observe student B

5   If student B is 'off-task', record on sheet
      Select student C for observation
5   Observe student C
5   If student C is 'off-task', record on sheet
      Select student D for observation
      Observe student D
5   If student D is 'off-task', record on sheet
20   Spent in observing teacher behaviour not relevant to the analyses
      in this book. Select student E for observation.
60 seconds in total

This sequence was repeated throughout the lesson. During a 50-minute lesson, then, 200 student observations were made. Pupils were monitored in a systematic way so that all pupils in the class were observed for a similar number of intervals.

Inter-observer reliability

Classroom observations
In each centre two observers were trained in the use of the observational instrument. However, apart from when reliability checks were being completed, only one observer was used in each centre. Inter-observer reliability checks were carried out during four complete lessons in one centre and three in the other, when the second observer in each centre sat in on the lessons and independently coded the behaviours. Reliability coefficients, calculated by the frequency ratio method, of 0.85 and 0.89 were obtained in Centre A and Centre B respectively for the coding of student time on-task.

Classroom recordings
Inter-observer reliability for the classroom recordings was calculated by sending tape recordings of five separate lessons from one centre to the other. A research assistant in the second centre independently listened to the tapes and recorded the frequencies of the target behaviours. The frequency ratio method was then used to compare the frequencies obtained in the two centres. Both the positive comments for good behaviour and negative comments for poor behaviour had reliability coefficients of 0.78.

Outcome measures for the first school effectiveness study

We began our development of the outcome measures by considering the amount of time available in which to test. Given that we had to work within the time available in the shortest period operated in any school in the study and had to limit the number of testing occasions so that we did not make unreasonable demands on the schools, we decided to restrict the testing to two 50-minute sessions, including the time needed to give out the booklets, give instructions, collect the booklets in, etc.

We began by considering the possibility of producing achievement tests based on the syllabuses in the 'basic subjects' such as English, mathematics and science. However, we quickly decided not to pursue this option for a number of reasons. Firstly, in two 50-minute sessions we would be restricted to testing in no more than two subject areas unless we adopted a smorgasbord approach in which we sampled a few items from each of several subject areas to provide a global achievement score. Secondly, the development costs involved in a test of this type would be substantial because items would have to be written, trialled, analysed, revised, re-trialled, etc. Thirdly, we were limited in terms of the item types available to us because the costs involved in marking constructed response type questions (such as essays for the large numbers in our sample) were beyond our budget. Fourthly, the students in the cohort were to sit School Certificate in 1996, and their results in the School Certificate examinations would provide us with quality data in the various School Certificate subjects in approximately 12 months time.

Consequently, we decided to test the students on four measures which we had already produced or which we could put together with little expense and which concentrated on cognitive and affective abilities and achievements which might be predicted to enhance learning at school. Students with good verbal reasoning abilities, good vocabularies, good study skills and positive self concepts might be predicted to be able to profit more from their secondary school studies than those with less of these attributes. These measures were included in two booklets, each with three sections, one of which in each booklet gathered information not relevant to the contents of this book. A description of the relevant sections of both booklets is given below.

Booklet A

Verbal Analogies
The Verbal Analogies test as described above.

Study Skills
A Study Skills test made up of items from the Progressive Achievement Tests of Study Skills (Reid *et al*. 1978), with the kind permission of the publishers, the New Zealand Council for Educational Research. Students sitting the PAT tests are administered Form A in odd-numbered years so, to avoid having the students resit items they might already have sat earlier in the year, the Part 8 items of Form B were inspected with a view to taking two sets of items from each of the three tests in the series. That is, we wanted to

take two tests from each of *Study Skills 1: Knowledge and Use of Reference Materials*; *Study Skills 2: Reading Maps, Graphs, Tables and Diagrams*; and *Study Skills 3: Reading Study Skills*. The PAT Study Skills tests sometimes make use of colour in graphs, diagrams and the like, and the materials we selected had to be capable of being reproduced in black and white without causing problems because we were unable to afford colour printing. We eventually settled on six sets of questions:

1 A set of six five-option multiple choice questions about a table of contents from a book on the Earth's changing face. The book contained 12 chapters, picture credits, preface, bibliography, glossary and index; the questions asked the students to select the page numbers on which various kinds of information could be found. For example, one question asked on which pages the structure of a volcano would most likely be found.

2 A set of eight questions involving location skimming. Five minutes were given to find the answers to the eight questions in a passage of about 800 words in six paragraphs. Four questions involved identifying the paragraphs in which certain types of information could be found, and the other four questions required the answers to particular detailed questions in five-option multiple choice format.

3 A set of five five-option multiple choice questions about a graph showing the books issued in a school library each term from 1972 to 1975. The graph was a set of five frequency polygons, each of which showed the number of books of one type (adventure, hobbies, animal, war and sport) issued during the period. For example, one question asked the students to select the type of book for which the number of books issued during the period had varied least.

4 A set of five five-option multiple choice questions about a bar graph and associated table giving information about berryfruit in the 1970–1 season. The graph showed percentages of six berryfruits produced in the season which were sold as fresh fruit or for processing, while the table gave the same information expressed in tonnages plus other information such as net area under cultivation and yield per hectare. For example, one question asked which crop was sold in the greatest quantity for processing.

5 A set of eight five-option multiple choice questions about an excerpt from a dictionary. For example, one question asked the students to select the meaning of the word 'gill' which is pronounced differently from the others.

6 A set of eight questions on outlining. This comprised four paragraphs each of approximately 100 words on the Plain of Shinar (as the area between the Tigris and Euphrates rivers used to be known) accompanied by an incomplete outline of six or seven points. The students had to select from given statements those that best completed each outline.

When we ran a pilot administration of the tests to check on the timing we realized that it would be difficult for students to finish Test A in the time available but we decided to leave the questions on outlining in the test with a view to not scoring them if too many students failed to finish. This in fact turned out to be the case; we did not score the outlining questions, so the final test comprised 32 items in five sets.

Booklet B

Self Concept
The Self Concept scale described above.

Vocabulary
A 55-item vocabulary test adapted from the Progressive Achievement Tests of Reading (Reid and Elley 1991), with the kind permission of the publishers, the New Zealand Council for Educational Research. We again chose Part 8, Form B for the reasons given above when discussing the Study Skills test. Because of the limited time available we wanted to shorten the test slightly. We therefore eliminated the ten easiest items (using the item statistics for Part 8 given in the manual) on the grounds that the students in the study were at the end of their fourth-form year when sitting the test although it was developed for use at the beginning of the fourth-form year. The ten items deleted all had difficulty indices above 70. The 45 remaining items involved a sentence with a word underlined. The students had to select from five given alternatives the word which means the same or most nearly the same as the underlined word. For example:

He carried a large *staff* in his hand

(A) box (B) heap (C) pole (D) flag (E) bag

The tests in Booklets A and B were administered to the fourth-form classes in the Smithfield schools in late November and early December 1995.

1996

Questionnaire

At the beginning of 1996 a third questionnaire was sent to the Smithfield sample. Among other things this questionnaire asked the parents to indicate the number of times they had contacted the school their son or daughter was attending, for each of a number of reasons, during 1994 and 1995. For example, they were asked to indicate how often they had contacted the school to discuss their child's academic progress.

Attendance data

From the schools we also gathered information on the 1994 and 1995 attendance records of each of the Smithfield students. Attendance is an obvious variable to include in any attempt to account for school outcomes. Clearly, students are unlikely to learn adequately if, for whatever reason, they are absent from school for long periods of time. We gathered information on the number of half-days that the Smithfield students had attended secondary school in 1994 and 1995.

While typically schools were open for about 380 half-days each year, not all schools in the study were open for the same number of half-days. Consequently, we divided the number of half-days a student was present at school by the number of half-days it was possible for that student to attend that school and multiplied by 400 to place all schools on the same scale.

One issue with the attendance data was deciding what to count as possible attendance days. It was decided that exam leave and any other days when the schools were not in session (such as the day most schools were 'closed' for a one-day strike) would be removed from the set of possible attendance days. Information, in the form of half-days attended, was recorded for the Smithfield students on the remaining days.

Examination of the attendance records of the Smithfield schools showed that a few pupils had changed schools during 1994–5. We decided that a reasonable cut-off point should be set that would exclude pupils who had spent too much time outside the school in which they sat the outcome tests, but not exclude pupils who had spent the major proportion of their time in that school. We settled on a maximum of 130 half-days spent in a school other than the one in which the outcome measures were sat for a student to remain in the study. Essentially, this means that anyone spending more than Term 1 of their third-form year in a school other than the one in which they sat the outcome measures was eliminated from the school effectiveness analyses.

1997

School Certificate results

In May 1997 each of the schools in the project was visited and arrangements were made to gather information on the 1996 attendance records of the Smithfield students. In addition, the principals were asked to sign a consent form giving the project permission to approach the New Zealand Qualifications Authority to obtain lists of results for the fifth-form students sitting external examinations in 1996 in their schools.

The New Zealand Qualifications Authority was sent the consent forms obtained from the Smithfield schools in May 1997 and we were duly sent a hard copy of the 1996 School Certificate results obtained by the students in the Smithfield schools. The results are all given in percentage marks, with the exception of Te Reo Maori where there are two marks, each on a five-point scale, one for the written part and one for the oral part. These marks were converted to 'percentage marks' as explained below.

It soon became obvious that not all students in the Smithfield sample had simply taken School Certificate subjects. Enquiries with NZQA and the Smithfield schools revealed that a few students who attempted School Certificate also attempted some Sixth Form Certificate subjects in their third year at high school. NZQA supplied us with information on the students in the Smithfield sample taking School Certificate and Sixth Form Certificate subjects concurrently in 1996.

To convert the Sixth Form Certificate (SFC) grades (which are on an eight-point scale) to percentage marks so they can be analysed along with the other School Certificate marks we used a table supplied by NZQA. This table shows the School Certificate mark range in each School Certificate subject corresponding to each of the Sixth Form Certificate grades. For example, the entry for mathematics is as follows.

SFC Grade mathematics

	1	2	3	4	5	6	7	8
SC score Range	100–88	87–83	82–76	75–69	68–59	58–47	46–35	34–1

For each Sixth Form Certificate subject for which there is a School Certificate equivalent, the Sixth Form Certificate grade was converted to a School Certificate mark by taking the mid-point of the interval for the grade obtained by the student in that Sixth Form Certificate subject. For Sixth Form Certificate subjects for which there is no School Certificate equivalent, such as drama, the mean values of the intervals were calculated for all the subjects in the School Certificate list as follows.

SFC Grade other

	1	2	3	4	5	6	7	8
SC score Range	100–84	83–79	78–73	72–66	65–57	56–48	47–37	36–1

The mid-points of these mean values were then used to assign the School Certificate marks for these Sixth Form Certificate grades.

For Te Reo Maori (Maori language), a table obtained from NZQA allowed the marks for the oral and written parts of the School Certificate examination to be converted to Sixth Form Certificate grades. For example, School Certificate marks of 2 for oral and 3 for written convert to a Sixth Form Certificate grade of 5. These Sixth Form Certificate grades were converted to School Certificate marks using the mid-points of the mean values described above.

In addition to sitting School Certificate some students in some schools had also obtained unit standards credits, usually at Level 1 although occasionally at Level 2. Information about the unit standards credits obtained in the Smithfield schools was obtained from NZQA, and it seemed reasonable to count these unit standards where appropriate. Given that some schools had a number of students obtaining credit on the Framework while other schools did not, we would be disadvantaging the schools in which students obtained unit standards credit if we simply ignored credit on the Framework because it was difficult to handle. However, precisely how to handle the unit standards credits was not at all straightforward.

We began by deciding that 'double dipping' would not be appropriate. Perusal of the NZQA printouts made it clear that some schools were getting credit on the Framework for their students in a subject while preparing them for the School Certificate examinations in that subject. So, for example, one student was awarded 12 credits in Level 1 history unit standards but he also had 50 per cent in School Certificate history. To count the unit standards credits on top of the School Certificate marks would be double dipping, so we ignored the unit standards.

Other students though had unit standards credits in subjects they had not sat for in School Certificate. For example, in one school several students had not sat the School Certificate mathematics examination but these students had unit standards credits in mathematics. For example, one boy in this school had 11 credits in Level 1 mathematics unit standards as follows:

05223	Use formulae and equations to solve problems	2 credits
05224	Use decimals and percentages to solve problems	2 credits
05225	Use fractions, ratio and proportions to solve ...	2 credits
05228	Measure and use calculations to solve problems	2 credits
05230	Carry out an investigation and interpret data	3 credits

Because this student had not taken mathematics for School Certificate, the unit standards credits were in addition to any School Certificate marks he had obtained. The problem was how to count this achievement in a manner which would allow us to include it in our analyses.

We inspected the unit standards printouts and found one school which had clearly put all of its students through unit standards in history as well as the School Certificate examinations in history. Fifty-four students in this school had taken history for both qualifications. The correlation between the number of unit standards credits in history and School Certificate history marks was 0.83, which is a high correlation and suggests that the students probably had the opportunity to obtain a significant number of unit standards credits. The high fliers in history who got high School Certificate history marks appear to have obtained all or nearly all the unit standards offered, while the students whose achievement in history was much lower obtained only a limited number of unit standards credits and got only modest School Certificate marks. The regression equation to predict School Certificate history marks from the unit standards credits was:

School Certificate history = 22.62 + 2.11 (history unit standards credits)

The New Zealand Qualifications Authority offered to help us check out the procedure we had used for history by providing a data set on 124 students who had taken mathematics both for School Certificate and unit standards in two non-Smithfield schools. The correlation between unit standards credits in mathematics and School Certificate marks in mathematics was 0.79, which is very similar to the correlation obtained in history. The regression equation to predict School Certificate marks from unit standards credits was:

School Certificate mathematics = 37.12 + 1.68 (mathematics unit standards credits)

The intercept is somewhat higher than the intercept for history and the regression coefficient is a little lower. It was decided to 'split the difference' between the two samples by averaging the values predicted for School Certificate using each subject. So, for example, a student gaining 25 unit standards credits was predicted to obtain 75 per cent in School Certificate with the history sample and 79 per cent in School Certificate with the mathematics sample. Twenty-five unit standards credits therefore converted to $(75 + 79)/2 = 77$ per cent.

Attendance

We gathered attendance data for the 1996 year using the same procedures used to gather attendance during 1994 and 1995.

The composition sample

The composition data set was collected to address the theoretical debate about the effects of market policies on *choice and school intakes*. To illuminate this debate, we collected data on student enrolment patterns in the 11 secondary schools in Green City over the period 1990–5. Along with data on the gender, socioeconomic status and ethnic backgrounds of students, we also collected information on the residential addresses of students. The resulting data set enabled us to develop a picture of enrolment shifts between schools.

Data collection

We initially wanted to collect data on the Year 9 (first year) intakes of all our target secondary schools from 1990–5. However, given the likely amount of work involved, we decided only to collect retrospective data for the target secondary schools in one urban centre. Nevertheless, this has involved the development of a comprehensive data set on some 12,600 students, a sizable task in itself.

Identifying the third-form intakes for 1993–5 from the March 1993–5 rolls was straightforward, but for earlier years the procedure proved to be more complex. In November 1992 the schools were asked to supply computer printouts of information on all students in their current third to fifth forms. The November 1992 rolls included some students who had arrived after the third form and omitted other students in the original third-form intakes who had already left. Students who had arrived later than the third form were therefore identified by computer printouts of all new students for each year or by records on the date of first attendance. In many cases schools were able to provide the names of the secondary schools students who had transferred from other schools and these were also recorded. Students who, on the other hand, had already left the school were also identified by a variety of means. Some schools had retained paper files of third-form rolls of previous years which could be directly compared to the current roll to identify students who had left. In other schools we used computer or card files to identify students who had left.

The 11 target secondary schools in Green City were all either state or integrated (Catholic) schools. State and integrated schools form over 90 per cent of Green City's secondary school provision. The target schools include some from the inner city area and others from a wedge of the city which includes both middle and working class suburbs. In principle then, the schools can be seen as comprising a local market because, although the suburbs are some miles from the city centre, proximity to public transport affords the opportunity for students to travel in both directions. Approximately 80 per cent of all students living in the centre of Green City attended the schools in our study, while for the suburban region we had a higher coverage of about 90 per cent. The more comprehensive coverage in the suburbs usefully allows us to track shifts from one school to another.

Measurements

We collected the following information on the 12,621 students: gender, residential address, ethnic background, occupations of both parents or caregivers and when the student had left the school (where applicable).

Residential addresses

For the purpose of coding residential addresses, the metropolitan region surrounding the schools was divided into 15 geographical areas, drawn along the boundaries of the former school zones. In cases where these zones were particularly large, the areas were further subdivided. Together with areas outside the metropolitan region, 17 categories for residential areas were used. No residential address was known for 1 per cent of the students, most of whom had already left the school.

Ethnic background

Ethnic background information was provided by the school and was invariably drawn directly from student enrolment cards where ethnic background was self-identified. Five categories were used: Maori, Pacific Island Polynesian, Asian, European/Pakeha and Other. Where school records identified a student as having more than one ethnic origin, the order of priority during coding was: Maori, minority group, European/Pakeha. For 3 per cent of the students we were unable to gain information on their ethnic background. In most cases these students had already left the school.

Socioeconomic status

Collecting reliable data on the occupations of both parents or caregivers proved to be difficult in some schools. Three main problems occurred, all of which required specific solutions. Firstly, although most schools collected occupational data on enrolment forms and recorded the information on computer, there were numerous gaps in the computer data. Checking the original enrolment forms showed that these gaps were because spaces on enrolment forms had been left blank. We are unsure whether parents had not provided the information because they simply preferred not to answer the question, were unemployed, or one or both parents were absent. Secondly, two schools had not asked for occupational information at all, while another school had asked for it in a way that was insufficiently clear to be codeable. A third problem was that the computer codes used by some schools overgeneralized occupational categories to the point of being uncodeable.

The difficulties were approached on a school-by-school and sometimes on a year-by-year basis, in ways which eventually secured adequate data from all years in all schools. Several schools updated their records by sending home a form. The fact that schools increasingly need occupational data themselves for equity funding purposes was advantageous in securing their cooperation. In other cases we went directly to the enrolment forms rather than computer records when these were clearly inadequate. In one instance a school allowed us to distribute a questionnaire to the pupils themselves about their parents' occupations as this was seen to be more effective than sending a questionnaire home to parents. As far as we can tell, the students, assured of confidentiality, were frank.

In cases where clear occupational data were not available from schools in one way or another or were insufficiently clear, electoral rolls were consulted using residential addresses as a check. Occupations were coded into the most recent version of the Elley and Irving index (Irving 1991a). We extended the index for our purposes with categories for (i) beneficiaries and unemployed, and (ii) homemakers or retired. The distinction between (i) and (ii) was made because of the likely socioeconomic difference between these groups.

Despite all our efforts, for 8 per cent of the students no occupational information could be found for either of the parents or caregivers. As is the case with missing data on other variables, most of these students had already left the school.

As for the main cohort, we used a family-based indicator for SES. Hence for cases where two parents or caregivers were in paid employment, we averaged their scores on the Elley and Irving scale. For solo parents who were in paid employment, and for families with one parent or caregiver in paid employment, the Elley and Irving score of that parent was used as the indicator of family SES. Unemployment was also looked at on a family basis, so that 'unemployed families' include (i) solo parents who were not in paid employment and (ii) two-parent families where neither of the parents or caregivers was in paid employment.

Basic descriptors

The overall characteristics of the students in the data set are shown in Table 6.1.

An assumption that underlies our study is that changes in school composition did not result from substantive demographic shifts. Although we have no independent demographic data to justify this assumption, it can be seen that the overall characteristics of the first-year intakes for the 11 schools were very stable throughout the period studied. The total number of students dropped only slightly over the years, following the national trend (Ministry of Education 1992). Proportions of indigenous Maori and minority Pacific Island Polynesian students remained stable at around 13 per cent for both groups. The socioeconomic backgrounds of the students fluctuates only marginally over the period. The general picture, then, is one of stability from year to year which makes it most likely that any composition changes experienced by schools were primarily the result of between-school processes rather than underlying demographic shifts.

Interviews with principals

Interviews with the principals of the target secondary schools in Green City were held over the period November 1992 to February 1993. The interviews, which were reasonably open-ended, centred on the impact of de-zoning on schools and market activities undertaken by the schools.

Questions asked included:

- What do you think are the main ways that the recent reforms have affected your college?
- I'd like to talk a little about the removal of zoning from secondary schools. Can you explain to me the original arrangements for your college? What effect has the removal of zoning had? What is your present enrolment scheme? Do you envisage any further change?
- Tell me about the 'clientele' of the school, the students and families who attend. Is the nature of the roll changing? Do you want the school to expand? If so, where would that expansion come from? What constraints are there on the growth of the school?
- What do you regard as the advantages and disadvantages of the school in the new, more competitive, environment? Are you marketing the school? What problems are there? What changes in school policy have resulted? How is the need to market the school affecting the day-to-day running of the school?

The transcribed interviews have produced some useful anecdotal evidence about the impact of de-zoning and market competition which is analysed in conjunction with the composition data and parent interviews.

The telephone sample

The first phase of the Smithfield Project had two aims: firstly, to collect baseline data for the Smithfield sample (which was done by initial questionnaire) and by the collection of school achievement and aptitude data: secondly, to address the question: 'What are the consequences of the creation of education markets for parental choice?'

In order to answer this question we began to explore the supply-side of the market by the collection of composition data and by interviewing principals from our target secondary schools in Green City.

We also wanted to focus on the demand-side of the market to understand the processes by which parents 'choose' schools for their children. It was decided to conduct phone interviews with a selected sample of parents in the cohort who were themselves in the process of making this decision. The extensive information obtained from these interviews enabled us to elaborate on the issue of parental choice of schooling and complemented the data obtained from the Smithfield sample questionnaires. It is from the telephone sample that the data in relation to Tables 4.1 and 4.2 were collected.

Data collection

Most research on how parents choose schools is based on retrospective data and therefore deals primarily with the outcomes of the decision-making process. We felt that the decision-making process itself needed to be unpacked in greater detail to do justice to the complexities of educational decision making. From a theoretical perspective it also seemed important to try and disentangle choice of school (as made by parents) from the choice of students (as made by schools). To do this we focused in considerable depth on the decision-making process itself by conducting phone interviews with a sub-sample of the parents in the Smithfield sample. It was as part of these interviews that the questions relating to Tables 4.1 and 4.2 were asked.

Timing

The interviews with parents were conducted to focus on the 'demand-side' of the education market. We hoped to limit the impact of the 'supply-side' on the decision-making process by conducting the interviews prior to parents actually applying to and being accepted or rejected for schools. In this way, the possible impact of enrolment decisions made by schools on parental choice could be minimized. Also, we felt that efforts by schools to market themselves by, for example, open evenings and open days, might have an impact on parental choice. The interviews were therefore undertaken between April and June (1993), with an emphasis on the earlier weeks, at a time prior to any marketing strategies being used by the schools. In doing so, we hoped to gauge parental awareness, knowledge of, and interest in the education market prior to their active engagement with that market.

Format

We chose an interview approach to gain an in-depth understanding of the decision-making process itself, about which little is known. At the same time, we also wanted to find out what impact socioeconomic status, gender and ethnic background might have on educational decision making. We were aware of the need to undertake quantitative analyses in order to identify patterns and to make generalizations on the basis of the data. This had implications for both the size and the composition of the sample.

Clearly, then, there was a tension between the detailed nature of the data we wanted to collect, the number of parents to be interviewed, and practicalities in terms of time and money required. A compromise was found by deciding to conduct around 500 phone interviews rather than a much smaller number of face to face interviews. Although we were aware of the limitations of using phone interviews, a relatively open question style was chosen so as not to pigeonhole responses excessively. Where possible, the structure and formulation of questions was geared towards making coding and analyses easier later on. After the interviews were conducted, much effort was taken to code the responses of the more open questions in order to do justice to the important subtleties of educational decision making. It should also be noted that limited verbatim anecdotal material was retained.

Given that some respondents were not on the telephone and that a telephone approach might not be very appropriate for Pacific Island and Maori families, an additional 50 interviews were done face to face by Maori and Samoan interviewers. Otherwise the interviews were done by three interviewers in one urban centre and four in the other. Most of the interviews took place in the evenings, and only parents who had indicated on the initial consent form that they were willing to be contacted were approached. Because the rural cohort was established later than the urban cohort, no interviews were conducted for the rural area.

Process

For the telephone interviews, families were contacted during the day if possible and in the evenings if they were unavailable during the day. In most cases, parents and caregivers were able to be interviewed the first time they were contacted. In cases where the time of calling was not a good one, the interviewer arranged another time to call back.

When the interview schedule was designed, we also discussed the issue of who should be spoken to: female or male caregivers. In the end we decided that the interviewer should ask to speak to one of the parents or caregivers of the named child, without any further specification. The person who answered the phone was therefore mostly the person with whom the interview took place. In a few cases the phone was handed over to another person when it was made clear what the interview was about. We recorded the gender of the respondents so that it can be used when analysing the data. The majority of the respondents, 79 per cent, were mothers/female caregivers.

Interviewers introduced themselves and gave an explanation of the nature and purpose of the interview. They then asked whether the person they were speaking to had filled in the initial questionnaire: this was the case for 83 per cent of the respondents. Respondents were also given an assurance of confidentiality.

At the close of the interview, respondents were given the opportunity to ask any further questions or make additional comments and were offered the contact phone number of the project. The phone interviews lasted about 20 minutes on average, although some interviews took up to one hour.

Content

The interview schedule was designed to elicit several types of information, notably (i) influences on decision making, (ii) the nature of decision making, and (iii) other background information. We examine these in turn.

Influences

Our concern was to get a feel for the constraints and possibilities parents perceived with respect to enrolling their children in secondary schools. In order to explore better these kinds of considerations we asked in which school(s) parents intended to enrol their child and why. We were concerned that an abstract ranking of significant factors would be inappropriate and misleading. For the most part, therefore, questions of educational priorities and possibilities were asked in the context of discussions about particular schools. In addition, some abstract questions were asked, which enabled us to elaborate on the partly methodological and partly theoretical issue of how the kind of questioning might affect the findings.

Part of the theoretical debate about parental choice has centred around the issue of 'information imperfections' and the working of a market (Bridge 1978; Clune and Witte 1990; Clark 1993). Questions were therefore included on how parents find out (or intend to find out) about schools.

The nature of decision making

Another concern was to investigate the related processes by which different kinds of families made decisions about schools. Here we were concerned with issues such as who, within families, actually makes the decision, to what degree enrolment at a particular school is a conscious or taken-for-granted decision, and so on.

Other information

We also collected additional baseline data such as the current occupation and highest level of education obtained by parents. This enabled us to create alternative measures of SES against which to compare our current measures. Also questions were included on the perception of parents about their child's achievement in reading and maths, and the aspirations of parents for their child.

Sampling

The fairly limited empirical research on parental choice to date has shown
different and at times contradictory results (see Maddaus 1990). This is
especially the case regarding the impact of (travel) distance and SES background on choice. These contradictions may well result from differences in
local sociogeographic characteristics and/or the socioeconomic background of those being interviewed. These considerations called for a case
study approach on the basis of sociogeographic characteristics of particular
areas. However, we also wanted the sample to be representative of the entire
cohort with regard to gender, socioeconomic and ethnic background of the
students whose parents were to be interviewed. This was because, as mentioned earlier, we wanted to be able to make at least *some* generalizations.

The sampling design we decided upon was essentially based on a series of
seven case studies, all with slightly different sociogeographic characteristics. This approach enabled us to highlight the impact of type and composition of secondary schools available to particular communities, rather than
considering these to be factors that need to be controlled for statistically.
The areas and their characteristics included:

- an area where the only local school is co-educational and predominantly
  white working class, but other schools involve considerable travel;
- an area where the local schools are co-educational, predominantly working class and non-Pakeha, but other schools involve considerable travel
  and also have enrolment schemes;
- an area where the local schools are single sex, predominantly working
  class and non-Pakeha, and other schools are close but out of zone;
- an area which is served by two state co-education schools with similar
  middle class and Pakeha-dominated characteristics, but one has a relatively liberal character while the other is more traditional in its approach;
- an area where most students from diverse socioeconomic and ethnic
  backgrounds appear to attend the relatively mixed local school, except
  for a few students who attend schools some distance away;
- an area where there is a wide choice of secondary schools available
  nearby;
- an area which, although suburban, is relatively remote from any secondary schools.

Parents within each area were defined as those whose child was attending
one of the feeder primary and intermediate schools in that area and who
had given consent to be involved in the Smithfield Project and who were
willing to be contacted. The number of parents interviewed within each of
these areas varies from 45 to 150, according to the size of the area under
study and the complexities of educational decision making within them
which we predicted prior to the interviews.

To enable us to make generalizations, parents were sub-sampled in such a way that the total number of interviews (550) is representative of the socioeconomic background of the entire cohort. Because the socioeconomic composition of the cohort in each of the urban centres is slightly different, stratification was done for each centre separately. We also made sure that equal numbers of parents of boys and girls were interviewed within each area. Sampled parents from Maori and Pacific Island backgrounds in two of the case study areas, 50 in total, were approached by a Maori and Samoan interviewer respectively. Most of these interviews, at the request of the respondents, were carried out face to face rather than by phone.

Response rates

The non-response rate in one case study area and for the Pacific Island interviews would have exceeded that for the other case studies had we done nothing about it. Therefore, but only in these two cases, replacements were found for those not able to be contacted. This applied to a total of 12 parents. All in all, 534 interviews were successfully completed, giving a non-response figure of 3 per cent (N = 16). The non-responses were mainly the result of disconnected phones, failure to make contact after repeated efforts, and students having already left the area.

Determining school circuits

Since it was not appropriate to determine school circuits according to school status in New Zealand in the way the King's group had, the circuits for this study were determined according to judgements made about the social class mix of students within schools. An exploratory classification of the schools in the two urban centres according to three circuits (high, middle and low) was made as a result of intra-group discussion by the Smithfield team. For the core of high circuit schools there would be little that would be considered controversial, since they comprised private or, by common wisdom, elite single-sex schools. In Central City, one co-educational school located in a high SES residential area, was included. This school was also oversubscribed and operated an enrolment scheme. Inevitably this exploratory classification contained an element of arbitrariness since there were no clear divisions between schools according to SES. All schools recruit from all SES groups, although – and this is the significant point – in varying proportions. The key question, then, is how are these varying proportions arrived at when nominally everyone has equal choice. In the event, our analysis of choice-making over time provided an explanation of how the SES composition of schools is determined. In this sense circuits of schooling should be seen as a consequence of the way opportunities are structured under choice regimes.

The place of single-sex schools within the circuits could have proved problematic in that while the circuits were determined by our judgements of the socioeconomic mix of the school intake, arguably, choice of single-sex schools could operate independently of social class considerations. We have, therefore, taken great pains in our analysis to test this particular view. In many respects the low circuit schools chose themselves because they were so clearly marked out by their sociogeographic location. In retrospect, a better way of determining circuits might have been to ask a panel of local real estate agents!

Notes

Chapter 1

1 Whether education can improve economic prosperity depends on the way the economy and society are structured. See Brown and Lauder (1999).

2 The sources for these international comparisons were Robitaille and Garden (1989); Irving (1991b); Keeves (1992) and OECD (1994). For a discussion of the question of declining standards in the United States see Ravitch (1995).

3 More powerfully, Brian Haig (1991) has called the entire enterprise of meta-analysis into question as being methodologically misconceived.

4 Few studies have examined the longer-term impact of schools. In research on the performance of students from different school types at university in New Zealand, Hughes, Lauder and Strathdee (Hughes *et al*. 1996b) found that students from state schools outperformed their private and Catholic school counterparts when at university. In the United States, Coleman and Hoffer (1987) found that Catholic schools provide higher education students with some advantage.

5 We found Gintis's (1995) analysis of the formal properties of perfectly competitive markets vis-à-vis education markets particularly helpful to this part of our discussion.

Chapter 3

1 For a discussion of this issue within the context of state and market provision for education see Dale (1997).

2 One innovation that, after prolonged struggle now has achieved consensus, at least within the education community and among policy makers, is the development of Maori immersion schools, *Te Kohanga Reo* and *Kura Kaupapa* schools. This is an example of the establishment of culturally autonomous schools. However, this is a small and under-resourced sector in New Zealand education.

Chapter 4

1 The difference in Ns between Tables 4.1 and 4.2 and 4.3 *et seq.* is due to the first two tables being constructed from answers to the telephone sub-sample of the 1994 parent questionnaire. The telephone sub-sample is representative of the parent questionnaire sample. See the Appendix.

2 Schools which interview usually apply a variety of criteria in determining the suitability of out-of-zone applicants. These include: family association with the school; ability of the school to meet the learning needs of the student; and preference for the type of education offered (for example, co-educational or single sex).

3 We investigated the chance of an application to a high circuit school being accepted by SES background. We used analysis of covariance which allowed us to control for achievement. The probability of being accepted after adjusting for achievement was 0.89 for high SES students, 0.85 for middle SES students and 0.73 for low SES students. We then repeated the analysis for each of our four ethnic groups in turn. It appears that ethnicity mediates the effects with a highly significant SES effect for Pakeha but not for the other three ethnic groups. For example, Maori had a low probability of acceptance whatever their SES background. We discuss ethnicity in detail later in this chapter.

4 Schools were considered local when students lived within the original zone boundaries of the school. Schools which were clearly not the local school and for which travel was required were considered adjacent. To get to distant schools students bypassed their local school and at least one other in a way that involved considerable travel.

5 A further point to note is that the middle circuit schools appear to remain well mixed in terms of their socioeconomic intake. This raises an interesting question about why high SES parents might choose middle circuit schools for their children. For a discussion of this issue see Ball *et al.* (1994).

6 It should be noted that we cannot be wholly certain (for example) that the 54 per cent in Table 4.6 are all from the 59 per cent in Table 4.3, which they would need to be before we could say that 93 per cent of high SES parents who 'prefer' a high circuit school have their son or daughter attending one. We tested our assumption by tracking 10 per cent of the students from each SES group and found that the relative percentages hold true. The same issue applies where we compare tables in other parts of the chapter.

7 We again used analysis of covariance to investigate the probability of an application to a high circuit school being accepted. This time we were concerned with the probability of acceptance by ethnicity after controlling for achievement and SES. The adjusted probabilities for acceptance were 0.87 for Pakeha, 0.84 for Pacific Island, 0.76 for Other and 0.64 for Maori; the ethnicity effect is significant ($p = 0.002$).

Chapter 5

1 There were five families in the original study carried out by Sue Watson (1997). All confirmed the general findings reported in this chapter.

2 Students enter secondary school at the age of 13 in New Zealand.

Chapter 6

1 The concept of polarization can be understood and measured in a variety of ways. How it is interpreted will depend upon the particular policy questions and issues that are of concern. For example, in previous publications (Lauder *et al.* 1994; Waslander and Thrupp 1997) we used a broad measure of polarization known as the dissimilarity index. This measure can understate the nature and effects of polarization because it does not distinguish between situations in which many schools have a small imbalance and those in which a few schools have a major imbalance. We have found that as the more affluent in a neighbourhood bypass their local schools for schools they consider more desirable there is a real risk of spirals of decline developing and leaving a small rump of 'ghetto' schools. The dissimilarity index and other general measures obscure such polarizing effects. Defined in the way we have used it in this report, polarization refers to (i) the degree of high SES flight from working class schools, (ii) the relative opportunities of different SES groups within a neighbourhood to exercise choice, and (iii) the exit from working class schools inducing a spiral of decline.

Chapter 7

1 Each of these points is contestable. For example, Harker and Nash (1996) looked at School Certificate English, mathematics and science in New Zealand and found that nearly all the variance was between individuals and relatively little was between schools. After they had dropped two outlier schools from their original sample of 37 schools they suggested that only between 5 to 9 per cent of the variance was between schools. When they analysed this variance Harker and Nash found that two-thirds of it could be accounted for by the individual-level independent variables they studied (sex, initial ability, SES and ethnicity) and that adding school-level independent variables (school averages on initial ability, SES and ethnicity) accounted for very little further between-school variance. Indeed, adding school-level independent variables *reduced* the between-school variance explained in English. When summarizing their findings Nash and Harker (1997: 3) said: 'The statistical findings suggest that once the character of a school's intake has been taken into account no systematic differences can be detected in the performance of schools when School Certificate marks are used as the criterion. The hypothesis that the "ability" or social class composition of a school has an independent effect on a school's performance is shown to be doubtful.'
2 The results on these four measures were converted to T-scores and the mean T-score calculated.
3 As with the PAT tests the scores on these measures were converted to T-scores and the mean T-score found.
4 We kept the vocabulary load of these items as low as possible, with 85 per cent of the words used being classified at Level 1 or Level 2 on the Wright list of the 10,000 most common words in English prose (Wright 1965). To minimize the influence of reading abilities on the results of this test, it was read to the students.
5 School Certificate is an examination with a long history. First introduced in the 1930s, it became prominent in the 1940s. Until 1968 the qualification was

obtained by scoring 200 or more marks in English and three other optional subjects. In 1968 the system changed to a single-subject system in which students could take any number of papers up to six and pass each independently of the others. No subject was compulsory. Beginning in 1975, a controversial system of inter-subject scaling was introduced which led to a clear hierarchy of subjects, with some having pass rates approaching 90 per cent and others having pass rates below 40 per cent. That is, in some subjects almost 90 per cent of the candidates passed while in others over 60 per cent failed. Scaling was abandoned in the 1990s but the system still operates on the basis of historical means and the pass rates still vary; in subjects which had high pass rates under scaling, the papers are set and the marking schedules devised to obtain high pass rates.

6 The percentages of the total variances which are between schools in both our study of School Certificate and Harker and Nash's are almost certainly underestimates of the true levels in our samples for the reasons advanced by Harker and Nash (1996). For example, the schools in both studies differ in the proportion of the students who actually sit School Certificate, and this has not been accounted for in either study.

7 At the beginning of this chapter we footnoted the findings of Harker and Nash in New Zealand, who suggested that relatively little of the total variance in School Certificate English, mathematics and science is between schools as opposed to between individuals. In addition, they suggested that virtually none of the between-school variance could be accounted for by the contextual variables they investigated.

Now, the differences between the two studies are extremely important because they lead to vastly different conclusions regarding school effects. If we take the Harker and Nash figures and extrapolate from them we can paint the following picture. Typically, around 95 per cent of the variance in School Certificate performance is between individuals and only about 5 per cent is between schools. The between-school variance in English may be a bit higher, but it is less than 10 per cent. However, schools differ in terms of the individual characteristics of their students on important variables such as ethnicity, SES, initial ability and gender. When cognizance is taken of these individual-level independent variables, about two-thirds of the between-school variance can be accounted for. Aggregating these individual-level variables to the school level does not appreciably improve the percentage of the Level 2 variance that can be accounted for. It can be concluded that the differences between schools are minor and can be largely accounted for in terms of the characteristics of the students attending those schools operating at the individual level. Therefore, it is not possible to select successful schools on the basis of any of the variables studied. Parents who use league tables to select schools for their children are behaving irrationally because league tables do not take account of the schools' intakes and are consequently misleading. Schools at the top of the tables are likely to be there simply because of the initial characteristics, achievements and abilities of their students operating at the individual level. Sending a child with different characteristics, achievements and abilities to such schools will not improve that child's performance in comparison with what would be achieved at other schools.

8 On the basis of our findings we calculate that about 8 per cent of the total variance is related to school-level variables. If we take both of our studies and 'average out'

the findings for the six cognitive outcomes then around 16 per cent of the variance is between schools. Of this variance about 45 per cent is accounted for by the Level 1 independent variables studied and about 45 per cent is explained by the Level 2 variables studied. If we make the assumption that the unexplained variance would be equally split between other Level 1 and Level 2 variables not included in the studies, then about half the between-school variance is accounted for by Level 2 variables.

9 As we have previously noted, the Level 2 variable POSCOM was significantly related to performance in School Certificate mathematics and science. Now the interesting thing about this variable is that it is negatively related to outcomes. On psychological theories with any currency one would expect that positive teacher comments would be positively related to outcomes. While it is easy to understand how teacher praise can be punishing for the occasional child of a shy disposition, we would need to rewrite the texts on educational psychology if we could show that positive teacher comments are generally punishing. So how can this effect be explained? The most likely explanation is that teachers whose students are struggling because of their status on the individual-level variables and the school mix variables related to outcomes are trying particularly hard to overcome the handicaps under which their students labour by engaging in behaviours designed to foster achievement. So they praise their students more frequently than teachers in advantaged situations who do not need to use positive comments to reinforce or motivate their students. In all probability, using positive comments has a beneficial effect, but not enough to offset the detrimental effects of other variables, and so positive teacher comments show up in the results as negatively related to outcomes. If this interpretation is correct it would be foolish to suggest that teachers are in control of the comments they make and should desist from making positive ones for fear of limiting the achievement of their charges.

Chapter 8

1 We owe this insight to Gerald Grace.

Appendix

1 One school declined to take part in the study.
2 A follow-up study provided the justification for including people responding Kiwi or New Zealander in this way (see Hughes *et al.* 1996a).

References

Ambler, J. (1994) Who benefits from educational choice? Some evidence from Europe, *Journal of Policy Analysis and Management*, 13(3): 454–76.

Anastasi, A. (1988) *Psychological Testing*, 6th edn. New York: Macmillan.

Ball, S. (1990) 'Education, inequality and school reform: values in crisis'. Inaugural lecture. King's College, London.

Ball, S., Gewirtz, S. and Bowe, R. (1994) *School Choice, Social Class and Distinction: The Realisation of Social Advantage in Education*. Centre for Educational Studies. London: King's College.

Ball, S., Bowe, R. and Gewirtz, S. (1997) Circuits of schooling: a sociological exploration of parental choice in social class contexts, in A. H. Halsey, Hugh Lauder, Phil Brown and Amy Stuart Wells (eds) *Education: Culture, Economy and Society*. Oxford: Oxford University Press.

Barney, D. (1975) *Who Gets to Pre-school: The Availability of Pre-school Education in New Zealand*. Wellington: New Zealand Council for Educational Research.

Benton, R. (1987) *How Fair is New Zealand Education? Part 2: Fairness in Maori Education*. Wellington: New Zealand Council for Educational Research.

Bernstein, B. (1997) Class and pedagogies: visible and invisible, in A. H. Halsey, Hugh Lauder, Phil Brown and Amy Stuart Wells (eds) *Education: Culture, Economy and Society*. Oxford: Oxford University Press.

Bourdieu, P. (1997) The forms of capital, in A. H. Halsey, Hugh Lauder, Phil Brown and Amy Stuart Wells (eds) *Education: Culture, Economy and Society*. Oxford: Oxford University Press.

Bowe, R., Ball, S. and Gold, A. (1992) *Reforming Education and Changing Schools*. London: Routledge.

Bowe, R., Ball, S. and Gewirtz, S. (1997) 'Parental choice', consumption and social theory: the operation of micro markets in education, *British Journal of Educational Studies*, 42: 38–52.

Bowles, S. and Gintis, H. (1976) *Schooling in Capitalist America*. London: Routledge.

Bridge, G. (1978) Information imperfections: The Achilles' Heel of entitlement plans, *School Review*, 86(3): 504–29.

Broadfoot, P., Osborn, M., Gilly, M. and Paillet, A. (1988) What professional responsibility means to teachers: national contexts and classroom constants, *British Journal of Sociology of Education*, 9(3): 265–87.

Brophy, J. and Good, T. (1986) Teacher behaviour and student learning, in M. Wittrock (ed.) *Handbook of Research on Teaching*, 3rd edn. New York: Macmillan.

Brown, M. (1998) The tyranny of the international horse race, in R. Slee, G. Weiner and S. Tomlinson (eds) *School Effectiveness for Whom? Challenges to the School Effectiveness and School Improvement Movements*. London: Falmer Press.

Brown, P. (1987) *Schooling Ordinary Kids*. London: Tavistock Press.

Brown, P. (1997a) Cultural capital and social exclusion: some observations on recent trends in education, employment and the labour market, in A. H. Halsey, Hugh Lauder, Phil Brown and Amy Stuart Wells (eds) *Education: Culture, Economy and Society*. Oxford: Oxford University Press.

Brown, P. (1997b) The third wave: education and the ideology of parentocracy, in A. H. Halsey, Hugh Lauder, Phil Brown and Amy Stuart Wells (eds) *Education: Culture, Economy and Society*. Oxford: Oxford University Press.

Brown, P. and Lauder, H. (1997) Education, globalization and economic development, in A. H. Halsey, Hugh Lauder, Phil Brown and Amy Stuart Wells (eds) *Education: Culture, Economy and Society*. Oxford: Oxford University Press.

Brown, P. and Lauder, H. (1999) *Collective Intelligence and the Future of Society in the Global Economy* (forthcoming).

Brown, P. and Scase, R. (1994) *Higher Education and Corporate Realities: Class Culture and the Decline of Graduate Careers*. London: UCL Press.

Brown, P., Halsey, A., Lauder, H., Stuart Wells, A. (1997) The transformation of education and society, in A. H. Halsey, Hugh Lauder, Phil Brown and Amy Stuart Wells (eds) *Education: Culture, Economy and Society*. Oxford: Oxford University Press.

Bryk, A., Raudenbush, S. and Congdon, R. (1996) *Hierarchical Linear and Nonlinear Modeling with the HKM/2l and HLM/3L Programs*. Chicago: Scientific Software International Inc.

Buchanan, J. and Tullock, G. (1962) *The Calculus of Consent*. Ann Arbor, MI: University of Michigan Press.

Buchanan, J. and Wagner, R. (1977) *Democracy in Deficit*. New York: Academic Press.

Chubb, J. and Moe, T. (1990) *Politics, Markets and America's Schools*. Washington, DC: The Brookings Institute.

Chubb, J. and Moe, T. (1992) *A Lesson in School Reform from Great Britain*. Washington DC: The Brookings Institute.

Chubb, J. and Moe, T. (1997) Politics, markets and the organisation of schools, in A. H. Halsey, Hugh Lauder, Phil Brown and Amy Stuart Wells (eds) *Education: Culture, Economy and Society*. Oxford: Oxford University Press.

Clark, E. (1993) *OECD School Choice Study in New Zealand, A Report to the Ministry of Education, Wellington*. Wellington: Ministry of Education.

Clune, W. and Witte, J. (eds) (1990) *Choice and Control in American Education*, vol. 1. Philadelphia, PA: Falmer Press.

Codd, J., Gordon, L. and Harker, R. (1997) Education and the role of the state: devolution and control post-Picot, in A. H. Halsey, Hugh Lauder, Phil Brown and

Amy Stuart Wells (eds) *Education: Culture, Economy and Society*. Oxford: Oxford University Press.

Coleman, J. (1990a) Choice, community and future schools, in W. Clune and J. Witte (eds) *Choice and Control in American Education*, vol. 1. New York: Falmer Press.

Coleman, J. (1990b) *Equality and Achievement in Education*. Boulder, CO: Westview Press.

Coleman, J. (1992) Some points on choice in education, *Sociology of Education*, 65: 260–2.

Coleman, J. and Hoffer, T. (1987) *Public and Private High Schools: The Impact of Communities*. New York: Basic Books.

Coleman, J., Campbell, E., Hobson, C., McPartland, J., Mood, A., Weinfeld, F. and York, R. (1966) *Equality of Educational Opportunity*. Washington, DC: Government Printing Office.

Coleman, J., Hoffer. T. and Kilgore, S. (1982) *High School Achievement*. New York: Basic Books.

Connell, R., Dowsett, G., Kessler, S. and Ashenden, D. (1982) *Making the Difference*. Boston, MA: Allen and Unwin.

Dale, R. (1997) The state and the governance of education: an analysis of the restructuring of the state–education relationship, in A. H. Halsey, Hugh Lauder, Phil Brown and Amy Stuart Wells (eds) *Education: Culture, Economy and Society*. Oxford: Oxford University Press.

Darling-Hammond, L. (1997) Restructuring schools for student success, in A. H. Halsey, Hugh Lauder, Phil Brown and Amy Stuart Wells (eds) *Education: Culture, Economy and Society*. Oxford: Oxford University Press.

David, M. (1993) *Parents, Gender and Education Reform*. Cambridge: Polity Press.

David, M. (1997) Diversity, choice and gender, *Oxford Review of Education*, 23(1): 77–87.

David, M., West, A. and Ribbens, J. (1994) *Mother's Intuition? Choosing Secondary Schools*. London: Falmer Press.

Department of Trade and Industry (1997) *Competitiveness: A Benchmark for Business*. London: DTI.

Dewey, J. (1916) *Democracy and Education*. New York: Macmillan.

Dore, R. (1976) *The Diploma Disease*. London: Allen and Unwin.

Elley, W. (1991) *How Well Do New Zealand Students Achieve by International Standards?* Canterbury, NZ: University of Canterbury, Education Department.

Elley, W. and Reid, N. (1971) *Progressive Achievement Tests of Listening Comprehension*. Wellington: New Zealand Council for Educational Research.

Elley, W. B. and Irving, J. C. (1985) The Elley-Irving socioeconomic index 1981 census revision, *New Zealand Journal of Educational Studies*, 20(2): 115–28.

Fischer, C., Hout, M., Jankowski, M., Lucas, S., Swidler, A. and Voss, K. (1996) *Inequality by Design: Cracking the Bell Curve Myth*. Princeton, NJ: Princeton University Press.

Flew, A. (1987) *Power to the Parents*. London: The Sherwood Press.

Frank, R. and Cook, P. (1995) *The Winner-Take-All Society*. New York: Free Press.

Frank, R. and Cook, P. (1997) Tax and the winner-takes-all society, *Employment Policy Institute*, 10(10), Jan/Feb.

Freeman, R. (1995) The limits of wage flexibility to curing unemployment, *Oxford Review of Economic Policy*, 11(1): 63–72.

Friedman, M. and Friedman, R. (1980) *Free to Choose*. London: Penguin.

General Accounting Office (USA) (1994) *Elementary School Children: Many Change Schools Frequently, Harming their Education*. Report to the Hon. Marcy Kaptur, House of Representatives. Washington, DC: General Accounting Office.

Gerstner, L., Semerad, R., Doyle., D. and Johnston, W. (1994) *Reinventing Education: Entrepreneurship in America's Public Schools*. New York: Dutton.

Giddens, A. (1991) *Modernity and Self-Identity: Self and Society in the Late Modern Age*. Cambridge: Polity Press.

Gilder, G. (1981) *Wealth and Poverty*. New York: Basic Books.

Gintis, H. (1995) The political economy of school choice, *Teachers College Record*, 96(3): 492–511.

Glass, G. and Matthews, D. (1991) Are data enough? Review of politics, markets and America's schools, *Educational Researcher*, April, 24–7.

Glovinsky, S. (1971) *Alum Rock Union Elementary School District Feasibility Study, Final Report*, September.

Goldstein, H. (1993) Review of politics, markets and America's schools, *British Educational Research Journal*, 19(1): 116–18.

Goldthorpe, J. (1997) Problems of meritocracy, in A. H. Halsey, Hugh Lauder, Phil Brown and Amy Stuart Wells (eds) *Education: Culture, Economy and Society*. Oxford: Oxford University Press.

Goodman, A., Johnson, P. and Webb, S. (1997) *Inequality in the UK*. Oxford: Oxford University Press.

Gottschalk, P. (1997) Inequality, income growth and mobility: the basic facts, *Journal of Economic Perspectives*, 11(2): 21–40.

Gottschalk, P. and Smeeding, T. (1997) Cross national comparisons of earnings and income inequality, *Journal of Economic Literature*, 35: 633–87.

Grace, G. (1995) *School Leadership: Beyond Educational Management*. London: Falmer Press.

Green, A. (1997) Educational achievement in centralised and decentralised systems of education, in A. H. Halsey, Hugh Lauder, Phil Brown and Amy Stuart Wells (eds) *Education: Culture, Economy and Society*. Oxford: Oxford University Press.

Hacker, A. (1997) *Money, Who Has How Much and Why*. Scribners: New York.

Haig, B. (1991) Meta-analysis, methodology and research integration, *International Journal of Educational Research*, 15: 569–86.

Halsey, A., Heath, A. and Ridge, J. (1980) *Origins and Destinations, Family, Class and Education in Modern Britain*. Oxford: Clarendon Press.

Halsey, A., Heath, A. and Ridge, J. (1984) The political arithmetic of public schools, in G. Walford (ed.) *British Public Schools: Policy and Practice*. London: Falmer Press.

Hanushek, E. (1986) The economics of schooling: production and efficiency in public schools, *Journal of Economic Literature*, 19 (September) 1141–77.

Hanushek, E. (1989) The impact of differential expenditures on school performance, *Educational Researcher*, 18(4): 45–65.

Hanushek, E. (1994) *Making Schools Work: Improving Performance and Controlling Costs*. Washington, DC: The Brookings Institute.

Harker, R. and Nash, R. (1996) Academic outcomes and school effectiveness: Type 'A' and Type 'B' effects, *New Zealand Journal of Educational Studies*, 32(2): 143–70.

Hayek, F. (1976) Law, legislation and liberty: vol. 2, *Rules and Order*, 1–23. London: Routledge.

Hedges, L., Laine, R. and Greenwald, R. (1994) Does money matter? A meta-analysis of studies of the effects of differential school inputs on student outcomes, *Educational Researcher*, 23(3): 5–14.

Herrnstein, R. and Murray, C. (1994) *The Bell Curve: Intelligence and Class Structure in American Life*. New York: The Free Press.

Hillgate Group (1987) *The Reform of British Education*. London: Claridge Press.

Hills, J. (1995) *Inquiry into Income and Wealth, Vol II: A Summary of the Evidence*. York: Joseph Rowntree Foundation.

Hirsch, F. (1977) *The Social Limits to Growth*. London: Routledge.

Ho, E. and Willms, D. (1996) Effects of parental involvement on eighth-grade achievement, *Sociology of Education*, 60: 126–40.

Hughes, D. and Lauder, H. (1991) Human capital theory and the wastage of talent in New Zealand, *New Zealand Journal of Educational Studies*, 26(1): 5–20.

Hughes, D., Lauder, H., Dupuis, A., Watson, S. and Strathdee, R. (1996a) *A Question of Ethnicity: The Meanings of 'New Zealander'*. The Smithfield Project, Phase Two, Fifth Report to the Ministry of Education. Wellington: Ministry of Education.

Hughes, D., Lauder, H. and Strathdee, R. (1996b) First-year university performance as a function of type of secondary school attended and gender, *New Zealand Journal of Educational Studies*, 31(1): 13–28.

Hughes, D., Lauder, H., Watson, S., Hamlin, J. and Simiyu, I. (1996c) *Markets in Education: Testing the Polarisation Thesis*. The Smithfield Project, Phase Two, Fourth Report to the Ministry of Education. Wellington: Ministry of Education.

Hughes, D., Lauder, H., Watson, S., Strathdee, R., Simiyu, I. and Hamlin, J. (1997) *School Effectiveness: An Analysis of Differences Between Nineteen Schools on Four Outcome Measures Using Hierarchical Linear Modelling*. The Smithfield Project, Phase Two, Sixth Report to the Ministry of Education. Wellington: Ministry of Education.

Hughes, D., Lauder, H., Simiyu, I., Watson, S., Strathdee, R. and Hamlin, J. (1999) *Do Schools Make a Difference? Hierarchical Linear Modelling of School Certificate Results in 23 Schools*. The Smithfield Project, Phase Three, Ninth Report to the Ministry of Education. Wellington: Ministry of Education.

Hutchison, D. (1993) School effectiveness studies using administrative data, *Educational Research*, 35: 27–47.

Hutton, W. (1995) *The State We're In*. London: Jonathan Cape.

Irving, J. (1991a) *Update of the Elley and Irving Scale*. Wellington: Ministry of Education.

Irving, J. (1991b) *The Monitoring of Aacdemic Standards in the Basic Subjects in New Zealand Schools Vis-A-Vis New Zealand's International Compatriots and Major Trading Partners*. Wellington: Ministry of Education.

Irving, J. and Elley, W. (1977) A socioeconomic index for the female labour force in New Zealand, *New Zealand Journal of Educational Studies*, 12(2): 154–63.

Jencks, C. (1985) How much do high school students learn? *Sociology of Education*, 58(2): 128–35.

Jencks, C., Smith, M., Ackland, H., Bane, M., Cohen, D., Gintis, H., Heyns, B. and Michaelson, S. (1972) *Inequality: A Reassessment of the Effects of Family and Schooling in America*. New York: Basic Books.

Johnson, P. and Reed, R. (1996) Intergenerational mobility among the rich and the poor: results from the national child development survey, *Oxford Review of Economic Policy*, 12(1): 127–42.

Jones, A. (1989) The cultural production of classroom practice, *British Journal of Sociology of Education*, 10: 19–31.

Jones, A. (1990) 'I just wanna decent job'. Working-class girls' education: perspectives and policy issues, in H. Lauder and C. Wylie (eds) *Towards Successful Schooling*. London: Falmer Press.

Jones, G. (1985) Sexual tyranny: male violence in a mixed secondary school, in G. Weiner (ed.) *Just a Bunch of Girls: Feminist Approaches to Schooling*. Milton Keynes: Open University Press.

Keeves, J. (1992) *The IEA Study of Science III: Changes in Science Education and Achievement: 1970 to 1984*. Oxford: Pergamon Press.

Kelsey, J. (1995) *The New Zealand Experiment: A World Model for Structural Adjustment?* Auckland: Auckland University Press.

Kohn, M. (1969) *Class and Conformity*, Homewood, IL: The Dorsey Press.

Lange, D. (1988) *Tomorrow's Schools*. Wellington: Department of Education.

Lareau, A. (1992) Gender differences in parent involvement in schooling, J. Wrigley (ed.) *Education and Gender Equality*. London: Falmer Press.

Lareau, A. (1997) Social class differences in family–school relationships: the importance of cultural capital, in A. H. Halsey, Hugh Lauder, Phil Brown and Amy Stuart Wells (eds) *Education: Culture, Economy and Society*. Oxford: Oxford University Press.

Lauder, H. (1990) The New Right revolution and education in New Zealand, in S. Middleton, J. Codd and A. Jones (eds) *New Zealand Educational Policy Today*. Wellington: Allen and Unwin.

Lauder, H. (1997) Education, democracy and the economy, in A. H. Halsey, Hugh Lauder, Phil Brown and Amy Stuart Wells (eds) *Education: Culture, Economy and Society*. Oxford: Oxford University Press.

Lauder, H. and Hughes D. (1990a) Social origins, destinations and educational inequality, in J. Codd, R. Harker and R. Nash (eds) *Political Issues in New Zealand Education*. Palmerston North: Dunmore Press.

Lauder, H. and Hughes, D. (1990b) Social inequalities and differences in school outcomes, *New Zealand Journal of Educational Studies*, 25: 37–60.

Lauder, H. and Yee, B. (1987) Are teachers being proletarianized? Some theoretical, empirical and policy issues, in S. Walker and L. Barton (eds) *Changing Policies, Changing Teachers*. Milton Keynes: Open University Press.

Lauder, H., Hughes, D. and Fitzgerald, N. (1992a) *The Evaluation of Non-Cognitive School Outcomes: Transition Education: A Case Study*. Final Report in Fulfilment of Contract Number 41/17/220 between the New Zealand Department of Education and the University of Canterbury. Christchurch: Department of Education.

Lauder, H., Hughes, D., Dupuis, A. and McGlinn, J. (1992b) *To Be Somebody:*

Class, Gender and the Rationality of Educational Decision-Making. Wellington: Ministry of Education.

Lauder, H., Hughes, D., Waslander, S., Thrupp, M., McGlinn, J., Newton, S. and Dupuis, A. (1994) *The Creation of Market Competition for Education in New Zealand*. The Smithfield Project, Phase One, First Report to The Ministry of Education. Wellington: Ministry of Education

Lauder, H., Hughes, D., Watson, S., Simiyu, I., Strathdee, R. and Waslander, S. (1995) *Trading in Futures: The Nature of Choice in Educational Markets in New Zealand*. The Smithfield Project, Phase One, Third Report to the Ministry of Education. Wellington: Ministry of Education.

Lee, V. and Marks, H. (1992) Who goes where? Choice of single-sex and coeducational independent secondary schools, *Sociology of Education*, 65: 226–53.

Levačić, R., Hardman, J. and Woods, P. (1998) *Competition as a Spur to Improvement? Differential Improvement in GCSE Exam Results*. Manchester: Paper presented to the International Congress for School Effectiveness and Improvement, January.

Levin, H. and Kelly, C. (1997) Can education do it alone? in A. H. Halsey, Hugh Lauder, Phil Brown and Amy Stuart Wells (eds) *Education: Culture, Economy and Society*. Oxford: Oxford University Press.

MacDonald, M. (1980) Socio-cultural reproduction and women's education, in R. Deem (ed.) *Schooling for Women's Work*. London: Routledge and Kegan Paul.

Maddaus, J. (1990) Parental choice of school: what parents think and do, *Review of Research in Education*, 16: 267–96.

Mahony, P. (1985) *Schools for the Boys? Co-Education Reassessed*. London: Hutchinson.

McCulloch, G. (1991) School zoning, equity and freedom: the case of New Zealand, *Journal of Educational Policy*, 6(2): 155–68.

McPherson, A. and Willms, D. (1987) Equalisation and improvement: some effects of comprehensive reorganisation in Scotland, *Sociology*, 21: 509–39.

Middleton, S. (1992) Gender equity and school charters: theoretical and political questions for the 1990s, in S. Middleton and S. Jones (eds) *Women and Education in Aotearoa*. Wellington: Bridget Williams Books.

Ministry of Education (1991a) *Directory of Primary, Secondary and Tertiary Institutions*. Wellington: Ministry of Education

Ministry of Education (1991b) *Education Statistics of New Zealand 1991*. Wellington: Ministry of Education.

Ministry of Education (1992) *Education Statistics of New Zealand 1992*. Wellington: Ministry of Education.

Ministry of Education (1993) *Education Statistics of New Zealand 1993*. Wellington: Ministry of Education.

Ministry of Education (1994) *Education Statistics of New Zealand 1994*. Wellington: Ministry of Education.

Ministry of Education (1995a) *Directory of Primary, Secondary and Tertiary Institutions*. Wellington: Ministry of Education.

Ministry of Education (1995b) *Education Statistics of New Zealand 1995*. Wellington: Ministry of Education.

Ministry of Education (1996) *Directory of Primary, Secondary and Tertiary Institutions*. Wellington: Ministry of Education.

Mislevy, R. (1995) What can we learn from international assessments? *Education, Evaluation and Policy Analysis*, 17(4): 419–37.

Moore, D. and Davenport, S. (1990) Choice: the new improved sorting machine, in W. Boyd and H. Walberg (eds) *Choice in Education: Potential and Problems*, Berkeley, CA: McCutchan.

Morris, B. (1997) Is your family wrecking your career? (and vice versa), *Fortune*, March 17, 41–9.

Mortimore, P., Sammons, P., Stoll, L., Lewis, D. and Ecob, R. (1988) *School Matters, The Junior Years*. Wells: Open Books.

Murray, C. (1984) *Losing Ground: American Social Policy 1950–1980*. New York: Basic Books.

Nash, R. and Harker, R. (1997) *Progress at School: Final Report to the Ministry of Education*. Palmerston North: Massy University.

Nash, R., Harker, R. and Charters, H. (1990a) *Access and Opportunity in Education*, First Phase Report. Palmerston North: Massey University.

Nash, R., Harker, R. and Charters, H. (1990b) Reproduction and renewal through education, in J. Codd, R. Harker and R. Nash (eds) *Political Issues in New Zealand Education*. Palmerston North: Dunmore Press.

National Commission on Excellence in Education (1983) *A Nation at Risk*. Washington, DC: NCEE.

New Zealand Qualifications Authority (1996) *Secondary Qualification Statistics*. Wellington: NZQA.

New Zealand Treasury (1987) *Government Management Vol. II: Education*. Wellington: New Zealand Treasury.

Newton, S. (1994) 'Gender identity construction and the choice of single-sex schooling for girls', MA thesis, Victoria: University of Wellington.

Nohria, N. and Eccles, R. (1992) *Networks and Organisations: Structure, Form and Action*. Boston, MA: Harvard Business School Press.

OECD (1994) *The United States 1993–1994*. Paris: OECD.

Offe, C. (1990) Reflections on the institutional self-transformation of movement politics, in R. Dalton and M. Koehler (eds) *Challenging the Political Order: New Social and Political Movements in Western Democracies*. New York: Oxford University Press.

Osborne, D. and Gaebler, T. (1993) *Reinventing Government: How the Entrepreneurial Spirit is Transforming the Public Sector*. New York: Plume.

Paterson, L. (1991) An introduction to multilevel modelling, in S. Raudenbush and J. Willms (eds) *Schools, Classrooms and Pupils*. London: Academic Press.

Peltzman, S. (1993) The political economy of the decline of American public education, *Journal of Law and Economics*, 36, April, 331–70.

Picot, B., Ramsay, P., Rosemergy, M., Wereta, W. and Wise, C. (1988) *Administering for Excellence*. Wellington: Department of Education.

Polanyi, K. (1957) *The Great Transformation*. Boston, MA: Beacon Press.

Powell, A., Farrar., E. and Cohen, D. (1985) *The Shopping Mall High School*. Boston, MA: Houghton Mifflin.

Purkey, S. and Smith, M. (1983) Effective schools: a review, *The Elementary School Journal*, 84: 427–52.

Raudenbush, S. and Willms, J. (eds) (1991) *Schools, Classrooms and Pupils*. London: Academic Press.

Ravitch, D. (1995) *National Standards in American Education*. Washington, DC: The Brookings Institute.

Reich, R. (1991) *The Work of Nations*. London: Simon and Schuster.

Reid, N. (1993) *Progressive Achievement Tests of Mathematics*. Wellington: New Zealand Council for Educational Research.

Reid, N. and Elley, W. (1991) *Progressive Achievement Tests of Reading*. Wellington: New Zealand Council for Educational Research.

Reid, N., Croft, C. and Jackson, P. (1978) *Progressive Achievement Tests of Study Skills*. Wellington: New Zealand Council for Educational Research.

Reid, N., Jackson, P., Gilmore, A. and Croft, C. (1981) *Test of Scholastic Abilities, Teachers' Manual*. Wellington: New Zealand Council for Educational Research.

Robitaille, D. and Garden, R. (1989) *The IEA Study of Mathematics II: Contexts and Outcomes of School Mathematics*. Oxford: Pergamon Press.

Rosario, J., Barnett, W. and Franklin, B. (1992) On politics, markets and America's schools, *Journal of Educational Policy*, 7(2): 223–35.

Rosenshine, B. (1983) Teaching functions and instructional programmes, *The Elementary School Journal*, 83: 335–51.

Sammons, P. (1995) Gender, ethnic and socioeconomic differences in attainment and progress: a longitudinal analysis of student achievement over 9 years, *British Educational Research Journal*, 2(4): 465–85.

Sennett, R. and Cobb, J. (1972) *The Hidden Injuries of Class*. Cambridge: Cambridge University Press.

Sexton, S. (1991) *A Report Commissioned on New Zealand Schools and Current Reforms*. Wellington: New Zealand Business Round Table.

Snook, I. (1987) The voucher system: an alternative method of financing education, *New Zealand Journal of Educational Studies*, 22(1): 25–34.

Solon, G. (1992) Intergenerational income mobility in the United States, *American Economic Review*, 82(3): 393–408.

Steinberg, L., Brown, B. and Dornbusch, S. (1996) *Beyond the Classroom: Why School Reform Has Failed and What Parents Need to Do*. New York: Simon and Schuster.

Stuart Wells, A. (1995) African-American students' view of school choice, in B. Fuller, R. Elmore and G. Orfield (eds) *School Choice: The Cultural Logic of Families, the Political Rationality of Schools*. New York: Teachers College Press.

Stuart Wells, A. and Serna, I. (1997) The politics of culture: understanding local political resistance to de-tracking in racially mixed schools, in A. H. Halsey, Hugh Lauder, Phil Brown and Amy Stuart Wells (eds) *Education: Culture, Economy and Society*. Oxford: Oxford University Press.

Teddlie, C., Kirby, P. and Stringman, S. (1989) Effective versus indifferent schools: observable differences in the classroom, *American Journal of Education*, 97: 221–37.

Theisen, G., Acohola, P. and Boakari, M. (1983) The underachievement of cross-national studies of achievement, *Comparative Educational Review*, 27(1): 46–68.

Thrupp, M. (1996) 'The school mix effect', unpublished PhD, Victoria, New Zealand: University of Wellington.

Thrupp, M. (1997) How school mix shapes school processes: a comparative study of New Zealand schools, *New Zealand Journal of Educational Studies*, 32(1): 53–82.

Thrupp, M. (1999) *Schools Making a Difference: Let's be Realistic*. Buckingham: Open University Press.

Thurow, L. (1993) *Head to Head: The Coming Economic Battle Among Japan, Europe and America*. London: Brealey.

Tomlinson, S. (1997) Sociological perspectives on failing schools, *International Studies of Sociology of Education*, 7(1): 81–100.

Tomlinson, S. (1998) A tale of one school in one city, in R. Slee, G. Weiner and S. Tomlinson (eds) *School Effectiveness for Whom? Challenges to the School Effectiveness and School Improvement Movements*. London: Falmer Press.

Tooley, J. (1996) *Education Without the State*. London: London Institute of Economic Affairs.

The Treasury (1987) *Government Management Vol. II: Education*. Wellington: Government Printer.

Tyler, S. (1979) Time-sampling: a matter of convention, *Animal Behaviour*, 27: 801–10.

Walkerdine, V. (1984) Some day my prince will come, in A. McRobbie and M. Nava (eds) *Gender and Generation*. London: Macmillan.

Waslander, S. and Thrupp, M. (1997) Choice, competition and segregation: an empirical analysis of a New Zealand secondary school market, 1990–1993, in A. H. Halsey, Hugh Lauder, Phil Brown and Amy Stuart Wells (eds) *Education: Culture, Economy and Society*. Oxford: Oxford University Press.

Waslander, S., Hughes, D., Lauder, H., McGlinn, J., Newton, S., Thrupp, M. and Dupuis, A. (1994) *An Overview of Research Activities*. The Smithfield Project, Phase One, Second Report to The Ministry of Education. Wellington: Ministry of Education.

Watson, S. (1997) Single-sex education for girls: heterosexuality, gendered subjectivity and school choice, *British Journal of Sociology of Education*, 18(3).

Weiss, M. (1993) New guiding principles in educational policy: the case of Germany, *Journal of Educational Policy*, 8(4): 307–20.

Whitford, D. (1997) Sale of the century, *Fortune*, February 17, 42–51.

Whitty, G., Power, S. and Halpin, D. (1998) *Devolution and Choice in Education*. Buckingham: Open University Press.

Wilkinson, R. (1996) *Unhealthy Societies*. London: Routledge.

Willis, P. (1977) *Learning to Labour*. Farnborough: Saxon House.

Willms, D. and Echols, F. (1992) Alert and inert clients: the Scottish experience of parental choice of schools, *Economics of Education Review*, 11: 339–50.

World Bank (1995) *Priorities and Strategies for Education: A World Bank Review*. Washington: World Bank.

Wright, C. (1965) *An English Word Count*. Pretoria: National Bureau of Educational and Social Research.

Index

MARKETS, CHOICE AND EQUITY IN EDUCATION

Sharon Gewirtz, Stephen J. Ball and Richard Bowe

- What has been the impact of parental choice and competition upon schools?
- How do parents choose schools for their children?
- Who are the winners and losers in the education market?

These important and fundamental questions are discussed in this book which draws upon a three year intensive study of market forces in education. The authors carefully examine the complexities of parental choice and school responses to the introduction of market forces in education. Particular attention is paid to issues of opportunity and equity, and patterns of access and involvement related to gender, ethnicity and social class are identified.

This is the first comprehensive study of market dynamics in education and it highlights the specificity and idiosyncrasies of local education markets. However, the book is not confined to descriptions of these markets but also offers a systematic theorization of the education market, its operation and consequences. It will be of particular interest to students on BEd and Masters courses in education, headteachers and senior managers in schools, and policy analysts.

Contents
Researching education markets – Choice and class: parents in the marketplace – An analysis of local market relations – Managers and markets: school organization in transition – Schooling in the marketplace: a semiological analysis – Internal practices: institutional responses to competition – Choice, equity and control – Glossary of terms – References – Index.

224pp   0 335 19369 2 (Paperback)   0 335 19370 6 (Hardback)

DEVOLUTION AND CHOICE IN EDUCATION
THE SCHOOL, THE STATE AND THE MARKET

Geoff Whitty, Sally Power and David Halpin

- What is the background to, and significance of, policies of devolution and choice in education that are currently fashionable in many parts of the world?
- What has been the actual impact of these policies on school managers, teachers, students and local communities?
- How might equity be preserved in systems of education where increased responsibility is delegated to the level of the school?

This book examines recent school reforms in England and Wales, the USA, Australia, New Zealand and Sweden. It suggests that, at the same time as appearing to devolve power to individual schools and parents, governments have actually been increasing their own capacity to 'steer' the system at a distance. Focusing particularly on the 'quasi-markets' favoured by the New Right, the authors review the research evidence on the impact of the reforms to date. They conclude that there is no strong evidence to support the educational benefits claimed by the proponents of the reforms and considerable evidence that they are enabling advantaged schools and advantaged parents to maximize their advantages. They argue that, if these damaging equity effects are to be avoided, there is an urgent need to redress the balance between consumer rights and citizen rights in education.

Contents

176pp   0 335 19711 6 (Paperback)   0 335 19712 4 (Hardback)